JEWEL ORNAMENT OF LIBERATION

Jewel Ornament of Liberation

THE CLEAR LIGHT SERIES

SHAMBALA BERKELEY

1971

This book is published in The Clear Light Series by
SHAMBALA PUBLICATIONS, INC.
1409 Fifth Street
Berkeley, CA. 94710

Cover design by Chögyam Trungpa

This book is published in the CLEAR LIGHT series dedicated to W. Y. Evans-Wentz. The series is under the joint editorship of Samuel Bercholz and Michael Fagan.

Published by arrangement with Rider & Co., London.
Made and printed in Great Britain.

ISBN 0-87773-026-1
LCC 72-146507

CONTENTS

FOREWORD

When I was asked to design the cover for the *Jewel Ornament of Liberation*, I chose the syllable AH because it is the sound representing all pervading speech as well as the seed syllable of *sunyata*. I thought it most appropriate for a book born from the energy aspect of a great and dedicated teacher as sGam.po.pa. was.

There have been many attempts made to present the Buddhist teachings of Tibet, and generally there are certain consistent misconceptions, reminiscent of the seven blind men describing the elephant. An example of this is the persistent idea of a lamaist cult with complicated practices leading to magic. This occurs particularly through the isolation and dramatization of certain details out of context: a partial view rather than showing the whole journey in the great vehicle.

The vividness of the book is due not only to Sgam.po.pa's philosophical studies as a Kadampa monk but also to his years of meditation experiences under Milarepa in which he managed to achieve the meeting point of meditation and intellectual activity. He exercised great skill in bringing together the Buddhist Tantric Yoga of Naropa and the Hinayana monastic discipline of Sarvastivadin.

The book is particularly good for students of Buddhism because it does not present the complex practices of visualization and other deeply involved symbolic practices, but quite wisely, within the keeping of the tradition, deals first with the neurotic aspect of the samsaric mind. With the understanding of the positive ideas of tatagatagarbha and the good working basis of the human body, the journey becomes a totally creative one. Both his understanding and the development of the realization of impermanence are concerned with training the mind rather than giving practices to the student which lead only to more 'insane' mental productions. Unfortunately, the latter occurs all too frequently in the presentation of Tibetan Buddhism to the western audience.

Throughout the evolutionary development of man searching for the Dharma in the West, many people, Buddhist or instinctively Buddhist, have been greatly inspired by this book and I am sure many more will benefit from it in the future. It is in the flow of karma that this book materialized in 1959 on the very eve of the destruction of the spiritual land of Tibet. Professor Guenther was instrumental in making available the only commentary and guide in English to the Bodhisattva tradition of Tibet, Japan and China. The book remains the classic text of all Buddhists.

I would also like to draw the reader's attention to an occasional difficulty with the text. As in some other ancient texts, certain details are perhaps more part of a past culture than valid facts, such as the concept of Mount Meru as the centre of the world, and so on. However, I highly recommend *The Jewel Ornament of Liberation* as a thorough and complete exposition of the stages of Mahayana.

As part of the lineage of sGam.po.pa's order of Karma Kargyu, I find it very auspicious to be writing the foreword to this new edition.

CHÖGYAM TRUNGPA

September, 1970
Tail of the Tiger
Buddhist Community
Barnet, Vermont

PREFACE

SIX YEARS AGO, when for the first time I accompanied a young Lama to his monastery to spend my vacation there, I was given several Tibetan texts for study. Among these was sGam.po.pa's 'Jewel Ornament of Liberation'. A casual perusal at that time revealed unique qualities of style and content which, I thought, if translated, might make it a classic in Buddhist literature.

The work belongs to the group of texts which are known as 'Stages on the Path' (*lam.rim*). They are manuals which guide the student from the elementary tenets of Buddhism to the profoundest realization of Buddhahood. sGam.po.pa's work seems to have been the first Tibetan text of this kind and it has remained famous to the present day. It deals with the whole of Buddhism in such a lucid manner that it can be studied and understood without constantly looking up long-winded and often rather obscure commentaries and sub-commentaries. It is therefore a real 'Jewel Ornament', a title which is an allusion to a particular type of literature known as 'adornments' (*alaṅkāra*) in Buddhist Sanskrit, because they give the choicest and most important subjects in a highly polished and rather concise form. Another outstanding feature of sGam.po.pa's work is that it is addressed to all people who are, or may become, spiritually inclined. It appeals to the layman as well as the monk and the philosopher who unceasingly pursues man's perennial quest for the meaning of life. As a practical guide the 'Jewel Ornament' never loses itself in theory and scholastic controversy. However, to the Western reader the lengthy description of the various hells and the imminence of death may seem fantastic and depressing. But this is because we have lost the belief in hells other than the world we live in and fail to see how the thought of death affects us and brings us back to that which is our very own. In the light of death, we are brought before ourselves and our real possibilities are revealed so that we can choose which path to follow: that of frustration or that of fulfilment and liberation.

The translation is based on a modern carefully executed Bhutanese block-print. Throughout the Tibetan text has been the final authority, although I have indicated the places where the quotations from the Tibetan translations of Buddhist Sanskrit texts in the bKa'.'gyur and bsTan.'gyur are found in the original Sanskrit works in my possession or accessible to me. But nowhere have I substituted a translation from Sanskrit for the Tibetan version. sGam.po.pa is full of quotations from works inside and outside the bKa'.'gyur and bsTan.'gyur. But since the practice has always been to quote from memory it sometimes happens that a verse is said to be found in a particular work where it is not or that only the general idea has been reproduced. This accounts for the divergences between some of the Tibetan and Sanskrit versions. In the notes I have quoted from various works of the bKa'.rgyud.pa school of Buddhism. Apart from giving additional references they are meant to specify the meanings of the technical terms.

It is a special source of satisfaction for me that during my repeated stays at bKra.śis chos.gliṅ dgon.pa in Lahoul I have been able to discuss the whole of the translation and the meaning of terms with my Guru and friend bLa.ma Dam.chos rin.chen. I am particularly grateful to him for lending me this work and many others for study and for his valuable oral instructions.

I received incidental help and advice from the Incarnate Lama Dar.mdo sprul.sku Thub.bstan lhun.grub legs.bzaṅ of 'Bras.spuṅs blo.gsal.gliṅ rgyal.roṅ and abbot of Budhgaya as well as from the famous scholar dge.bśes bsTan.'dzin rgyal.mtshan.

In identifying the titles of Tibetan works which are usually given in their conventional and abbreviated form and checking them with those in the Catalogue of the sDe.dge edition of the bKa'.'gyur and bsTan.'gyur published by the Tôhoku Imperial University (Sendai, 1934), I have been greatly assisted by my friend bLa.ma Rig.'dzin lhun.grub, Tibetan lecturer at Nava Nalanda Mahavihara.

To all of them I offer my sincere thanks.

Finally I have to express my debt of gratitude to my friend Joseph E. Cann, Esq., for his encouragement and, last not least, to my wife, Ilse Guenther, Ph.D., for her constant interest and help in the preparation of the various indices.

HERBERT V. GUENTHER

1958
Lucknow, U.P.
India

INTRODUCTION

sGam.po.pa holds a unique position among the many illustrious philosopher-saints of Tibet. He ranks next to The Buddha in authority, and whichever line of thought Mahāyāna Buddhists adopt as a guide for their way of life, he commands the highest respect of all. Tradition has it that he is an incarnation of Candraprabhakumāra who as the son of a rich householder in Rājagṛha (modern Rajgir in Bihar) had requested The Teacher to recite the Samādhirājasūtra. sGam.po.pa himself states that formerly he had been Candraprabhakumāra, and so his works are referred to as having been composed by Zla.'od gžon.nu, which is the Tibetan for Candraprabhakumāra.

sGam.po.pa, 'the man from sGam.po', equally well known as Dvags.po lha.rje, 'the physician from Dvags.po', as 'the incomparable Dvags.po lha.rje' (*mñam.med Dvags.po lha.rje*) and 'the renowned one of the human world' (*'Dzam.gliṅ grags.pa*), was born in the year A.D. 1079 as the second of three sons to sÑi.ba rgyal.po and his wife So.mo.gza' Che.lcam. In his youth he studied medicine and became quite a scholar in that science. An early marriage ended tragically by the death of his wife when he was just past twenty. On her death-bed she is said to have asked him not to remarry, but it is safe to assume that her sudden death made a deep impression on him so that he devoted himself to a religious life. This for him was not escapism but the continuance of his profession on a higher level: the alleviation of suffering on the worldly plane from the realm of the spirit.

At the age of twenty-six he received simultaneously the noviciate and the final monastic ordination. It seems that from this time onwards he bore the name bSod.nams rin.chen. First he was a follower of the bKa'.gdams.pa doctrine which originated with Dīpaṅkara Śrījñāna, commonly known as *jo.bo chen.po dbaṅ.ldan Atiśa*, whose 'Bodhipathapradīpa' he often quotes in his works. At this time his teachers were Bya.yul.pa, sÑug.rum.pa, and lCags.ri Goṅ.kha.pa. As the study of Buddhism is always bound up with meditation, in which he was instructed by the teacher Byaṅ.chub.sems.dpa', he spared no pains to meet Mi.la.ras.pa as soon as he had heard about the latter from some beggars. Mi.la.ras.pa then instructed him in the Vajrayāna discipline and in particular in the meditative practice of the mystic inner heat (*gtum.mo*) which, with other exercises developed and systematized by the mahāsiddha Nāropa,[1] are essential for the realization of the Tantrik goal Mahāmudrā (*phyag.rgya chen.po*). sGam.po.pa combined the teachings of the bKa'.gdams.pa and the experiences of Mahāmudrā in a unique manner, so that the two streams united (*bKa'.phyag chu.bo gñis 'dres*). He had many disciples and was the organizer of the bKa'.rgyud.pa order. He died in the year A.D. 1153.[2]

In all his works sGam.po.pa blends the theoretical exposition of the Sūtras with the experiential contents of the Tantras. He is never pedantic, but always simple and to the point in a way rarely met with among philosophers. While Indian pandits are mostly diffuse, sGam.po.pa, like all Tibetan scholars, orders and structures his material so that the important points stand out simply and clearly.

In his 'Jewel Ornament of Liberation', the full title of which is 'The Explanation of the Stages on the Mahāyānic Path towards Liberation, called a Jewel Ornament of Liberation or the Wish-Fulfilling Gem of the Noble Doctrine', sGam.po.pa deals with the whole of Buddhism as a way of life. He is convinced that every sentient being is capable of attaining enlightenment which is not so much a change from one extreme, Saṃsāra, to another, Nirvāṇa, but the ineffable experience in which both have ceased to dominate the thought of man so that he begins to live his life as transformed by pure transcendence.

Saṃsāra and Nirvāṇa are not entities, but interpretations of our experiences, and as such are both Śūnyatā, which again is an operational term, not an ontological concept. Although all sentient beings may attain enlightenment by their own efforts, because each is a potential Buddha, human existence is the most suitable occasion for such striving. It is not something self-evident, although we can only act as human beings. We must always be aware of human dignity and so respect others as equally worthy beings. By this awareness we gain confidence in being able to realize a thoroughly human and humane goal, and find the meaning of life. In this striving we are in need of spiritual friends. They may be found at any level, because, if Saṃsāra and Nirvāṇa as interpretations have their common root in transcendence, which from the ordinary point of view is just nothing (Śūnyatā), whatever and whomsoever we meet serves as a symbol and guide to transcendence. Since all our experiences, from the most sordid aspects of life to the most lofty ideals, are of a transitory nature, it is important for us always to be aware of this fact and not to build on them as a solid foundation which will only obscure our mind and expose us to unending sorrow. In this awareness the transitory does not lead us into despair, but serves as a lamp to the everlasting which no words can express and which pervades everything temporal. Subject to transitoriness all that we call the world, including gods, animals, spirits, denizens of hell, and demi-gods, is a constant source of dissatisfaction which has its origin in our actions (Karma), for what we poetically describe as the pangs of hell and the bliss of heaven is the accompanying feeling-tone of our actions.

Thus in whatever we do we are in duty bound to be aware of being human beings and of our task which must not be allowed to glide into a betrayal of human dignity but must be expressive of this dignity in benevolence and compassion. Mahāyāna Buddhism is not escapism, it is the unending task to make life liveable, and this is not achieved by running away from man or by attempting to slaughter him wholesale (in the mistaken belief that a civilized human is a dead one).

Although sGam.po.pa does not say so directly, it is evident from the whole of Buddhist training that what has been discussed so far and which is condensed into the four topics of (i) the difficulty of being and becoming a human being, (ii) the transitory nature of everything, (iii) the relation between our actions and our situation in life, and (iv) the general unsatisfactoriness of Saṃsāra, represents that aspect of Mahāyāna Buddhism which everyone is assumed to be capable of expressing in his individual life. Certainly, to become worthy of the name of a human being, even in its most elementary aspect, is no easy task from the Mahāyāna point of view.

But all this is not sufficient to attain enlightenment or to realize Buddhahood, for which a special training is needed. It begins with taking refuge in the Three Jewels, the Buddha, the Dharma, and the Sangha, which is of three orders: an outer order in which the Buddha is represented by an image, the Dharma by the Mahāyāna texts, and the Sangha by the Bodhisattvas, those who strive continuously for enlightenment; an inner order, where the Buddha is the patterning of our life, the Dharma the experience of Nirvāṇa and tranquillization, and the Sangha the Bodhisattvas who have reached the highest level of spirituality; and a mystic order, where Buddhahood alone is the refuge, as the foundation, path and goal of our life. Taking refuge in this Mahāyānic sense is always accompanied by the resolution to adopt an attitude which is directed towards enlightenment and the earnest endeavour to develop and cultivate such an attitude.

Since there is an intimate relation between our actions and our attitude, the resolution to strive for enlightenment naturally shows in what we do and is thus related to ritual acts. Ritual is essentially the active transformation of experience and human life is permeated with it. It is the expression of a human need, not the deplorable remnant of former superstitious ages, although it may become silly idolatry when its meaning and function is no longer understood. Man requires something to which he can turn in reverence; if he were not in need he would never have attempted to take refuge in something or someone. For his emotional balance he needs cathartic acts such as confessing all that he has done wrongly and also rejoicing in the good done by his fellow-beings. Man needs communication which should consist in making other human beings aware of their spiritual potencies, and when so doing he cannot run away and find some sheltered place of self-beguiling peace. Communication continues as long as there are sentient beings who suffer because they are unaware of their possibilities.

In his feeling of reverence, in his cathartic acts of confessing evil and rejoicing in the good done by others, in unending communication, man shatters the narrow world of his ego and transcends himself. In so doing, however, he would destroy himself and become a living example of insanity if he were to ascribe to himself the world he enters by breaking the walls of his ego-centred prison. Therefore everything that has been done and which was creative of symbols must be returned to the sphere where transformation of experience into symbols had its origin. If enlightenment is at the core of human life and if man lives out of enlightenment allowing it to be of decisive importance in all his actions by developing an attitude towards it, he must relate himself to, not alienate himself from, it. Transmutation of good, as this is technically known, is one of the most important acts of the ritual. In recognizing the needs of man instead of conceiving him as a phantasmagoria, Mahāyāna Buddhism has successfully overcome the Hīnayāna nihilism.

The interrelation between attitude and acts needs constant attention. Here the six 'perfections' strengthen an enlightened attitude which, in turn, makes the 'perfections' more and more perfect. Five of them, liberality, ethics and manners, patience, strenuousness, and meditative concentration, are overshadowed by and lead up to the sixth perfection: discriminating awareness born from wisdom.[3]

This last perfection makes us see Reality as it is. It abolishes the formidable superstitions in existence and non-existence, it liberates us from the philosophical systems of realism and mentalism (usually confused with and presented as idealism), and leads us beyond monism and pluralism. It is in the discussion of the perfection of discriminating awareness born from wisdom (*śes.rab*, Skt. *prajñā*) that sGam.po.pa blends the Sūtra and Tantra conceptions.

However, discriminating awareness is only the beginning, not the climax of our striving for enlightenment, because it makes us see

Reality so that we can follow it with open eyes. With this seeing the Buddhist Path starts, and every step we take leads to wider horizons termed spiritual levels, until it terminates in Buddhahood: potentiality has become actuality. As such, Buddhahood is no soporific state, but stretches out into all sentient beings as motive and goal.

The above represents the leading ideas of sGam.po.pa's 'Jewel Ornament of Liberation'. In the whole of Buddhist literature there is hardly any other work which in simple and concise form deals with the whole of Buddhism as a living experience and as a human task. It is therefore the manual of all who aspire to become a Lama in the bKa'.rgyud.pa order. May it be a guide to many others!

NOTES TO INTRODUCTION

1. Nāropa, the spiritual teacher of Mar.pa who, in turn, became the Guru of Mi.la.ras.pa, is famous for his unflagging zeal in serving his Guru Tilopa (Tillipa). The latter taught him among other disciplines the 'Six Topics' (*chos.drug*) which comprise the development of the mystic inner heat (*gtum.mo*), the experience of one's body as a phantom (*sgyu.lus*), the dream (*rmi.lam*) and the radiant light experiences (*'od.gsal*), the experience of the state between death and rebirth (*bar.do*), and the practice of transferring mind to higher spiritual levels (*'pho.ba*). According to Tilopa's 'Ṣaḍḍharmopadeśa' (Chos.drug.gi man.ṅag, bsTan. 'gyur, vol. sṅags pu, fol. 129b) these topics had been developed by former teachers. Thus the experiences of one's body as a phantom (*sgyu.lus*) and of radiant light (*'od.gsal*) go back to Nāgārjuna; the development of the mystic inner heat (*gtum.mo*) to Caryapa; the dream experience (*rmi.lam*) to Lavapa, and that of the state between death and rebirth (*bar.do*) as well as the practice of transferring mind to higher spiritual levels (*'pho.ba*) to Pukasiddhi.

2. For a further account of sGam.po.pa's life see 'The Blue Annals', vol. ii, pp. 451 seq. and my 'Dvags.po lha.rje's 'Ornament of Liberation' in 'JAOS', vol. 75, pp. 90 seq.

3. *śes.rab*, Skt. *prajñā* is one of the key terms of Buddhist philosophy. Since the latter is a way of life concerning the whole man rather than a mere intellectual pastime, *prajñā* is a most difficult term to define. It is usually translated by 'wisdom'. This is tolerably correct in so far as *prajñā* is the culmination of a disciplinary process which starts with ethics and manners (*śīla*) and proceeds through concentrative absorption (*samādhi*) to wisdom (*prajñā*). By etymology it is *dharmāṇāṃ*

pravicaya, 'analysis of events and/or entities'. In this analysis what is conducive to the spiritual life is selected. *Prajñā* therefore is really 'discrimination', which in Webster's 'Dictionary of Synonyms' means 'the power to select the excellent, the appropriate and the true'. But as a result of the previous training *prajñā* is more than ordinary discrimination. Unfortunately there is no functional term to express this 'more' in Western psychology.

In Webster's Dictionary 'wisdom' suggests 'an ideal quality of mind or character that is the result of a trained judgment exercised not only in practical affairs but in philosophical speculation, of wide experience in life and thought, of great learning and of deep understanding'. It is here that the weakness of 'wisdom' as a translation of *prajñā* stands out. We are wont to consider it as a 'result' not as a 'beginning', which appears to be corroborated by the Buddhist ideal of ethics and manners leading to concentrative absorption and then to wisdom.

For us philosophy is the climax of mental life, but in Buddhist Tantrism it is only a 'starting point', a means to an end which is conduct (*spyod.pa*, Skt. *caryā*) that yields the highest quality of satisfaction (*bde.ba chen.po*, Skt. *mahāsukha*). Both conduct and satisfaction are expressive of *ye.śes*, Skt. *jñāna*, 'transcending awareness', 'knowledge in itself', and not 'knowledge of'. *Prajñā* therefore represents a station on the path to *jñāna* and means 'analytical appreciative understanding'. But this is somewhat clumsy. In this work the translation by 'discriminating awareness born from wisdom' has been adopted throughout. This, though lengthy, is preferable to the inexact 'wisdom', as it preserves the basic meaning of 'discrimination' (*pravicaya*) and by linking it up with 'wisdom', it indicates the Buddhist conception of a hierarchy of intellectual-spiritual acumen. It is the wise man who sets out to transcend the world.

I

THE MOTIVE

Homage to saintly Mañjuśrī who was once a Prince![1]
Having bowed to the Victorious One, his Sons and the sublime experiences,[2]
As well as to the Gurus who are their foundation,[3]
In relying on Mi.la.ras.pa's and Atīśa's grace, I write for the benefit of myself and others
This Jewel of the Noble Doctrine which is like the Wish-Fulfilling Gem.

GENERALLY SPEAKING: the whole of reality is subsumed under the duality of Saṃsāra and Nirvāṇa. Saṃsāra is to be understood in the sense that its ultimate nature[4] is Śūnyatā, its causal characteristic[5] bewilderment[6] and its primary characteristic[7] its manifestation as misery.[8] The ultimate nature of Nirvāṇa is Śūnyatā, its causal characteristic is the end and dispersion of all bewilderment and its primary characteristic is liberation from all misery.

However, the question may arise: who is bewildered in this confusion called Saṃsāra? The answer is: all sentient beings of the three world-spheres.[9] Or, it may further be asked, from which fundamental stuff does this bewilderment come? And the answer is: from Śūnyatā. The motive behind this bewilderment is great ignorance and the bewilderment works in the mode of life of the six kinds of living beings.[10] Its similes are sleep and dream and it has existed since beginningless Saṃsāra. It is vicious because we live and act solely in misery. Can this bewilderment ever become transcending awareness born from wisdom?[11] It will do so as soon as unsurpassable enlightenment has been attained. But if you think that it will disperse by itself, you should remember that Saṃsāra is notorious for being without end.

You may further argue, since the status of Saṃsāra is bewilderment, great misery, endless duration and the absence of the possibility of being liberated by itself, what kind of enlightenment have people striven to attain since time immemorial and what is the use of such striving. The answer falls under the following heads:

Motive,[12] working basis,[13] contributory cause,[14]
Method,[15] result[16] and ensuing activity[17]—
These are the six general indicators of unsurpassable enlightenment
That judicious men[18] should know.

In other words, you should know the motive which is unsurpassable enlightenment; the individual which is the working basis for attaining that enlightenment; the contributory cause urging the latter to attain it; the method and result of such attainment and the resulting Buddha-activity.

These topics will be introduced in their proper sequence by the headings

(a) The motive is Tathāgatagarbha;
(b) The working basis is the most precious human body;
(c) The contributory cause are spiritual friends;
(d) The method are the instructions of spiritual friends;
(e) The result is Sambuddhakāya; and
(f) The activity (2b) is working for the benefit of others without preconceived ideas.[19]

So far these topics have been mentioned as constituting the body of doctrine; now they will be explained in detail as the limbs of that body.

(a) The first has been introduced by the words 'The motive is Tathāgatagarbha'.

However, if you wonder whether dejected people like ourselves will ever attain by our own exertions this unsurpassable enlightenment liberating ourselves from Saṃsāra which is by nature bewilderment, you may be reassured by remembering that if enlightenment can be won by hard work, it must be within our reach; for in all beings like ourselves the Buddha-motive, Tathāgatagarbha, is present. This is affirmed in the 'Tiṅ.ṅe.'dzin.gyi rgyal.po'i mdo' ('Samādhirājasūtra'):

> Tathāgatagarbha embraces and permeates all beings.

In the 'mDo mya.ṅan.las 'das chuṅ' ('Mahāparinirvāṇasūtra'):

> All beings are endowed with Tathāgatagarbha.

In the 'mDo mya.ṅan.las 'das.pa chen.po' ('Mahāparinirvāṇasūtra'):

> Just as butter exists permeating milk, so does Tathāgatagarbha permeate all beings.

And in the 'mDo.sde.rgyan' ('Mahāyāna-sūtrālaṅkāra' IX, 37):

> Tathatā, which becomes purified, although it is in itself undifferentiated in and for all beings,
> Is Buddhahood; because of it all sentient beings are endowed with its essence.

Now all beings are endowed with Tathāgatagarbha, because

Dharmakāya which is Śūnyatā, permeates them; because in the very nature of things[20] which is Tathatā, there are no differentiations, and in all sentient beings there are factors which allocate them to certain families. Thus is stated in the 'rGyud.bla.ma' ('Uttaratantra' I, 28):

> Because of the permeation of Sambuddhakāya, of the (3a) undifferentiatedness of Tathatā,
> And of the existence of families, all sentient beings are constantly endowed with Buddha-nature.

In the first instance, it has been said 'Dharmakāya which is Śūnyatā, permeates all beings'. This means that since The Buddha is essentially Dharmakāya and Dharmakāya Śūnyatā and since this Śūnyatā permeates all beings, the latter are endowed with Buddha-nature.

It has further been stated 'There are no differentiations in the very nature of things which is Tathatā'. This means that beings are endowed with Buddha-nature since in the Tathatā of Buddhas and of sentient beings there is no differentiation into good or bad, great or small, high or low.

Finally, 'In all sentient beings there are factors which allocate them to certain families'. This means that they live in the five types of Buddha-families given below:

> The Cut-off family,[21] the Dubious-family,[22]
> The Śrāvaka family,[23] the Pratyekabuddha family,[24]
> And the family of followers of the Mahāyāna way of life[25]—
> Under these five families beings are subsumed as belonging to Buddha-families.

The 'Cut-off family' are those who according to the great teacher Thogs.med (Asanga) have the six primary characteristics of insolence, shamelessness, mercilessness and so on. His words are:

> Seeing the vicious state of Saṃsāra they are not moved;
> Hearing of the excellences of the Buddhas they have no confidence;
> They have no respect for themselves or others, and no compassion;
> They are totally unrepentant, however wicked their lives may be—
> Abounding in these six negative qualities they have no chance of becoming Buddhas.

And in the 'mDo.sde.rgyan' ('Mahāyāna-sūtrālaṅkāra' III, 11):

> Some are surely working only evil;

Others are defeating positive qualities;
And yet others are without the normal good prospects for liberation;
He who is deficient in positive qualities is devoid of the motive of Buddhahood (3b).

But even those who are thus characterized and said to form the Cut-off family, because their minds have been intent on wandering in Saṃsāra for a long time, are not people who will never be able to attain enlightenment. They would do so if they would only exert themselves. This is stated in the 'sÑiṅ.rje padma dkar.po'i mdo' ('Mahākaruṇāpuṇḍarīkasūtra'):

Ānanda, if a man without the good fortune of being able to attain Nirvāṇa should throw only a flower up into the sky, when he has seen The Buddha, he would be endowed with the fruit of passing into Nirvāṇa. I call him bordering on, approaching Nirvāṇa.

The 'Dubious-family' are those whose future way of life depends on certain conditions. Those who rely on a spiritual friend who is a Śrāvaka, or who are friends and acquaintances of one and believe in the Śrāvaka way of life after they have perused the Śrāvaka-sūtras, will become members of that family and disclose themselves as such. Similarly when they meet a Pratyekabuddha or a follower of the Mahāyāna way of life they will become respectively either Pratyekabuddhas or followers of the Mahāyāna way of life.

The 'Śrāvaka family' are those who are afraid of Saṃsāra, yearn for Nirvāṇa and have little compassion. As has been said about them:

Having seen the misery of Saṃsāra they become afraid
And yearn for Nirvāṇa;
They do not delight in working for the benefit of sentient beings;—
Endowed with these three characteristics is the Śrāvaka family.

The 'Pratyekabuddha family' are those who in addition to these three characteristics are very arrogant, keep silent about their teachers and like to live alone in solitude. As has been said:

Shaken by Saṃsāra they run after Nirvāṇa;
They have little compassion and are extremely conceited;
They keep silent about their teachers (4a) and like to be alone—
These the wise should know as the Pratyekabuddha family.

These two families of Śrāvakas and Pratyekabuddhas represent two distinct ways of life, and although both of them attain their respective goals, the Nirvāṇa which they claim to have experienced is not the real one. In what state, then, do they abide? Though they stand on ground prepared by the habitual working of ignorance,[26] they remain in an essentially mental body[27] acquired through unsullied deeds.[28] Since at this stage meditative absorption[29] is unsullied, they cling to the idea that this is Nirvāṇa. You may now argue, if this Nirvāṇa is not the real one, the Exalted One should not have shown these two ways. Oh yes! He should have done so for the following reason. Suppose some Indian merchants go to fetch jewels from the outer sea, but in the middle of their journey, in some desert, they become exhausted and think that they cannot go on. Then as they are about to turn back, their leader by his miraculous power creates a huge city for their refuge. In the same way those of little courage take fright after hearing of the Buddha's spiritual awareness, thinking that it will be most troublesome to attain to Buddhahood, and that through their inability they will have to turn back. Then they find that they can stay where they are as Śrāvakas and Pratyekabuddhas now that these two ways of life have been shown to them.[30] As is stated in the 'Dam.chos padma dkar.po' ('Saddharmapuṇḍarīkasūtra' V, 74):

Thus all Śrāvakas
Think that they have attained Nirvāṇa.
To them the Victorious One says
That this is rest but not Nirvāṇa.

As soon as the Tathāgata learns that they are resting among the Śrāvakas and the Pratyekabuddhas, He urges them to attain Buddhahood (4b) by Body,[31] Speech,[32] and Mind.[33] 'By Mind' means that the radiance that emanates from Him awakens beings from their unsullied meditative absorption as soon as it touches the Śrāvakas and Pratyekabuddhas in their mental bodies. Thereafter He reveals His Body. 'By Speech' means that He says: 'Bhikṣus, you have not yet accomplished your work, you are not doers of your task, your Nirvāṇa is not the real one. Bhikṣus, now come to the Tathāgata, listen to and understand what He has to say.'[34] Thus He urges them on. This has been shown in the 'Dam.chos pad.dkar' ('Saddharmapuṇḍarīkasūtra' VII, 107):

Bhikṣus, today I declare:
Nirvāṇa has not yet been attained.
For the True spiritual awareness of the Omniscient One
You should rouse your energy and have great confidence.
Attain the True spiritual awareness of the Omniscient One!

Urged on in this way, Śrāvakas and Pratyekabuddhas prepare their minds for an attitude which is directed towards and centred in enlightenment,[35] and after having practised the Bodhisattva-life throughout countless aeons they become Buddhas. This is stated in the ''Phags.pa Laṅ.kar gśegs.pa'i mdo' ('Laṅkāvatārasūtra') and the 'Dam.chos pad.dkar' ('Saddharmapuṇḍarīkasūtra' V, 44):

> Śrāvakas do not pass into Nirvāṇa.
> They will all become Buddhas
> After having practised the Bodhisattva-life.

What, then, is the 'family of the followers of the Mahāyāna way of life'?

> Classification, essence, synonyms,
> Reason for the superiority over other families,
> Causal characteristic and distinctive marks[36]—these six topics
> Refer to the followers of the Mahāyāna way of life.

'Classification' here is twofold: the Self-existing[37] and (5a) the Evolved family.[38]

As to their respective 'essence', the Self-existing family has the power of setting up the Buddhadharmas,[39] is of beginningless time, and has been obtained by the very nature of all that is.[40] The Evolved family has the same power, but as a result of practising in the past the tenets of the good and wholesome.[41] Consequently both are endowed with the good fortune of Buddhahood.

The 'synonyms' of the term 'family' are seed, sphere and ultimate nature.

The 'reason for the superiority of the Mahāyāna over other families' is that those of Śrāvakas and Pratyekabuddhas are inferior, being purified only by the removal of one veil, namely, conflicting emotions.[42] The family of the followers of the Mahāyāna way of life is supreme, because it is purified by the removal of the double veil of conflicting emotions and primitive beliefs about reality.[43] Therefore this family is superior to and unsurpassed by all others.[44]

The 'causal characteristic' is the Awakened[45] and the Unawakened family.[46] The Awakened is characterized by the fact that the distinctive mark of the attainment of the goal (enlightenment) is visible, whereas in the Unawakened this is not visible, because the goal (enlightenment) has not yet been achieved.[47]

This awakening occurs when the family is free from adverse, and supported by favourable, conditions. Without this it is unawakened.

There are four adverse conditions: To be born in unfavourable circumstances[48] and without an inclination towards enlightenment; to be opinionated and to suffer from the evil of the double veil (of conflicting emotions and primitive beliefs about reality).

The favourable conditions are two. Outwardly, the teaching of the Noble Doctrine by others (5b) and inwardly, proper mindfulness,[49] aspiration for the good and wholesome[50] and so on.

The 'distinctive marks' are the signs which reveal the Bodhisattva family. As has been said in the 'Chos.bcu.pa'i mdo' ('Daśadharmaka-sūtra'):

> The family of judicious Bodhisattvas
> Is known by its signs
> As fire by its smoke
> And water by the ducks upon it.

The signs are that body and speech, independent of the influence of a spiritual friend, are by nature gentle and mind is very little affected by fraud and deceit, while there is love for all beings and inner purity. Thus in the 'Chos.bcu.pa'i mdo' ('Daśadharmakasūtra'):

> Gentle and not abusive,
> Without deceit and fraud,
> Full of love towards all beings—
> So is a Bodhisattva.

In other words, from time out of mind a Bodhisattva, in whatever he undertakes, acts out of compassion for all sentient beings, is devoted to the Mahāyāna, endures unheard-of hardships and practises the tenets of the good and wholesome which are the very nature of the Perfections.[51] In the 'mDo.sde.rgyan' ('Mahāyāna-sūtrālaṅkāra' III, 5) it is written:

> From the very beginning to apply oneself to one's work with compassion,
> Devoted interest[52] and patient endurance,[53]
> And to accomplish good—these virtues
> Are known as the distinctive marks of this family.

Under these circumstances, from among the five families, that of the followers of the Mahāyāna way of life possesses the proximate motive towards Buddhahood. Those of Śrāvakas and Pratyeka-buddhas, however, because they will only attain Buddhahood after a long time, possess the remote motive. The Dubious-family are those among whom some are in possession of the proximate, others of the remote, motive. Moreover the Cut-off family, who are intent on wandering in Saṃsāra, can ultimately attain enlightenment, because even they possess a very remote motive.

Therefore, since there exist these families in which sentient beings are grouped, beings (6a) are endowed with Buddha-nature. In this way, for the three reasons given above, it has been shown that there is Buddha-nature in all sentient beings.

Should you ask for a simile, the following will serve: As silver is found in and may be refined from its ore, sesame oil pressed from its seed and butter churned from milk, so in all beings may Buddhahood become a reality.

The first chapter, dealing with the Motive, from
The Jewel Ornament of Liberation or
The Wish-Fulfilling Gem of the
Noble Doctrine.

NOTES TO CHAPTER I

1. The Sanskrit original of this invocation, Mañjuśrī Kumārabhūta, is often translated 'Mañjuśrī the Youth'. This misses the associations the Tibetans have when they hear or read these words by which they understand the story of the Bodhisattva Mañjuśrī who as King Amba vowed to become a Bodhisattva. An allusion to this and to the Sūtra from which it has been taken is found in Atīśa's 'Bodhipathapradīpa', verses 25 seq., as well as on fol. 57b of this work.

2. Buddhist works open with an invocation of the Three Jewels by which in Hīnayāna Buddhism the Buddha is understood as the human teacher, the Dharma as his doctrine and the Sangha as the community of monks and nuns. sGam.po.pa, a follower of the Mahāyāna, gives a deeper interpretation. The Buddha is the indivisible unity of the Three Kāyas, of which the Dharmakāya represents the mental-spiritual realm, the Sambhogakāya the verbal-communicative realm, and the Nirmāṇakāya the overt action realm. The unity of these three Kāyas is termed Svābhāvikakāya (Tib. *ṅo.bo.ñid.kyi sku*), but should not be considered as an additional Kāya.

The Sangha are the eight foremost Bodhisattvas: Mañjuśrī, Vajrapāṇi, Avalokiteśvara, Kṣitigarbha, Nivaraṇaviṣkambhin,

Gaganagarbha, Maitreya, and Samantabhadra. The Dharma are the experiences of peace (*ži*, Skt. *śamatha*) and Nirvāṇa. This interpretation is given on fol. 42 seq.

3. *rtsa.bar gyur.pa bla.ma.* The *rtsa.ba'i bla.ma* as distinct from the *brgyud.pa'i bla.ma* who upholds the school tradition, instructs the pupil whose doubts are thus dispelled. He is set on the way so that by finding himself he may be able to help others. The necessity of a Guru is pointed out in the 'Lus.med mkha'.'gro'i chos.sde'i rnam. par bśad.pa chos.kyi ñiṅ.khu', fol. 4b: 'Venerable Mi.la.ras.pa said:

> "If farming is not done for its own sake,
> It is difficult to make others profit by it."'

These words show the necessity of a gifted teacher. Further, the best one is he who by comprehensive understanding of reality has found inner freedom and through his compassion is able to make others find it.

4. *raṅ.bžin*, Skt. *svabhāva*. This term must not be confused with what common sense calls 'the nature of a thing', which is the set of characteristics that belong to it. Unfortunately common sense is not clear about 'causal characteristics' belonging to a thing and 'primary characteristics' belonging to the states of that thing. See L. S. Stebbing, 'A Modern Introduction to Logic', p. 267. *raṅ.bžin* refers neither to the causal nor to the primary characteristics, but to that which cannot be conceptualized and which is also termed Śūnyatā. The world as our thoughts and beliefs about it is essentially a symbol of Śūnyatā or transcendence, which in Buddhism never becomes immanence. It is therefore possible to say that 'ultimate nature' is not ultimate (*raṅ.bžin.med*).

5. *rnam.pa*, Skt. *ākāra*. It is a characteristic mode of behaviour in relation to other things. See L. S. Stebbing, 'A Modern Introduction to Logic', p. 267.

6. *'khrul.pa*, Skt. *bhrānti*. Being synonymous with *gti.mug* (Skt. *moha*) and *ma.rig.pa* (Skt. *avidyā*) 'ignorance', it is essentially an emotive factor, forming a triad with *'dod.chags* (Skt. *rāga*) and *že.sdaṅ* (Skt. *dveṣa*). While *'dod.chags* and *že.sdaṅ* may be termed social affections and correspond to our likes and dislikes, *'khrul.pa* is a contemplative affection for which there is no equivalent in Western psychology. Further, *'dod.chags* and *že.sdaṅ* never work apart but always in conjunction with *gti.mug* (*ma.rig.pa*, *'khrul.pa*), while *'khrul.pa* can operate alone and without them. See 'Abhidharmakośa' II, 29, p. 167. Although essentially emotive, *'khrul.pa* is half-way between an emotion and a cognition. Its translation by 'error' has to be rejected,

because though etymologically it implies deviation, unlike error *'khrul.pa* does not imply culpability, since it does not suggest a guide, principle or the like to be followed. Similarly its translation by 'delusion' has to be rejected, because all that we divide into normal and delusive perceptions falls under the operation of *'khrul.pa.*

7. *mtshan.ñid,* Skt. *lakṣaṇa.* A primary characteristic is non-causal, though it is caused by the causal characteristic. See C. D. Broad, 'Mind and its Place in Nature', p. 432.

8. *sdug.bsṅal,* Skt. *duḥkha.* There is nothing pessimistic about Buddhism. The position of misery in human life is comparable to that of pain in an organism, indicating that something somewhere is not in order. Human life is goal-seeking, every step toward the goal bringing increasing happiness. Every goal-achievement has its appropriate reward of inner satisfaction and joy. Every deviation from this path violates the goal-seeking character of human life and is rewarded by suffering.

9. The three world spheres are Kāmadhātu, Rūpadhātu, and Ārūpyadhātu.

Primarily Kāmadhātu is the world of sensual desires and secondarily of sensuous objects. In this world sphere sentient beings have gross bodies and their thoughts are unconcentrated and utterly bewildered. To it belong the hells, the realm of spirits, the worlds of men and animals, and the six lower heavens of the Cāturmahārājikas, Trāyastriṃśas, Yāmas, Tuṣitas, Nirmāṇaratis, and Paranirmitavaśavartins. All these gods live and enjoy themselves in a very human way and are superior to man only by their powers, but not by their conduct or their chance of realizing liberation. See Chapters 2 and 4 of this work. 'Abhidharmakośa' III, 1, pp. 1 seq.; 69, p. 164; I, 22b–d, p. 43; II, 14, p. 132.

Rūpadhātu, lying above Kāmadhātu, is the realm of ethereal bodies where neither physical nor mental distress obtain, because of quiescence (*śamatha*) attained through meditative concentration (*dhyāna*) and because of the translucency (*accha, bhāsvara*) of bodies there. Rūpadhātu is the world of the four meditative concentrations (*dhyāna*). 'Abhidharmakośa' II, 12, pp. 129 seq.; III, 2, p. 2.

Ārūpyadhātu is the world of 'spiritual beings' which are absorbed in the contemplation of some unique idea such as the infinity of space, thought and vacuity. Or else they are submerged in a semi-ideational state where consciousness and its attendant functions are arrested. Although this world is said to be above Rūpadhātu, it cannot be placed anywhere. 'Abhidharmakośa' III, 3, p. 4; II, 14, pp. 132 seq. For the purely philosophical implications of Ārūpyadhātu see also my 'Philosophy and Psychology in the Abhidharma', pp. 193 seq., 337 seq.

10. The six types of beings are: denizens of hell, spirits, animals, human beings, lower gods and demons. See Chapter 5.

11. *ye.śes*, Skt. *jñāna*. For a full account see Chapter 20.

12. *rgyu*, Skt. *hetu*. 'Motive' is to be thought of simply as the power that moves an individual with a certain force. In this way it may be a drive which impels us on to a destination, but we are also drawn and pulled to a goal as yet unrealized. *rgyu* is a thoroughly dynamic term which implies both a drive and a goal. It has nothing to do with 'causes', whether they be material, efficient, formal or final. *rgyu* might be rendered freely as the goal-seeking character of life.

13. *rten*, Skt. *āśraya, ādhāra*. See Chapter 2.

14. *rkyen*, Skt. *pratyaya*. See Chapter 3.

15. *thabs*, Skt. *upāya*. See Chapters 4–19.

16. *'bras.bu*, Skt. *phala*. See Chapter 20.

17. *'phrin.las*, Skt. *samudācāra*. See Chapter 21.

18. *blo.ldan*, Skt. *matimān*. There is an intimate relation between *blo* (Skt. *mati*) and *śes.rab* (Skt. *prajñā*). *śes.rab* is discriminating awareness arising from wisdom, which paves the way to transcending awareness (*ye.śes*, Skt. *jñāna*). Transcending awareness alone experiences reality in its wholeness and is not dismembered by the description and acquaintance of ordinary knowledge. Life in a normal man is controlled by ignorance (*ma.rig.pa*, *avidyā*) which prevents discriminating awareness (*śes.rab*, *prajñā*) from developing. Undeveloped awareness is termed *blo* (Skt. *mati*). See 'Abhidharmakośa' I, 2, p. 3; II, 24, p. 154.

19. *rtog.med*, (*nirvikalpa*). Mentality, being an emergent characteristic, comprises several stages of which *rnam.par rtog.pa* (*vikalpa*), introduces the division into subject and object. Though this division is not obtained by inference, it is an interpretation which leads away from immediate experience. Apart from the epistemological conception, *vikalpa* also means 'being divided against oneself'. This should never be lost sight of, because it gives the epistemological problem a particular flavour. Emergence of mentality is described as follows:

'The twelve elements of the Law of Interdependent Origination (Pratītyasamutpāda) show that ignorance (*ma.rig.pa*) is the source of progressive, and knowledge (*rig.pa*) of regressive, development in which ignorance recedes. When therefore the momentary consciousness series (*śes.pa skad.cig.ma*) is investigated it is found to swing between the two poles. From the higher point of view as soon as the mind deviates from its own state of independence and self-sufficiency it becomes ignorant about Reality and its view of the latter is blurred. By this deviation which continues unhaltingly it then makes mistakes about the relation between the cause and effect of any action because its image of things is blurred. The first aspect is termed *rtog.pa* (*kalpanā*) "creative activity" or the most subtle stage, because this bewildered and active consciousness is and has always been uninterruptedly at work. The second aspect, postulating a mind dealing with sense fields and sense perceptions or with subject and object and clinging to duality, is characterized by a thorough-going split and termed *rnam.par rtog.pa* (*vikalpa*) or the subtle state. From this duality arises an unlimited variety of numbers or shapes. The infinite possibilities of a bewildering variety of appearance, all that becomes visible or is heard about in the three world-spheres, is termed *kun.tu rtog.pa* (*parikalpita*) "delusiveness" or the coarse state. Saṃsāra is built up from these three conditions. By understanding the nature of this momentary consciousness series oscillating in the manner described, the stream of creative activity (*rtog.pa'i rgyun*) is stopped; bewilderment is disentangled and this is Nirvāṇa.' 'rTen. 'brel kho.bo lugs.kyi khrid chos thams.cad.kyi sñiṅ.po len.pa', fol. 1 seq.

20. *chos.ñid* (*dharmatā*). It is synonymous with *raṅ.bžin* (*svabhāva*).

21. *rigs.chad.*(*kyi*) *rigs*. I have not been able to find a corresponding Sanskrit term. Sanskrit uses *agotraka* or *agotrastha*, 'having no family', 'not staying in any family'. In introducing a different term, sGam.po. pa was mindful of the humane idea expressed in 'Abhidharmakośa' IV, 80c, and its 'Bhāṣya' (p. 175), namely, that the foundation of all that is good and wholesome, which may temporarily have broken down, can be again restored so that none is lost for ever.

22. *ma.ṅes.*(*pa'i*) *rigs*, Skt. *aniyatagotra*.

23. *ñan.thos.*(*kyi*) *rigs*, Skt. *śrāvakagotra*.

24. *raṅ.rgyal.rigs* (*raṅ.saṅs.rgyas.kyi rigs*), Skt. *pratyekabuddhagotra*.

25. *theg.pa chen.po'i rigs*, Skt. *mahāyānagotra*.

26. *bag.chags*, Skt. *vāsanā*.

27. *yid.kyi raṅ.bžin.gyi lus*, Skt. *manomayakāya*. This means that a different spiritual outlook, which may lead to a different spiritual level, has been achieved. It does not imply the creation of a new body. See also 'Vijñaptimātratāsiddhi', pp. 271; 503.

28. *zag.pa.med.pa'i las*, Skt. *anāsravakarma*. It is activity which is not dominated by emotional instability.

29. *zag.pa.med.pa'i tiṅ.ṅe.'dzin*, Skt. *anāsravasamādhi*. It is the last of the four stages of meditative concentration. See 'Vijñaptimātratāsiddhi', p. 510.

30. This simile is taken from 'Saddharmapuṇḍarīkasūtra', p. 127.

31. *sku*, Skt. *kāya*. The Tibetan term *sku* as distinct from *lus* refers not to the physical aspect but to that ineffable factor in experience before we conceive of the perceived object as a 'body'. Sanskrit texts make no distinction between *kāya*, *deha* and *śarīra*.

32. *gsuṅ*, Skt. *vāk*.

33. *thugs*, Skt. *citta*.

34. Literal quotation from 'Saddharmapuṇḍarīkasūtra', pp. 128 seq.

35. *byaṅ.chub.kyi sems*, Skt. *bodhicitta*. What is necessary for changing an ordinary attitude into a new one with a spiritual goal, is discussed in Chapters 8 and 9.

36. *rtags*, Skt. *liṅga*.

37. *raṅ.bžin.gyis gnas.pa'i rigs*, Skt. *prakṛtistha*. 'Bodhisattvabhūmi', p. 3; 'Uttaratantra' I, 149

38. *yaṅ.dag.par bsgrubs.pa'i rigs*, Skt. *samudānīta*. 'Bodhisattvabhūmi', p. 3; 'Uttaratantra' I, 149.

39. The Buddhadharmas comprise ten powers (*bala*, Tib. *stobs*), four intrepidities (*vaiśāradya*, Tib. *mi.'jigs.pa*), three types of inspection (*smṛtyupasthāna*, Tib. *dran.pa ñer.bžag*), and Great Compassion (*mahākaruṇā*, Tib. *sñiṅ.rje chen.po*). See 'Abhidharmakośa' VII, 28, pp. 66 seq.

40. *chos.ñid.kyis thob.pa*, Skt. *dharmatāpratilabdha*. 'Bodhisattvabhūmi', p. 3. 'Vijñaptimātratāsiddhi', p. 562.

41. *dge.ba'i rtsa.ba*, Skt. *kuśalamūla*. 'Bodhisattvabhūmi', p. 3. 'Vijñaptimātratāsiddhi', p. 326. 'Abhidharmakośa' II, 25; and 'Bhāṣya' (p. 160).

42. *ñon.moṅs.pa'i sgrib.pa*, Skt. *kleśāvaraṇa*.

43. *śes.bya.ba'i sgrib.pa*, Skt. *jñeyāvaraṇa*.

44. 'Bodhisattvabhūmi', p. 3.

45. *sad.pa'i rigs*.

46. *mi.sad.pa'i rigs*.

47. 'Bodhisattvabhūmi', p. 3.

48. A detailed account is given in Chapter 2.

49. *tshul.bžin yid.la byed.pa*, Skt. *yoniśomanasikāra*.

50. *dge.ba'i chos.la 'dun.pa*, Skt. *kuśaladharmacchanda*. 'Vijñaptimātratāsiddhi', pp. 310, 320, 323, 344. 'Abhidharmakośa' V, 16, p. 36.

51. For a detailed analysis see Chapters 12 seq.

52. *mos.pa*, Skt. *adhimokṣa*.

53. *bzod.pa*, Skt. *kṣānti*. Being one of the Perfections this is discussed in Chapter 14.

2

THE WORKING BASIS

(b) 'The working basis is the most precious human body.'[1]

SINCE ALL BEINGS are endowed with Buddha-nature, do the other five forms of existence such as denizens of hell, spirits and the like, have the power to attain Buddhahood? No. The expression 'precious human body' means the body representing a unique occasion and effecting the right juncture and mind possessing three kinds of confidence. There are auspicious resources in an individual who is the working basis for the attainment of Buddhahood. The following may guide you:

Five headings relate to the excellent working basis:
Unique occasion, right juncture,
Trust, longing and lucidity.
The former two belong to the body, the latter three to mind.

'Unique occasion'[2] means to be free from the eight unfavourable conditions, listed in the 'mDo dran.pa ñer.bžag' ('Saddharmasmṛtyupasthāna'):

Denizens of hell, spirits, animals,
Members of the border tribes, long-living Gods,
Those with erroneous views and those born in a period where there is no Buddha
And the stupid. These represent the eight unfavourable conditions.

How are they unfavourable? It is the nature of denizens of hell to be constantly pained, of spirits (6b) to have their minds tormented and of animals to be utterly foolish. These three groups, ignorant of modesty and shame, have developed a wicked character and therefore cannot take the Dharma to heart.[3]

'Long-living Gods' means those who are imperceptive;[4] and since in this and its attendant state consciousness functions are interrupted in their proper working, the Dharma cannot be taken to heart. It also refers to the gods of the world of sensuality, because they are long-lived when compared to men. And it means that life as a god always represents an unfavourable condition, because the gods living in temporal happiness, do not strive for the good and wholesome.[5]

Therefore, it is only here and now in this slight misery of human existence that we find what is valuable for spiritual development; in other words, discontent with Saṃsāra and compassion towards all sentient beings are born; our haughtiness is curbed; and while refraining from evil deeds, we delight in whatever is good and wholesome. In the 'Byaṅ.chub.sems.dpa'i spyod.pa.la 'jug.pa' ('Bodhicaryāvatāra' VI, 21) it is written:

> Still another value of misery is
> That discontent dispels one's haughtiness;
> That compassion towards beings in Saṃsāra is born;
> And that one abstains from evil and delights in the good and wholesome.[5a]

Thus these four forms of existence do not present a unique occasion.

It may, however, be noted that although the members of the border tribes are human beings, they are spoken of as unsuited, because it is difficult to find a decent man among them.[6]

Those with erroneous views are equally unsuited, because they do not recognize that the good and wholesome is the cause of the temporal happiness of heaven and the ultimate bliss of liberation.[7]

He who is born in a world where there is no Buddha, is equally unsuited, because there is no one to show him what is, and what is not, to be done.[8]

So are the stupid, because they are unable to know for themselves what has been said to be good or evil.[9]

Thus, to be free from the eight unfavourable conditions is a most excellent and unique occasion.

'Right juncture'[10] (7a) refers to five events which affect us directly and to another five occurring through others and affecting us mediately, so that there are a total of ten. The five affecting us directly are:

> As a human being to be born in the central country and to possess all senses,
> Not to revert to inexpiable evil deeds and to have confidence in the foundation of spiritual life.[11]

'As a human being' means to have the same fate and fortune as other men and to have either the male or female organs.[12]

'To be born in the central country' implies a land where we can rely on virtuous people.[13]

'To possess all senses' is not to be an idiot or a mute and to have the good fortune to be able to realize the good and wholesome.[14]

'To have confidence in the foundation of spiritual life' is to believe that the Disciplinary Code (Vinaya) of the Noble Doctrine proclaimed by The Teacher (Buddha) is the foundation of all positive qualities.[15]

'Not to revert to inexpiable evil deeds' means not to commit heinous crimes in this life.[16]

The five events occurring through others and affecting us mediately are: (i) The appearance of a Buddha in this world;[17] (ii) the teaching of the Noble Doctrine;[18] (iii) the stableness of the elements of existence taught in the Noble Doctrine;[19] (iv) the attuning to this stableness[20] and (v) to have active compassion and love for the sake of others.[21]

Thus effecting the right juncture of ten events, five of which affect us directly and five, occurring through others, mediately, is most excellent.

These two factors of unique occasion and right juncture meet in the precious human body.

The latter is called precious, because it is similar to the Wish-Fulfilling Gem, as difficult to obtain and very useful. The 'Byaṅ.chub.sems.dpa'i sde.snod' ('Bodhisattvapiṭaka') says:

> It is difficult to become a human being,
> To receive the Noble Doctrine
> And for a Buddha to appear.

In the 'sÑiṅ.rje padma dkar.po'i mdo' ('Mahākaruṇāpuṇḍarīkasūtra'):

> It is difficult to be born human (7b) and to win the perfect and unique occasion. It is hard for a Buddha to appear in the world. It is difficult to have an aspiration for the good and wholesome, and to fulfil the vow of acquiring the good.

In the ''Phags.pa sDoṅ.po bkod.pa'i mdo' ('Gaṇḍavyūhasūtra', p. 116):

> It is difficult to turn away from the eight unfavourable conditions; to obtain birth as a human being and to win the pure perfect unique occasion;[22] it is hard for a Buddha to appear in the world. It is difficult to have all senses; to hear the Buddha's Dharma; to associate with virtuous people; to find truly spiritual friends; to receive methodical instruction and to live a proper life. It is difficult in the world of men to realize the meaning of the elements of existence taught in the Buddha's Dharma.[23]

And in the 'Byaṅ.chub.sems.dpa'i spyod.pa.la 'jug.pa' ('Bodhicaryāvatāra' I, 4):

> Unique occasion and right juncture are very hard to obtain.

A simile to illustrate the difficulty is given in the 'Byaṅ.chub. sems.dpa'i spyod.pa.la 'jug.pa' ('Bodhicaryāvatāra'):

> The Exalted One said:
> Just as it is difficult for a tortoise to put its neck
> Into the hole of a yoke tossed about in a great ocean,
> So also it is very hard to obtain existence as a human being.

The following is taken from the 'Yaṅ.dag.pa'i luṅ':[24]

> If this great earth should become water, a yoke thrown into it by a man would be tossed about to the four cardinal points by the wind. In a thousand years a one-eyed tortoise would not be able to put its neck into it (how much less chance is there for a being to be born human) (8a).

The term 'individual' is used because a human existence is difficult to win by those who are born in the three lower forms of life (denizens of hell, spirits, animals).

The reason for this difficulty is that the body which represents a unique occasion and effects the right juncture is obtained by the accumulation of merits. Those who are born in the three lower forms of life, however, not knowing how to accumulate the merits that accrue from good deeds, always act and live evilly. Therefore a human body can only be acquired by one who, though he is born in the three lower forms of existence, has very little evil and possesses an accumulation of merits accruing from good deeds that are to be experienced in some other form of life.

The great usefulness is pointed out in the 'Byaṅ.chub.sems.dpa'i spyod.pa.la 'jug.pa' ('Bodhicaryāvatāra' I, 4):

> Since man's aim is achieved.

'Man' is in Sanskrit *puruṣa*, which means by etymology to have power or ability. Since within the body which presents a unique occasion and effects the right juncture, there is the power or the ability to secure rebirth in higher forms of life and also to realize ultimate good, we speak of 'man'. Further, since this power is of three kinds, strong, mediocre and weak, man also is of three types, excellent, mediocre and inferior. This is declared in the 'Byaṅ.chub. lam.gyi sgron.ma' ('Bodhipathapradīpa', 1):

> Man is to be known in three ways:
> As inferior, mediocre and excellent.

The inferior man, without falling into the three lower forms of existence, has the capacity of attaining the state of either god or man.

He who by any means whatsoever
Provides the pleasures of Saṃsāra
For himself alone,
Is called an inferior man.[25]

The mediocre man can win a state of peace and happiness after he has freed himself from Saṃsāra.

He who turns his back to the pleasures of the world
And abstains from evil deeds,
But provides only for his own peace,
Is called a mediocre man.[26]

The excellent man (8b) has the capacity of attaining Buddhahood so that he is able to work for the benefit of all sentient beings.

He who seriously wants to dispel
All the misery of others,
Because in the stream of his own being[27] he has understood the nature of misery,
Is an excellent man.[28]

About the great usefulness of the human body the Teacher Candragomin has said:

Who can deprive of his fruit a man
Who, having obtained a human body, has gone to the end of the ocean of birth,
Who sows the good and wholesome as the seed of excellent enlightenment
And who has greater virtues than the Wish-Fulfilling Gem?
The Path[29] which can be traversed only by a man of great inner strength,
Cannot be followed by gods or serpent demons,
Not even by Garuḍas, Vidyādharas, Kinnaras, or Uragas.

This human body which presents a unique occasion and effects the right juncture, has the power to reject evil and to accomplish good, to cross the ocean of Saṃsāra, to follow the path towards enlightenment and to obtain perfect Buddhahood. Therefore it is superior to other forms of life such as gods and serpent demons, and it is even better than the Wish-Fulfilling Gem. It is called 'precious' because of the difficulty of obtaining this human body and because of its great usefulness.

Yet, though difficult to obtain and very useful, it easily breaks down, because there are many causes of death and without waiting it passes on to the future. Thus in the 'Byaṅ.chub.sems.dpa'i spyod.pa.la 'jug.pa' ('Bodhicaryāvatāra' II, 59):

> Living in pleasure and thinking:
> 'This moment I shall not die', is unwise.
> One should think: 'The time will certainly come
> When I shall become nothing.'

Therefore, because of the difficulty of its attainment, of the easiness of its breaking down (9a), and of its great usefulness, we should think of the body as a boat and by its means escape from the ocean of Saṃsāra. As is written:[30]

> Standing in the boat of the human body,
> You should cross the great flood of misery.
> Since later this boat is difficult to get,
> Do not sleep now, you fool.

Or, conceiving the body as a horse we should gallop on it away from the road of the misery of Saṃsāra. As is stated:

> Riding the human body as a racehorse,
> One should gallop away from the misery of Saṃsāra.

Or, thinking of the body as a servant we should urge it on to good and wholesome deeds. As is declared:

> This body of men like ourselves
> Is only to be used as a servant.

He who does so must have confidence, without which positive qualities do not grow in our continuously changing stream of life. This is affirmed in the 'Chos.bcu.pa'i mdo' ('Daśadharmakasūtra'):

> Positive qualities do not grow
> In men without confidence,
> Just as a green sprout
> Does not shoot from a burnt seed.

And in the 'Saṅs.rgyas phal.po che'i mdo' ('Buddhāvataṃsaka'):

> Worldly people with little confidence
> Are unable to understand the Buddha's enlightenment.

Therefore confidence has to be awakened, as is stated in the ''Phags.pa rgya.che rol.pa' ('Lalitavistara', p. 70):

> Ānanda, you must use confidence. That is the request of the Tathāgata.

It is of three kinds:[31] trusting,[32] longing[33] and lucid.[34]

'Trusting confidence' originates in the inevitable relation between Karma and its results, in the Truths of misery and its origination (9b). It is the conviction that as a result of good and wholesome deeds the pleasures, and of evil deeds the misery, of the world of sensuality arises, while through subliminal activity[35] the pleasures of the two worlds higher than that of sensuality emerge;[36] it is the conviction that the five constituents of sullied individual existence,[37] called the Truth of Misery, are obtained by having lived a life ruled by Karma and conflicting emotions, which two factors are called the Truth of the Origination of Misery.[38]

'Longing confidence' means that having recognized enlightenment to be something particularly valuable, we study the path for its attainment with eagerness.

'Lucid confidence' starts with the Three Jewels. It is a lucid mind interested in and eager for the Jewels of the Buddha as the teacher of the path, of the Dharma as being the path and of the Saṅgha as the spiritual friends helping to realize that path. Thus in the 'Chos.mṅon.pa' ('Abhidharma'):[39]

> What is confidence?—It is conviction about Karma, its results, the Truth and the Jewels; it is longing and a lucid mind.

Further, in the 'Rin.chen 'phreṅ.ba' ('Ratnāvalī') it is stated:

> He who does not out of acquisitiveness, hatred, fear
> And delusion forsake the Dharma,
> Is called a man with the courage of his convictions;
> He is an excellent vessel for ultimate good.

Here 'not to forsake the Dharma out of acquisitiveness' means not to renounce it from cupidity. For instance, someone might say: 'I will give you lavish food, wealth, women and royalty, but you must forsake the Dharma.' Yet you will not renounce it.

'Not to forsake the Dharma out of hatred' means not to renounce it from anger (10a). Suppose someone has done me great harm and I have the opportunity of hurting him in return. Yet I will not forsake the Dharma (and retaliate).

'Not to forsake the Dharma out of fear' means not to renounce it from terror. For instance, someone might threaten: 'If you do not forsake the Dharma I shall order three hundred soldiers daily to cut five ounces of flesh from your body.' Yet you will not renounce it.

'Not to forsake the Dharma out of delusion' means not to renounce it from stupidity. Suppose, someone argues: 'Neither Karma, its results nor the Three Jewels are true. What is the use of your practising the Dharma? Renounce it.' Yet you will not do so.

Thus he who proves his confidence under these four conditions is called a man with the courage of his convictions; and he is an excellent vessel for the realization of ultimate good.

When these three kinds of confidence are present, infinite benefits arise: the attitude of an excellent man is formed; the unfavourable conditions are given up; the senses are keen and bright; ethics and manners[40] are not violated; emotional instability is overcome; the realm of Māra is transcended; the path of liberation is gained; extensive merits are accumulated; many Buddhas are seen; there is the support of the Buddhas and other such inconceivably positive qualities are acquired. So also in the 'dKon.mchog ta.la'i gzuṅs' ('Ratnolkā-nāma-dhāraṇī'):

> The attitude of great men is developed
> When one has confidence in the Victorious One and in His Dharma,
> In the life and work of the Sons of The Buddha
> And in unsurpassable enlightenment.

Further, when there is confidence, the Buddhas, the Exalted Ones, come near (10b) and teach him the Dharma. As is stated in the 'Byaṅ.chub.sems.dpa'i sde.snod' ('Bodhisattvapiṭaka'):

> Thus when the Buddhas, the Exalted Ones, have recognized a Bodhisattva with the courage of his convictions as a worthy vessel for the Buddhadharmas,[41] they approach and teach him the way of a Bodhisattva.

In this way, the precious human body, which presents a uniquc occasion and effects the right juncture, and the human mind possessing three kinds of confidence, are the individual or the working basis for the attainment of unsurpassable enlightenment.

The second chapter, dealing with the Working Basis,
from the Jewel Ornament of Liberation or
The Wish-Fulfilling Gem of the
Noble Doctrine.

NOTES TO CHAPTER 2

1. See Chapter 1, p. 2.
2. *dal*, Skt. *ksaṇa*. The same definition is given in the 'rDzogs.pa chen.po kloṅ.chen.sñiṅ.thig.gi sṅon.'gro'i khrid yig kun.bzaṅ.

bla.ma'i žal.luṅ' (The Instruction in the Preparation for the Essence of the Great Ultimate or Great Achievement coming from the Mouth of Guru Samantabhadra), fol. 2a: 'On the whole, not to be born in the eight unfavourable conditions and to be able to realize the Noble Doctrine, is unique occasion. The reverse are the eight unfavourable conditions.' In the following chapters this work will be referred to by its abbreviated title 'rDzogs chen kun.bzaṅ bla.ma'. The verse quoted by sGam.po.pa is also cited in the 'rDzogs chen kun.bzaṅ bla.ma' and in Padma dkar.po's 'sṄon.'gro'i zin.bris' (Synopsis of the Preparatory Stage), fol. 2a.

3. In the 'rDzogs chen kun.bzaṅ bla.ma' these three lower forms of existence are described thus, fol. 12a: 'To be born in hell is an unfavourable condition for practising the Dharma, because such beings live in constant pain from heat and cold. So is the state of spirits because they suffer the pain of hunger and thirst and of animals and because they live in the misery of servitude and of harming each other.'

4. *'du.śes.med.pa*, Skt. *asaṃjñin*. The state in which these gods live is the fourth Ārūpya-meditation. They are mentioned in 'Vijñaptimātratāsiddhi', p. 283, and in 'Abhidharmakośa' II, 41, pp. 199 seq. where certain problems of a logical nature are discussed. See also 'Triṃśikā', p. 34, and my 'Philosophy and Psychology in the Abhidharma', p. 273.

5. In the 'rDzogs chen kun.bzaṅ bla.ma', fol. 12a, the same definition of *'du.śes.med.pa* is given as by sGam.po.pa, but on fol. 12b is added: 'By practising a meditative absorption in which no sense of good and evil obtains and conceiving this state as liberation, they are born as imperceptive gods and stay in this absorption for many great aeons. But when the Karma which effected this state has become exhausted, on account of their erroneous view (of conceiving a passing meditative state as final liberation), they are reborn in the lower forms of existence. Hence this state is an unfavourable condition for practising the Dharma.'

5a. Anyone who is not conversant with the multiple meaning content of Buddhist technical terms, is likely to misunderstand this passage and to read into it such opinions as are held by certain religionists, that suffering is a blessing in disguise and essential for the achievement of sanctity. Actually the term *sdug.bsṅal*, usually translated by 'misery' and 'unsatisfactoriness', not only indicates an unpleasant and often painful feeling tone, it also implies a 'problem situation' or what the psychologist (not necessarily Freudian) calls a 'conflict'. In this context sGam.po.pa's statement may be compared with J. Dewey's dictum, 'Conflict is the gadfly of thought'. It cannot be emphasized too strongly that Buddhism never mistook an acceptance of misery and of human plight for a duty to inflict suffering on others.

6. In the 'rDzogs chen kun.bzaṅ bla.ma', fol. 12a, is stated: 'To be born in the tribal area is an unfavourable condition for practising the Dharma, because there the doctrine of the Buddha does not obtain.' On fol. 12b a more exhaustive explanation is given: 'kLa.klo is a designation of the inhabitants of any of the thirty-two border regions beginning with kLo.kha.khra. It is the habit of the kLa.klo to call killing a virtue and so they count the slaughter of living beings as something good. Although the kLa.klos of the border regions look like human beings, their minds do not work properly and so they cannot be turned toward the Noble Doctrine.—Those who marry their mothers, following an evil practice of their ancestors, live a life contrary to the Dharma. Since it is a rule that those who live a life of vice by being highly expert in killing living beings, hunting deer and so forth, go into lower forms of existence, the status of being a tribesman is an unfavourable condition.' In his 'sÑon.'gro'i zin.bris', fol. 2a, Padma dkar.po remarks: 'With respect to their doctrines the tribesmen are tigers and leopards; with respect to their countries they are wild hordes and, though they appear in human form, like animals they do not know what may and must not be done.' The Persian practice of marrying one's mother is referred to in 'Abhidharmakośa' IV, 68, p. 147.

7. *log.lta*, Skt. *mithyādṛṣṭi*. Above all, to deny the relation between Karma and its effects is considered erroneous. 'Abhidharmakośa' IV, 79, p. 171. According to the 'rDzogs chen kun.bzaṅ bla.ma', fol. 13a: 'On the whole, the views of eternalism and annihilation which are outside the Buddha's doctrine are wrong. Those who thus deceive themselves have no interest in the true doctrine and are in poor condition to practise the Noble Doctrine. Here in Tibet, ever since the Second Buddha from O.rgyan (Padmasambhava) has entrusted its protection to the twelve brTan.ma, there are no such believers. But since there are Buddhists who lean to similar beliefs and who assume an enduring self (*pudgala*), they present an unfavourable condition for realizing the Noble Doctrine in a proper way. An example is offered by Bhikṣu Legs.pa'i.skar.ma who, although he had attended the Exalted One for twenty-five years, had no confidence and due to his erroneous view was finally reborn as a spirit in a flower-garden.'

8. In the 'rDzogs chen kun.bzaṅ bla.ma', fol. 13a, is stated: 'A

world without a Buddha means to be born in a dark age. To be born in those empty spheres into which no Buddha has come, is an unfavourable condition because not even the name of the Three Jewels is heard there and the Noble Doctrine does not appear.'

9. 'rDzogs chen kun.bzaṅ bla.ma', fol. 13a seq.: 'If one is born as a *lkugs.pa*, one's stream of life is unsuited for work and hence one has not the ability to hear, study, practise and realize the Dharma. The term *lkugs.pa*, on the whole, designates those who are mute (and dumb). They present an unfavourable condition, because they are deficient in the human characteristics of speech and understanding. Those who are mentally *lkugs.pa* present an unfavourable condition because due to complete stupidity they cannot understand the message of the Dharma.'

10. *'byor*, Skt. *sampad.*

11. In the 'rDzogs chen kun.bzaṅ bla.ma,' fol. 13b, this verse is attributed to Nāgārjuna.

12. The 'rDzogs chen kun.bzaṅ bla.ma', fol. 13b seq., stresses the 'right juncture of the working basis of a human body' (*mi'i lus rten.gyi 'byor.pa*) in the following words: 'To realize the peace afforded by the True and Noble Doctrine it is absolutely necessary to have become a human being. If one has not obtained a human body, it may be argued that existence as an animal is the best type of life among the three lower forms of existence. But the animals which are found in the countries of men, however beautiful and valuable they may be, do not even understand the words: "If you say Oṃ-maṇi-padme-hūṃ once, you will become a Buddha", and cannot repeat them. If they are about to die from cold they know no better than to wait crouching for death. But if one is a human being, however weak one may be, one finds a cave, collects fuel, kindles a fire and knows how to warm one's face and hands. Since animals do not know how to do this they cannot realize the Dharma. Although gods and other divine beings possess beautiful bodies, they have not the good fortune of receiving the most perfect Doctrine in their form of existence, because they are not a suitable vessel for preserving one of the two forms of the Prātimokṣa.' For Prātimokṣa see Chapter 8 of this work.

13. As long as Buddhism flourished in India, the central country was Budhgaya, where The Buddha attained enlightenment and there were some twenty-four centres of teaching (*gnas.chen ñer.bži*). sGam.po.pa, as the text shows, calls a central country any place where spiritual values are alive. Padma dkar.po says in his 'sÑon. 'gro'i zin.bris', fol. 2a: 'With respect to the country, Budhgaya and the other centres in India are the places where the doctrine of

The Teacher is pure.' A more exhaustive definition is given in the 'rDzogs chen kun.bzaṅ bla.ma', fol. 14a seq.: 'The central country means the physical and spiritual centres. The former is Budhgaya (*rdo.rje.gdan*) in India south of Tibet, the place where a thousand Buddhas in an auspicious aeon have found enlightenment, which even in a thousand aeons does not perish and is beyond the harmful influences of the elements, which remains like a mould cast into the sky, and which is said to be adorned in its centre by the Bodhi-tree. This is the physical centre of the important cities of the sacred country. Spiritual centre means any place where the teaching of The Buddha, the Noble Doctrine, obtains. Where this is not found, the country is a wild one. After The Buddha, as long as the teaching existed in India, that country was both the physical and spiritual centre. Since nowadays it has been reported that Budhgaya has been taken by the infidels and that the teaching is no more, India is spiritually a wild country. Tibet, the land of the snow mountains, on the other hand, was a wild country before The Buddha, because civilization was low and the teaching had not spread. Later with the spread of civilization many incarnate rulers came and during the reign of Lha.tho.ri.gñan.bstan the sPaṅ.skoṅ.phyag.brgya.ma and the Sātstsha'i.brkos.pho fell from Heaven and so Tibet attained the status of the spiritual centre.'

14. 'rDzogs chen kun.bzaṅ bla.ma', fol. 15a seq.: 'If one is deficient in any of the five senses, one is not suited for the discipline of religious life. Since one has not the good fortune of meeting the Body of the Victorious One, the place of devotion and reverence, of seeing or hearing the precious Scriptures, the realm for study and pondering, one is not a suitable vessel for the true doctrine.'

15. 'rDzogs chen kun.bzaṅ bla.ma', fol. 15b: 'Since it is impossible to protect ourselves against the misery of Saṃsāra and evil existences if we have no confidence in the teaching of The Buddha, the place of confidence, and if we only have faith in the great power of other worldly gods and serpent demons and in the teaching of outsiders and infidels, the attainment of confidence which is the knowledge that the teaching of the Victorious One in Śāstras and Realizations, is the cause of being protected and the unfailing vessel for the true Dharma.'

16. 'rDzogs chen kun.bzaṅ bla.ma', fol. 15b: 'The term "reverting to inexpiable evil deeds" is usually applied to those who having been born in families who live by hunting, prostitution, and other forms of gaining a livelihood, from childhood on commit inexpiable evil deeds. But it really includes all actions contrary to the Dharma,

whether done by body, speech or mind. Since one is very likely to be born in such a family in the future, it is necessary not to act contrary to the Dharma.'

17. 'rDzogs chen kun.bzaṅ bla.ma', fol. 15b: 'There is no Dharma for those born in an unenlightened age without a Buddha, but since He has come in this age, The Teacher is a particular right juncture.'

18. 'rDzogs chen kun.bzaṅ bla.ma', fol. 16a: 'Since there is no advantage if the teaching is not propounded even if a Buddha has come, because the Dharmacakra has been turned in three ways, the teaching is the right juncture of the Noble Doctrine.'

19. *chos bstan.rnams gnas.pa*, Skt. *dharmāṇām (yathopa)diṣṭānāṃ sthiti*. sGam.po.pa here gives a deeper interpretation than is found in other works. Obviously he had in mind the famous passage, 'Whether Tathāgatas appear in the world or not, the nature of the elements of existence remains unaltered'. See for instance 'Abhidharmakośa' III, 28, p. 77; 'Saṃyuttanikāya' II, 25; 'Sekoddeśaṭīkā', p. 71; 'Daśabhūmikasūtra', p. 65.

The 'rDzogs chen kun.bzaṅ bla.ma', fol. 16a, declares: 'Since there is no advantage if the teaching disappears even if the Dharma has been explained, because the measure of duration is fulfilled the continuation of the teaching is the right juncture of time.'

20. *chos gnas.pa.rnams.kyi rjes.su 'jug.pa*, Skt. *sthitadharmānusārin*. Here too sGam.po.pa gives a different interpretation. Since the nature of all elements of existence is such that it has never been created and since it is wrong to introduce a division into Reality, everything is attuned to this ultimate nature or Reality. The 'rDzogs chen kun.bzaṅ bla.ma', fol. 16a, has: 'Since there is no advantage if one does not follow the teaching even if it continues to exist, the entering the gate of the teaching is in itself a right juncture.'

21. 'rDzogs chen kun.bzaṅ bla.ma', fol. 16a: 'Since one does not know the ultimate essence of the Dharma if one is not taken hold of by spiritual friends who are a suitable condition for such realization, even if one follows the doctrine, the fact of being supported by them is the right juncture of deep compassion.' Padma dkar.po, in his 'sÑon.'gro'i zin.bris', fol. 2b, agrees with the 'rDzogs chen kun.bzaṅ bla.ma'. He explains the five topics as meaning the appearance of a Buddha in this world, the teaching of the Dharma by him, the continuation of his teaching, the initiation into his teaching and the acquisition of all that is conducive to practising the Dharma.

22. The Sanskrit text has *durlabhā ksaṇasampadviśuddhiḥ*. However, the Tibetan translator did not understand *sampad* as *'byor* (see note 10), but as *phun.sum.tshogs.pa* 'most perfect'.

23. *chos daṅ rjes.su mthun.pa'i chos.la nan.tan byed.pa,* Skt. *dharmā-nudharmapratipatti.* The double connotation of dharma has to be noted. The first *dharma* (*chos*) refers to the Doctrine proclaimed by The Buddha, while the second *dharma* (*chos*) relates to the elements of existence discussed in the Doctrine. See 'Vijñaptimātratāsiddhi', p. 624; 'Madhyamakavṛtti', pp. 488, 579.

24. This Sūtra is also known as Yaṅ.dag rtsa.ba'i luṅ. It is not found in the bKa'.'gyur. The same simile is used and extensively elaborated in the 'rDzogs chen kun.bzaṅ bla.ma', fol. 22a seq. As a further example of the difficulty in obtaining a human body, verse 59 of Nāgārjuna's 'Suhṛllekhā', using the same images, is mentioned. In his 'sÑon.'gro'i zin.bris', fol. 2b, Padma dkar.po also employs this simile and adduces another one from the 'Garbhāvakrāntisūtra': 'When one scatters a handful of mustard seed over the eye of a needle suspended in midair, it may happen that a seed passes into the eye of the needle, but it is much more difficult to obtain the body of a human being.'

25. 'Bodhipathapradīpa', 3.

26. ibid. 4.

27. *rgyud,* Skt. *santati, santāna.* An individual, which in other systems is imagined as a combination of matter and a permanent mental principle (*ātman*), is in reality a continuously changing stream of that which from one viewpoint is believed to be matter and from another a mind. However, what we call the mental and the material occurs in a unity of organization. Organization is something dynamic.

28. 'Bodhipathapradīpa', 5.

29. The various aspects and stages of the Path are discussed in Chapter 19.

30. 'Bodhicaryāvatāra' VII, 14. This verse is also quoted in the 'sÑon.'gro'i zin.bris', fol. 2b. In the 'rDzogs chen kun.bzaṅ bla.ma', fol. 24a, the simile of the human body as a boat is expressed in the following way:

> 'If good, this body is a boat to liberation;
> If bad, it is an anchor in Saṃsāra;
> This body is a servant of both good and evil.'

31. The triple division of confidence (*dad.pa,* Skt. *śraddhā*) is particular to the Vijñānavāda school of Buddhism. See 'Triṃśikā', p. 26; 'Abhidharmasamuccaya', p. 6; 'Vijñaptimātratāsiddhi', p. 320. The 'Abhidharmakośa' II, 25, and its 'Bhāṣya', p. 156, only know the third definition given in the text.

32. *yid ches.pa'i dad.pa*, Skt. *abhisampratyaya.* In the 'rDzogs chen kun.bzaṅ bla.ma', fol. 121b, trusting confidence is defined as follows: 'Trusting confidence is to feel assurance deep in one's heart after having learned about the unusual qualities and sustaining power of the precious Three Jewels. When, after having learned that in all times and under all circumstances the precious Three Jewels are an unfailing help, the feeling of certitude which comes from conscience (*yid khyed śes.kyi dad.pa* "confidence of a mind that knows you") without hoping or aspiring for anything else except being aware of the Three Jewels as an unfailing help, whether you feel happy or sad, whether you are ill or are feverish, dying or alive, and whatever work you may have to do, this is trusting confidence. As is said by O.rgyan rin.po.che:

> By conscience spiritual sustenance settles on you
> And when your mind does not harbour doubts, whatever you think of will come true.'

33. *'dod.pa'i dad.pa*, Skt. *abhilāṣa.* According to the 'rDzogs chen kun.bzaṅ bla.ma', fol. 121a: 'Longing confidence is the birth of the desire to be freed from the reported misery of evil existences in Saṃsāra; it is the birth of the desire to attain the bliss of heaven and emancipation one has heard about; it is the birth of the desire to realize the advantages of the good and wholesome about which one has heard; it is the birth of the desire to renounce the evil of the vice one has seen.'

34. *daṅ.ba'i dad.pa*, Skt. *cetasaḥ prasāda.* According to the 'rDzogs chen kun.bzaṅ bla.ma', fol. 121a: 'Lucid confidence is the birth of confidence after a clear mind has been led to the idea that (the sustaining power of) Compassion has not descended on us when we are deprived of such chances as visiting monasteries in which there are many worshipful objects representing the Body, Speech and Mind of the Victorious One, or meeting face to face virtuous people who are spiritual teachers and friends, or hearing their qualities and life stories.'

35. *mi.g'yo.ba'i las*, Skt. *āneñjya karman.* In his explanation sGam. po.pa follows the 'Bhāṣya' ad 'Abhidharmakośa' III, 28 (p. 84). See also 'Abhidharmakośa' IV, 45, p. 106.

36. i.e., Rūpadhātu and Ārūpyadhātu. See Chapter 1, note 9.

37. *zag.bcas.kyi phuṅ.po lṅa*, Skt. *sāsravapañcaskandha.*

38. The Truth of Misery is a name for individual existence. It is not mere unpleasant feeling (*duḥkhā vedanā*), although this also is present as an indicator that somewhere something is not in order. The

Truth of the Origination of Misery is the working of Karma and conflicting emotions. As Sthiramati in his 'Triṃśikāvijñaptibhāṣya', p. 38, points out: 'Karma and conflicting emotions are the cause of Saṃsāra, and conflicting emotions are the main cause. Under this domineering influence Karma is able to outline a new existence.' The idea expressed by sGam.po.pa is found in 'Madhyamakavṛtti', pp. 475 seq.

39. sGam.po.pa has combined two definitions. The first part is found in the 'Bhāṣya' ad 'Abhidharmakośa' II, 25 (p. 156), the second in 'Abhidharmasamuccaya', p. 6.

40. *tshul.khrims,* Skt. *śīla.* A detailed analysis is given in Chapter 13. Not only are ethics and manners of primary importance for the acquisition of a human body in the cycle of existences, they are also the motive power (*rgyu,* Skt. *hetu*) of human life and of all spiritual development. In his 'sÑon.'gro'i zin.bris', fol. 1 seq., Padma dkar.po declares: 'By holding up ethics and manners as a cause, one obtains a human body as the result. They mean the intention to refrain from the ten types of unwholesome deeds and all that is connected with the latter. As has been stated:

> An attitude of restraint, once it has been adopted,
> Is called Perfection of ethics and manners. ('Bodhicaryāvatāra' V, 11cd.)

Since there are very few people who know how to abstain from evil deeds, the result or a human body is difficult to obtain. Venerable Mi.la.ras.pa affirmed:

> As to this jewel, the human body presenting a unique occasion and effecting the right juncture,
> There are very few people who support ethics and manners.'

41. See Chapter 1, note 39.

3
MEETING SPIRITUAL FRIENDS

(c) 'The contributary cause are spiritual friends.'[1]

THIS MEANS THAT although you may possess the most perfect working basis, but are not urged on by spiritual friends as a contributary cause, it is difficult to set out on the path towards enlightenment, because of the power of inveterate propensities due to evil deeds committed repeatedly in former times. Therefore you have to meet spiritual friends. This necessity is outlined in the following index:

Five headings refer to the meeting with spiritual friends:
Reason, classification,
Primary characteristics of each group,
The method of meeting them and the benefits.

There are three reasons for meeting them, scriptural authority, necessity and simile.

'Scriptural authority' is found in the ' 'Phags.pa sdud.pa' ('Prajñāpāramitāsaṃcayagāthā', fol. 18b):

Virtuous disciples having respect for the Guru
Should always be in touch with wise Gurus
Because from them the virtues of a wise man spring.

And in the ' 'Phags.pa brGyad.stoṅ.pa' ('Aṣṭasāhasrikā-prajñāpāramitā'):

Thus a Bodhisattva Mahāsattva who wishes to attain unsurpassable enlightenment must first (11a) approach, then meet and honour spiritual friends.

'Necessity' means that you who have the quality of being an individual able to attain omniscience, must meet with spiritual friends, because you yourself do not know how to accumulate merits and how to tear the two veils of conflicting emotions and primitive beliefs about reality. This is indisputable. In general, the Buddhas of the past, present and future make it clear why friends are necessary, while the Pratyekabuddhas illustrate the fact that without friends the ultimately real remains unattainable. And so for people like ourselves who intend to attain perfect Buddhahood it is necessary to accumulate all those merits which are subsumed under merit proper and spiritual awareness,[2] but the means of accumulating them depends on spiritual friends; and it is equally necessary to tear the two veils of conflicting emotions and primitive beliefs about reality, but the means of doing so again depends on these friends.

The 'similes' are that spiritual friends are like a guide when we travel in unknown territory, an escort when we pass through dangerous regions and a ferry-man when we cross a great river.

As to the first, when we travel guideless in unknown territory there is the danger of going astray and getting lost. But if we go with a guide then there is no such danger, and without missing a single step we reach the desired place. So also, when we have set out on the path towards unsurpassable enlightenment and are going towards the spiritual level of the Samyaksambuddha, if there is no spiritual friend belonging to the Mahāyāna way of life to act as our guide, then there is danger of losing our way in paths of the Non-Buddhists[3] (11b), of going astray in the way of life of the Śrāvakas, and of getting lost on the paths of the Pratyekabuddhas. But if we walk with a spiritual friend as our guide, then there is no danger and we arrive at the city of the Omniscient One. This is stated in the 'dPal.'byuṅ.gi rnam.thar':[4]

> Spiritual friends are like guides, because they set us on the path of the perfections.

In the second simile dangerous regions are haunted by thieves and robbers, wild beasts and other noxious animals. When we go there without an escort, there is the danger of losing our body, life or property; but when we have a strong escort we reach the desired place without loss. So also, when we have set out on the path towards enlightenment, accumulated merits and spiritual awareness and are about to go to the city of the Omniscient One, if there is no spiritual friend to act as an escort, there is danger of losing our stock of merits either from within ourselves, by preconceived ideas[5] and emotional instability, or from outside, by demons, wrong guides and other treacherous people, and there is also the danger that we may be robbed of our life which is approaching pleasurable forms of existence.[6] As has been stated:[7]

> When the crowd of robber-like emotions,
> Gets a chance to do so, it will steal the good one has acquired
> And even take the life which is on its way towards pleasurable
> forms of existence.

But if we have spiritual friends to escort us, we do not suffer the loss of our stock of the good and wholesome, are not robbed of our lives that are approaching pleasurable forms of existence, and we arrive at the city of the Omniscient One. This is affirmed in the 'dPal.'byuṅ.gi rnam.thar':[8]

> All the merits of a Bodhisattva are guarded by spiritual friends (12a).

And in the 'dGe.sñen.ma Mi.g'yo.ba'i rnam.thar':[9]

> Spiritual friends are like an escort, because they conduct us to the city of the Omniscient One.

Finally in the third simile when we cross a great river, if we have boarded a boat without a boatman, we are either drowned or carried away by the current and do not reach the other shore; but if there is a boatman we land safely by his efforts. So also, when we cross the ocean of Saṃsāra, if there are no spiritual friends to act as boatmen, though we have boarded the ship of the Noble Doctrine, we are either drowned in Saṃsāra or carried away by its current. As has been said:[10]

> One does not reach the other shore without an oarsman in the boat;
> Although one may have all qualities complete, without a Guru one does not arrive at the end of the world.

Therefore, when we are in touch with spiritual friends who are like boatmen, we reach the dry shore of Nirvāṇa, the other side of Saṃsāra. This is expressed in the 'sDoṅ.po bkod.pa'i mdo' ('Gaṇḍavyūhasūtra', p. 463):

> Spiritual friends are like a boatman, because they make us cross the great river of Saṃsāra.

And so we must meet with spiritual friends who are like a guide, an escort and a boatman.

The classification of these friends is fourfold: (i) in the form of an ordinary human being, (ii) as a Bodhisattva living on a high level of spirituality, (iii) the Nirmāṇakāya, and (iv) Sambhogakāya of the Buddha. These four types are related to our spiritual standing in life (12b).

Since at the beginning of our career it is impossible to be in touch with the Buddhas or with Bodhisattvas living on a high level of spirituality, we have to meet with ordinary human beings as spiritual friends. As soon as the darkness caused by our deeds has lightened, we can find Bodhisattvas on a high level of spirituality. Then when we have risen above the Great Preparatory Path[11] we can find the Nirmāṇakāya of the Buddha. Finally, as soon as we live on a high spiritual level we can meet with the Sambhogakāya as a spiritual friend.

Should you ask, who among these four is our greatest benefactor, the reply is that in the beginning of our career when we are still living imprisoned by our deeds and emotions, we will not even see so much as the face of a superior spiritual friend. Instead we will have to seek an ordinary human being who can illumine the path we have to follow with the light of his counsel, whereafter we shall meet superior ones. Therefore the greatest benefactor is a spiritual friend in the form of an ordinary human being.

As to the primary characteristics of the four types you must know that The Buddha is most perfect in renunciation, because he has torn and discarded the two veils of conflicting emotions and primitive beliefs about reality, and is most perfect in knowledge, because he possesses the two kinds of omniscience.[12]

You must understand that in Bodhisattvas living on a high level of spirituality and acting as spiritual friends these qualities of renunciation and knowledge are also present from the first level up to the tenth.

Finally, Bodhisattvas living on a higher level of spirituality than the eighth, possess ten powers by which to receive sentient beings into their fold. These are power (i) over the length of life, (ii) mind and (iii) necessities, (iv) over Karma (13a), (v) birth, (vi) creative imagination,[13] (vii) resolution, (viii) miracles, (ix) knowledge, and (x) presentation.

(i) 'Power over the length of life' means to be able to live as long as one desires,

(ii) 'over mind' to be able to enter a state of meditative absorption at will, and

(iii) 'over necessities' to be able to shower down a rain of immeasurably valuable necessities on sentient beings.

(iv) 'Power over Karma' means to be able to improve the effect of Karma that has to be experienced in some world sphere, continent, form of life, manner of birth or place in life,

(v) 'over birth' to be able to be born in the world of sensuality without spiritually departing from meditative concentration; and, having taken birth in the world of desires not to be affected by its evil, and

(vi) 'over creative imagination' to be able to turn water into earth and to accomplish similar phenomena.

(vii) 'Power over resolution' means to be able to determine to fulfil one's own and others' interests perfectly and also to accomplish this resolution,

(viii) 'over miracles' to be able to perform innumerable miracles in order to instil yearning into sentient beings, and

(ix) 'over knowledge' fully to know the Dharma, its purpose, its intrinsic meaning and its implication.

(x) 'Power over presentation' means to be able fully to satisfy the minds of all sentient beings by a single discourse on the Dharma in their respective languages, expounding it as in the Sūtras and other works in various words, inflections and grouping of letters, just giving them what and how much is necessary.

The primary characteristics of a spiritual friend in the form of an ordinary human being consist of either eight, four or two (13b) qualities. Of the first the 'Byaṅ.chub.sems.dpa'i sa' ('Bodhisattvabhūmi') says:

> A Bodhisattva is known as a spiritual friend perfect in every way if he is endowed with eight qualities: (i) to possess a Bodhisattva's discipline in ethics and manners, (ii) to be well versed in the Bodhisattvapiṭaka, (iii) fully to comprehend the ultimately real, (iv) to be full of compassion and love, (v) to possess the four intrepidities,[14] (vi) to have patience,[15] (vii) to have an indefatigable mind and (viii) to use right words.

The second group is referred to in the 'mDo.sde.rgyan' ('Mahāyāna-sūtrālaṅkāra' XII, 5):

> To be very learned, to dispel doubts,
> To be agreeable and to point out reality in two ways—
> Are the most perfect instructive qualities
> Of Bodhisattvas.

This means that (i) such a man is a great teacher by virtue of his immense learning, (ii) by his profound discriminating awareness he dispels others' doubts, (iii) by performing the deeds of a virtuous man he is praiseworthy, and (iv) he points out the ultimately real by its primary characteristics of having defiling and purifying elements.[16]

The third group is mentioned in the 'Byaṅ.chub.sems.dpa'i spyod.pa.la 'jug.pa' ('Bodhicaryāvatāra' V, 102):

> A spiritual friend is always
> Well versed in the message of the Mahāyāna,
> And not even for the sake of his life
> Will he give up the excellent behaviour of a Bodhisattva.

In other words a spiritual friend is (i) well versed in the message of the Mahāyāna and (ii) follows the precepts of a Bodhisattva.

The three ways of remaining in touch with a spiritual friend once you have found him are: (i) by receiving him respectfully and serving him, (ii) by showing him devoted interest and reverence, and (iii) by establishing for yourself the validity of his instruction and acquiring a primary understanding of it.[17]

(i) 'Remaining in touch with him by receiving him respectfully', means to fold your hands and rise quickly in his presence (14a), to bow down before and circumambulate him, to speak at the proper time and out of a loving disposition, to gaze at him ever and again with a mind that cannot be satisfied by one look; as the spiritual friend was respectfully received by the merchant Nor.bzaṅs. Also in the 'sDoṅ.po bkod.pa'i mdo' ('Gaṇḍavyūhasūtra')[18] is written:

> Be insatiable to gaze at spiritual friends because it is difficult to behold them, hard for them to appear and not easy to meet them.

'By serving him' is meant to provide him, regardless of trouble, with proper food, garments, bed-clothes, bedsteads, medicines and other necessities for life such as grain and butter; as the spiritual friend was served by the venerable rTag.tu.ṅu (Sadāprarudita). In the 'dPal.'byuṅ.gi rnam.thar'[19] we read:

> The enlightenment of a Buddha is obtained by serving spiritual friends.

(ii) 'To remain in touch with him by showing him devoted interest and reverence' is to think of a spiritual friend as the Buddha, not to disobey his commands, and to awaken in yourself devoted interest, reverence and confidence; as was done by pandit Nāropa.[20] Also in the 'rGyal.ba'i yum' ('Ekākṣarīmātā-nāma-sarvatathāgata-prajñā-pāramitā') it is stated:

> You must in earnestness awaken reverence for spiritual friends; you must be bounteous towards them and please them.

Further, in your own way and status in life you must know how to act as a friend, as may be seen from the 'rGyal.po Me'i rnam.thar'.[21]

(iii) 'To remain in touch with him by establishing the validity of his instruction and to acquire a primary understanding of it' (14b), means to realize the validity of his words while you come to understand his instruction by hearing and thinking about it and by making it a living experience.[22] For by so doing he is extremely pleased. As is declared in the 'mDo.sde.rgyan' ('Mahāyāna-sūtrālaṅkāra' XVII, 12):

> He who understands the instruction as it has been given to him
> Makes the spiritual friend's mind extremely pleased.

When such a friend is pleased, we attain Buddhahood, as is related in the 'dPal.'byuṅ.gi rnam.thar':[23]

> When spiritual friends are pleased, one attains the enlightenment of all Buddhas.

Asking a spiritual friend for the Dharma is done in three ways: (i) the preliminary step, (ii) the actual situation and (iii) the consequence.

(i) The preliminary step is to make the request with a mind bent upon enlightenment.

(ii) The actual situation is to ask as if you were ill, to regard the Dharma as the medicine and the spiritual friend as the physician and to follow the Dharma as the cure of the disease.[24]

(iii) As a consequence the defects of being like a pot turned upside down, with a leaky bottom or filled with poison, are eliminated.[25]

The benefits of being in touch with such friends may be learned from the 'dPal.'byuṅ.gi rnam.thar':[26]

> Oh son of a good family, Bodhisattvas to whom spiritual friends are closely attached, will not fall into lower forms of life. Bodhisattvas who are well guarded by them will not fall into the hands of evil individuals. Bodhisattvas who are well purified by them will not turn away from the Mahāyāna way of life. Bodhisattvas who are well supported by them go beyond the spiritual level of ordinary human beings.

And from the 'rGyal.ba'i yum' ('Ekākṣarīmātā-nāma-sarvatathāgata-prajñāpāramitā'):

> A Bodhisattva Mahāsattva to whom spiritual friends are well attached, quickly attains unsurpassable fully perfected enlightenment.

The third chapter, dealing with Meeting Spiritual Friends,
from the Jewel Ornament of Liberation or
The Wish-Fulfilling Gem of the
Noble Doctrine.

NOTES TO CHAPTER 3

1. See Chapter 1, p. 2.

2. According to 'Mahāyāna-sūtrālaṅkāra' XVIII, 38, merits and knowledge are necessary for rising to higher levels of spirituality and for living in the world without being subject to the degrading influences of conflicting emotions:

> The equipment of Bodhisattvas are unsurpassable merits and knowledge:
> The former serve to make him rise in Saṃsāra, the latter to pass through it without being emotionally and intellectually unbalanced.

3. *mu.stegs*, Skt. *tīrthika*.

4. The story of dPal.'byuṅ, Skt. Śrīsambhava, forms the fiftieth chapter of the 'Gaṇḍavyūhasūtra'. The passage quoted by sGam.po. pa is found there on p. 463.

5. *rnam.rtog*, Skt. *vikalpa*. See Chapter 1, note 19.

6. i.e. Rūpadhātu and Ārūpyadhātu. See Chapter 1, note 9.

7. 'Bodhicaryāvatāra' V, 28.

8. 'Gaṇḍavyūhasūtra', p. 461.

9. The story of dGe.bsñen.ma Mi.g'yo.ba, Skt. Upāsikā Acalā, forms the nineteenth chapter of the 'Gaṇḍavyūhasūtra'. The passage quoted is found there on p. 171.

10. 'Jñānasiddhi' XIV, 4.

11. The Preparatory Path (*tshogs.lam*, Skt. *sambhāramārga*) is divided into a smaller, mediocre, and great one. See Chapter 19.

12. A detailed discussion of this problem is given in Chapter 20.

13. *mos.pa*, Skt. *adhimukti*. See 'Daśabhūmikasūtra', p. 70.

14. *mi.'jigs.pa*, Skt. *vaiśāradya*. The intrepidities have been won by knowledge (*jñāna*). Where that reigns no fear is possible. The four intrepidities are the certitude that the whole of reality has been understood; that all disturbing and sullying factors have lost their power for ever; that those factors which are a hindrance to spiritual development have been pointed out; and that the path out of the misery of Saṃsāra has been shown. See 'Abhidharmakośa' VII, 32 and 'Bhāṣya', p. 75.

15. *bzod.pa*, Skt. *kṣānti*. For a detailed discussion of its meaning see Chapter 14.

16. This problem has been discussed in 'Vijñaptimātratāsiddhi', pp. 214 seq.

17. *bsgrub.pa*, Skt. *sādhana*; *nan.tan*, Skt. *pratipatti*. Both terms have the meaning of 'attainment', yet the difference is that *bsgrub.pa* refers

to the validity of a proposition giving an incontestable proof of its correctness to any logical investigation, while *nan.tan* is the first intellectual understanding which then has to give way to a direct understanding and experience (*rtogs*, Skt. *samaya*, *adhigama*). *bsgrub.pa* and *nan.tan* belong to the sphere of logic and discursive thought. They rank lower than knowledge by experience, because as the Mādhyamikas insist, logic is unable to cognize reality in its real nature.

18. Cp. 'Gaṇḍavyūhasūtra', p. 460.

19. This passage is not found in the Sanskrit version of the 'Gaṇḍavyūhasūtra'.

20. The hardships which Nāropa and Sadāprarudita took upon themselves in order to win enlightenment are a favourable topic in Tibetan literature. A lengthy account of their sufferings is given in the 'rDzogs chen kun.bzaṅ bla.ma', fol. 103 seq. On fol. 116 seq. that of Venerable Mi.la.ras.pa is also related. Even nowadays Nāropa's life is mentioned as an example of how deeply interested and indefatigable we must be if we are ever to achieve anything. His life is constantly contrasted with modern superficiality, its half-baked 'ideas' and desire for the limelight.

21. The story of rGyal.po Me, King Anala, forms the seventeenth chapter of the 'Gaṇḍavyūhasūtra'. In order to make people renounce evil and set out on the path of good he upheld civil order and punished criminals.

22. *sgom.pa*, Skt. *bhāvanā*. This term implies concentrated attention to that which has been observed to be the nature of things. It is never discursive.

23. 'Gaṇḍavyūhasūtra', p. 460.

24. The same simile is found in 'Gaṇḍavyūhasūtra', p. 464, where nine others are given in addition.

25. These three defects are discussed in the 'rDzogs chen kun.bzaṅ bla.ma', fol. 5 seq.:

'The three defects comparable with those of a pot are: not to listen is the defect of a pot turned upside down; not to bear in mind what you have heard is that of a pot with a leaky bottom; to be affected by emotional instability is that of a poisonous pot.

'The first simile means: When you listen to the explanation of the Dharma, you must listen to the voice of him who explains it without the perceiving faculty of your ears straying to some other sound. When you do not listen in this way, it is as if juice is poured on a pot with its opening down, for, though your body is present in the teaching room, you do not hear a single word of the Dharma.

'The second simile means: When you do not bear in mind the Dharma which you are going to hear, though the words have reached the perceiving and hearing faculties, it is as if juice is poured into a pot with a leaky bottom—however much you may pour, nothing will remain there; and however much of the Dharma you may have heard you do not know how to instil it into your mind and how to take it to heart.

'The third simile means: When you hear the explanation of the Dharma, but listen to it with ideas concerned with the will to live and the desire for fame or with thoughts affected by the five poisons that stem from the three emotionally upsetting forces of cupidity, aversion and bewilderment, not only will the Dharma not become beneficial to your mind, it will even turn into its very opposite, and this is like healthy juice poured into a poisonous pot.

'Therefore the saints in India said:

> When hearing the Dharma you must be like deer listening to the sound of music (6a): when thinking about it, like a man from the north shearing sheep: when making it a living experience, like a man getting drunk: when establishing its validity like a Yak eating grass hungrily and when you come to possess its fruition you must be free from clouds like the sun.

'When you hear the explanation of the Dharma, like deer enamoured of the sound of the lute and though shot by a stray hunter with a poisoned arrow, unable to understand or think what has happened, you must listen to the Dharma with the hairs on your body rising with joy, with eyes filled with tears, with hands folded, and not distracted by other thoughts. But if, when you are in the teaching hall, your mind runs after its own thoughts, the doors of your senses are opened to idle talk, your mouth is busy and your eyes roam hither and thither, you should remember that such conduct is improper; concentrate with devotion and count the beads of your rosary. When you listen in this way, you will bear in mind the meaning of what is explained, and having made it unforgettable, you will constantly take it to heart. The great Śākyamuni also declared:

> Although I showed you the means of liberation,
> You must know that it depends on you alone.

'Since the teacher who explains the Dharma to the disciple teaches him how to listen properly, how to renounce evil (6b), acquire the good and wholesome and take the teaching to heart, the disciple, on the other hand, must bear the teaching unforgettably in his mind, take it to heart and realize its meaning. But if he does not bear it in mind, then, although there may be benefit from listening to it, if he does not understand a small part of the meaning, it is as if he had not heard the Dharma.

'If you are affected by conflicting emotions, though you bear in mind the teaching, the Dharma does not become pure and effective. As has been stated by the incomparable Dvags.po lha.rje:

> If you do not practise the Dharma properly,
> It creates the condition for falling into evil existences.

'Thus he who has unwholesome thoughts such as erroneous conceptions about the Guru and the Dharma, who abuses his friends when they are not obstructing him, and who shows arrogance and contempt, must renounce these unwholesome elements, since they create the condition for evil existence.'

26. 'Gaṇḍavyūhasūtra', p. 462.

4

THE INSTRUCTION IN THE TRANSITORINESS OF THE COMPOSITE

(d) 'The method are the instructions of spiritual friends.'[1]

SINCE WE HAVE Buddha-nature as our driving force, as our working basis the precious human body which we have obtained from beginningless time in the course of generations, and as a contributary cause (of our development) the spiritual friends we have met, how is it that we have not already obtained Buddhahood? The fault lies in people like ourselves having come under the power of four obstacles by which the attainment of Buddhahood is prevented. They are: attachment to sensuous experiences during this life,[2] to sensual pleasures in this world,[3] to self-complacency[4] and ignorance about the means of realizing Buddhahood. Who, then, dispels these four obstacles? He who listens to the instructions of spiritual friends and takes them to heart. They are summarized below:

> There are four topics of instruction:
> Concentrated attention[5] to transitoriness and
> To the vicious state of Saṃsāra as a result of our own actions;
> The development of benevolence and compassion;
> And those factors which set up an enlightened attitude.

In other words, they are: (i) instruction in the development of concentrated attention to the significance of transitoriness and (ii) to the vicious state of Saṃsāra resulting from our actions, (iii) of benevolence and compassion and (iv) in the formation of an enlightened attitude.

Concentrated attention to the significance of transitoriness is the remedy for attachment to sensuous experiences in this life; similar attention to the vicious state of Saṃsāra due to our actions removes attachment to sensual pleasures in this world; the development of benevolence and compassion (15b) is the remedy against attachment to self-complacency, while the factors which set up an enlightened attitude remove ignorance about how to realize Buddhahood. These factors are experiences, which start with taking refuge in the Three Jewels[6] and lead up to concentrated attention to the meaning of the two types of non-individuality.[7] They are also those experiences which you have on the five paths[8] and ten levels of spirituality.[9]

Furthermore, some of them are the working basis,[10] others the frame of reference[11] and still others the method[12] for the formation of an enlightened attitude; others again are the training[13] in, the usefulness and the result, of the formation of an enlightened attitude. So there is nothing in Mahāyāna which does not fall under the scope of the formation of an enlightened attitude. Consequently all instructions therein originate with and depend on spiritual friends. As is stated in the 'sDoṅ.po bkod.pa'i mdo' ('Gaṇḍavyūhasūtra'):

> Spiritual friends are the birth-place of all good.

And,

> Omniscience depends upon instruction by them.

In this chapter we will deal with the development of concentrated attention to the significance of transitoriness as a remedy against attachment to sensuous experiences during this life. Generally speaking, it consists in the empirical fact that everything composite is transitory. The Buddha himself (16a) has declared:

> Bhikṣus, everything composite is transitory.

However, you may ask, how is transitoriness to be understood? The reply is that the end of every hoarding is spending, of every rising falling, of every meeting parting and of all living dying.[14] This is expressed in a verse in the 'Ched.du brjod.pa'i tshoms' ('Udānavarga' I, 20):

> The end of every hoarding is spending,
> Of every rising falling,
> Of every meeting parting and
> Of all living dying.

How, then, is this concentrated attention to the significance of transitoriness to be developed?

> Three headings indicate
> The development of concentrated attention:
> Classification, method,
> And profitableness.

Classification is twofold: transitoriness (i) of the world as the outer vessel and (ii) of sentient beings as the inner essence.

(i) Transitoriness of the world as the outer vessel is of two kinds: (a) that of gross and (b) subtle matter.

(ii) Transitoriness of sentient beings as the inner essence is also twofold: (a) that of others and (b) of myself.

The method of developing concentrated attention to the significance of transitoriness is:

(ia) the contemplation of the transitoriness of gross matter in this world as the outer vessel.

From the lower cosmic circle of Wind up to but excluding the fourth stage of meditative concentration, there exists nothing of a permanent nature nor anything solid or unchanging. Sometimes what is below the first stage of meditative concentration is destroyed by cosmic Fire, what is below the second stage by cosmic Water and what is below the third stage by cosmic Wind. After the destruction by Fire there is no ash, just as oil is completely consumed by a flame. After the destruction by Water there is no sediment, just as salt is dissolved in water. After the destruction by Wind not even a particle is left (16b), just as dust is carried away by the wind. As is stated in the 'Chos.mṅon.pa.mdzod' ('Abhidharmakośa' III, 102):

> Destruction by Fire takes place seven times, by Water once.
> When the latter has occurred seven times,
> The rest is destroyed by Wind.

The fourth stage of meditative concentration is destroyed neither by Fire, Water nor Wind, but by death and by the transmigration of beings therein. Therefore it is said:[15]

> The palaces of impermanence
> Arise and disappear together with the beings therein.

Further, the destruction of the universe by Fire is foretold in the 'dPa'.sbyin.gyis žus.pa'i mdo' ('Vīradatta-Gṛhapatiparipṛcchāsūtra'):

> When one aeon has passed, this universe
> Which is of the nature of space will become space.
> Even the mountains will be destroyed and burnt completely.

(ib) Transitoriness of the subtle is due to the change of the four seasons, is seen in the rising and setting of the sun and moon, and is witnessed in fleeting moments.

Of these 'transitoriness due to the change of the four seasons' means that by the power of spring in this vessel-like world, the soil becomes soft and reddish while grass, trees and vegetables sprout; but this is only transitory and comes about by the change of season. In the summer the soil becomes humid and green, while grass, trees and vegetables spread their stems and leaves. In autumn it becomes hard and yellow, while grass, trees and vegetables ripen into their fruits; finally in the winter it becomes frozen and whitish, while grass, trees and vegetables dry up and become brittle; but in each case this is only transitory and comes about by the change of season.

'Transitoriness seen in the rising and setting of the sun and moon' means that by the power of the rising day (17a) this vessel-like world is illumined by light and brightness, but with the coming of night it is dissolved in darkness. This also is transitory and a symbol of change.

'Transitoriness witnessed in fleeting moments' means that this vessel-like world which existed at an earlier moment does not do so at a later one. That it seems to continue in the same way is because something else similar arises, like the stream of a waterfall.

(ii) Of the two kinds of transitoriness of sentient beings as the inner essence, (a) that of others is as follows. All sentient beings in the three world-spheres are transitory. As is stated in the ''Phags.pa rGya.che rol.pa' ('Lalitavistara', p. 173):

> The three world-spheres are transitory like a cloud in the sky.

(b) Transitoriness of myself, means that I too am powerless to remain and have to depart. This can be known in a double way: (1) in discerning it in our own stream of life and (2) by drawing the conclusion from that of others.

(1) In the first case, the development of concentrated attention comprises (i) concentration on death and (ii) the signs thereof, (iii) on life as it draws to its end and (iv) on separation.

(i) 'Concentrated attention to death' is the thought that I shall not remain in the world for long, but will have to move on to another life.

(ii) 'Concentrated attention to the signs of death' is the thought that life is drawing to an end, breathing stops, the body becomes a corpse and mind must wander forth.[16]

(iii) 'Concentrated attention to life as it draws to its end' is the thought that a year has just passed and a month gone by; that since yesterday a day has lapsed; that now a moment has just passed and that in this way life becomes shorter every second (17b). In the 'Byaṅ.chub.sems.dpa'i spyod.pa.la 'jug.pa' ('Bodhicaryāvatāra' II, 40) it is said:

> Without waiting day or night, this life is continuously on the losing side;
> And while the remainder decreases and its very existence comes to naught, why should people like myself not die?

(iv) 'Concentrated attention to separation' is the thought that my present friends, wealth and body, all of which I esteem so much, will not always be with me, but will quickly depart. As is said in the 'Byaṅ.chub.sems.dpa'i spyod.pa.la 'jug.pa' ('Bodhicaryāvatāra' II, 35):

> Should I not have known that
> I would have to give up everything and depart from hence?

This concentrated attention to death should be developed in the following ninefold manner deriving from the three main heads of (A) the certainty of my death; (B) of my not knowing when it will come; and (C) of nothing following me to the hereafter.

(A) There are three reasons for this certainty: I must die because (i) there is no one who has not done so before, (ii) the body is composite and (iii) life ebbs from moment to moment.

(i) The first reason is given by the Teacher rTa.dbyaṅs (Aśvaghoṣa):

> It is doubtful whether you will hear
> Or see anyone
> Who did not die, who had been born,
> Either on earth or in the heavens.[17]

Thus all the sages of old who had magic powers[18] and infinite supernatural knowledge,[19] had to die without having found a place of refuge, where there is no death or where liberation might be obtained, to say nothing of people like ourselves. Therefore:

> The great sages with their five kinds of miraculous knowledge,
> Though they were able to walk far in the sky,
> Could not go to a place
> Where there is no death.[20]

But this is not all. Even the saintly Pratyekabuddhas and the Great (18a) Śrāvakas, the Arhants, had in the end to give up their bodies, to say nothing of people like ourselves. As is said in the 'Ched.du brjod.pa'i tshoms' ('Udānavarga' I, 23):

> When even the Pratyekabuddhas
> And the Śrāvakas of the Buddha
> Had to give up their bodies,
> What about ordinary people?

Finally, since the Nirmāṇakāya of the Perfectly Enlightened One, adorned with the major and minor marks of beauty and possessing the nature of the Vajra, had to be given up, what can be said of people like ourselves. The Teacher dPa'.bo (i.e. Aśvaghoṣa) said:

> When even the Body of the Buddha,
> The Vajrakāya adorned with the major and minor marks,

Is transitory,
What can one say about other embodied people
Whose bodies are without solidity like weeds?[21]

(ii) The certainty of death due to the body being composite, means that since everything that is composite is transitory, it is also perishable. As is stated in the 'Ched.du brjod.pa'i tshoms' ('Udānavarga' I, 1):

Alas! everything composite is transitory,
Subject to birth and death.[22]

Therefore, since this body is not non-composite, it is transitory and there is certainty of death.

(iii) This certainty because life ebbs from moment to moment, means that life continually passes away and so approaches death. Though this may not be conspicuous all the time, yet it can be compared with an arrow shot by an archer, water falling over a steep cliff or a person led to a place of execution.

The first simile is to be understood in the sense that life not pausing a moment quickly approaches death, just as an arrow shot by a skilful archer does not stay in one place in the sky, but swiftly reaches its destination. As is said:

Just (18b) as an arrow shot by a skilful archer,
As soon as he has pulled the string,
Does not wait but quickly reaches its target,
So also is the life of men.

The second simile makes it still clearer that man's life cannot wait but is like water falling over a steep cliff, which rushes on without pausing a single moment. As is stated in the ''Dus.pa rin.po.che tog' ('Mahāsannipātaratnaketudhāraṇī'):

Friends, this life passes quickly.
It is the rapid stream of a turbulent waterfall over a steep cliff.
The fool not recognizing this,
Stupidly lets himself be fooled by the sense objects.

And in the 'Tshoms' ('Udānavarga' I, 31):

Like the current of a great river,
Never turning back, it moves on.

The third simile means that we are like a prisoner being led to a place of execution, who with every step comes closer to death. As is written in the ''Phags.pa lJoṅ.śiṅ.gi mdo':

Just as a prisoner being led to a place of execution,
With every step comes nearer to death.[23]

And in the 'Tshoms' ('Udānavarga' I, 12):

Just as people who are about to be executed,
With every step they make,
Draw closer to the execution,
So also is the life of men.

(B) For the certainty of death without my knowing when it will come, there are also three reasons: because (iv) my span of life is not fixed, (v) the body is without solidity and (vi) there are many causes of death.[24]

(iv) It may be said that, although the life of beings or of men in other continents may be of determinate length, this is not so for people like us in Jambudvīpa. This is stated in 'Chos.mṅon.pa. mdzod' ('Abhidharmakośa' III, 78):

Here it is indeterminate; it is ten years at the end (of a cycle of aeons) and immeasurable at its beginning.

That some live longer than others is shown in the 'Tshoms' ('Udānavarga' I, 7–8):

Some die in the womb,
Others the moment they are born (19a),
Or while crawling
Or running about.
Some grow old and some die young,
And some in the prime of youth,
In due course they all pass on.[25]

(v) The fact that the body is without solidity means that there is no single solid substance in it apart from the thirty-six impure components. As is stated in the 'sPyod.'jug' ('Bodhicaryāvatāra' V, 62–3):

First open this heap of skin with your intellect,
Then separate the flesh from the network of bones with the scalpel of discriminating awareness.
Having opened the bones also look into the marrow
And see for yourself
Whether there is anything solid.

(vi) The fact that there are many causes of death means that there is nothing that does not become such a cause for ourselves as for others. As is written in the 'bŚes.sbriṅ' ('Suhṛllekha', 55):

This life has many dangers; it is more unstable
Than a bubble blown about by the wind.
With breath coming and going, it is the greatest miracle
That one ever awakens from sleep.[26]

(C) There are also three reasons for the fact that we die without being followed by anything: (vii) our wealth, (viii) friends (ix) and body do not accompany us.

(vii) That our wealth does not follow us is expressed in the 'sPyod.'jug' ('Bodhicaryāvatāra' VI, 59):

However much one may have acquired
And however long one may have enjoyed it with pleasure,
Like a man whose seams have split open,
One departs naked and empty-handed.

Thus wealth besides not following us is a great danger for life here and hereafter. The danger here is that we quarrel over it and that the misery of becoming its slave by guarding it arises; and in the life hereafter as a result of this misery we are born in (19b) evil existences.

(viii) That our friends do not follow is also stated in the 'sPyod. 'jug' ('Bodhicaryāvatāra'):

When the hour of death has come,
One's own children are no refuge,
Neither are father, mother or friends.
There is none to whom you can turn for refuge.

Thus friends besides not following us are a danger for life here and hereafter. The danger here is that we are afraid they may die and, overpowered by such fear, we come to great misery; as a result of which in the life hereafter we are born in evil existences.

(ix) That our body does not follow means that neither it nor its qualities accompany us. In the first place we should realize that however strong and powerful we may be, we do not escape death; however swiftly we may run, we cannot outrun it; and however learned and eloquent we may be, we cannot talk death away. We are like someone who cannot stop or catch hold of the sun when it sets behind a mountain.

That the body as such does not follow us is expressed in the 'sPyod.'jug' ('Bodhicaryāvatāra'):

This body gained with many difficulties
And preserved by food and clothing,
Will not accompany you. Birds and dogs will eat it.

It will be consumed by a blazing fire.
Drowned in water
Or hidden away in a grave in the earth.

Thus the body besides not accompanying us is also a danger for life here and hereafter. Here it is unable to stand disease, to suffer heat, cold, hunger or thirst; is afraid of being killed, fettered or flayed, and from this fright there comes great misery; as a result of which in the life hereafter (20a) we are born in evil existences.

(2) To draw the conclusion of our death from the stream of life of others, is the development of concentrated attention on death by having seen, heard or remembered that someone has died.

Having seen somebody dying means the following. When the body of one of our relatives, who formerly was strong, had a radiant face, was feeling well and never gave a thought to death, is today stricken with a deadly disease, when his strength gives way and he cannot sit; when his face becomes colourless, parched and grey; when he feels pain and is helpless by this affliction of disease and fever being unable to endure his suffering; when medicines and medical treatment do not take effect and all medical devices and religious ceremonies are of no avail; when he knows that he must die and is without strength to work; when for the last time he is surrounded by his friends, takes his last meal and speaks for the last time, then we should think: 'I also am essentially the same, of the same nature, and character and not beyond this nature.'

Then immediately after his breathing has stopped, however handsome he may have been and however much he has been seen fit to stay indoors, no one will have him in the house, be it only for one day. He is laid down on a stretcher, bound and tied crosswise, and the corpse carriers take him out; some people of his household embrace the corpse and pretend affectionately to cling to it, others weep and pretend to be dejected, others again fall to the ground in a faint, while still others say that the body is but earth and stone and that you, acting in such a way, have little sense. As soon as the corpse has been carried over the threshold and we see that it will never return to the house, we should recollect all this and think that we come to the same end.

Thus, when the corpse has been brought to the cemetery and thrown there (20a), and when we see it devoured by dogs, jackals and other wild beasts and its bones scattered, we should recollect all this and think that this will also happen to us.

Having heard that someone has died we should remember and think that this will also happen to us.

Bearing in mind that in our country, village or house an old man, young person or friend has died, we should remember this and think that it will also happen to us in a short time. Therefore it is said in a Sūtra:

> Since it is uncertain which will come earlier,
> Tomorrow or the world hereafter;
> Without striving for tomorrow
> One should get ready for the hereafter.[27]

The advantage of having developed concentrated attention to the significance of transitoriness is that by having understood[28] that everything composite is transitory, you turn away from hankering after this life. Moreover, confidence is nourished, you strive energetically, and by having become free from attachment and aversion, the foundation is laid for the comprehensive understanding[29] of the ultimate sameness of all constituents of reality.[30]

The fourth chapter, dealing with the Instruction in the Transitoriness of the Composite, from The Jewel Ornament of Liberation or The Wish-Fulfilling Gem of the Noble Doctrine.

NOTES TO CHAPTER 4

1. See Chapter 1, p. 2.

2. This could be freely translated by 'optimism', i.e. the assumption that determinate qualities will continue to exist unchanging and thereby provide a solid basis for what may be called a philosophy of life. Optimism, however, is false to the immediately apprehended fact that all determinate things are transitory. The only way to secure peace of mind is not to fall a victim to this common error. It may be noted that pessimism, the opposite of naïve optimism, is just as erroneous.

3. In other words, hedonism or the elevation of a passing pleasure into an immortal principle. Hedonism like optimism is equally false to immediate experience.

4. Self-complacency is a term for the Hīnayāna egotistic Nirvāṇa. For a further discussion see Chapter 7.

5. *sgom.pa*, Skt. *bhāvanā*. Literally this term means 'to bring into existence' in the sense that all to which we pay the closest attention becomes a living experience. It is preceded by 'hearing' (*thos.pa*, Skt. *śruta*) and by 'pondering over that which has been heard' (*bsam.pa*, Skt. *cintā*). But without *sgom.pa* nothing can be achieved.

6. A detailed account is given in Chapter 8.

7. The two types of non-individuality are *gaṅ.zag.gi bdag.med* (Skt. *pudgala-nairātmya*) and *chos.kyi bdag.med* (Skt. *dharma-nairātmya*). The former is the realization that the complete individual (*gaṅ.zag*, *pudgala*) or the Self (*ātman*), defined in various determinate ways since the time of the Upaniṣads, is but a congeries of driving forces (*saṃskārāḥ*) or a series of elements in interaction (*skandhadhātu-āyatana*), and that as a unique unchanging and immortal principle it is unwarranted and not capable of resisting criticism. This type of *nairātmya* is recognized in Hīnayāna Buddhism. Mahāyāna Buddhism realizes that the constituting elements (*dharma*) also are equally unwarranted as ultimate entities and incapable of resisting criticism.

8. See Chapters 8 and 19.

9. See Chapters 8 and 19.

10. The basis is the human being. See Chapters 2 and 8.

11. See Chapter 9.

12. See Chapter 9.

13. See Chapter 10.

14. The same idea is found in Padma dkar.po's 'sÑon.'gro'i zin.bris', fol. 4a.

15. 'Bhāṣya' ad 'Abhidharmakośa' III, 101, p. 216.

16. The same triple division, but increased by a fourth topic, is found in the 'sÑon.'gro'i zin.bris', fol. 3a: 'In the development of concentrated attention to transitoriness due to death there are four subjects: after birth death is unavoidable; it is unknown when it will come; there are many causes for it; and we die without anything following us. The thought that after birth death is unavoidable means to be aware that as soon as we are born we hurry into the presence of the Lord of Death without tarrying a single moment. As has been said by Dam.pa:

> Since death comes to what is born
> Without delay use this stream of life as a servant (for realizing ultimate good), oh man from Ḍiṅ.ri.'

17. The same verse is quoted in the 'sÑon.'gro'i zin.bris', fol. 4b and in the 'rDzogs chen kun.bzaṅ bla.ma', fol. 26b.

18. *rdzu.'phrul*, *ṛddhi*. It refers to certain phenomena produced by meditation. See 'Abhidharmakośa' VII, 48, and 'Bhāṣya' (pp. 112 seq.).

19. *mṅon.śes*, *abhijñā*. See 'Abhidharmakośa' VII, 45, and 'Bhāṣya' (pp. 107 seq.), also VII, 42, and 'Bhāṣya' (pp. 97 seqq.). There are six supersensible cognitions and faculties, of which the first five may be possessed by ordinary beings, the sixth belongs exclusively to the Āryas, who are spiritually advanced. The six are: miraculous powers (such as multiplying oneself, walking through walls and so on); hearing human and divine voices far and near; knowing others' thoughts; recollection of former lives; the vision of beings passing away and then reincarnating; and the awareness that all disturbing elements have lost their power of keeping us on low planes.

20. According to the 'rDzogs chen kun.bzaṅ bla.ma', fol. 29a, this verse is taken from the 'Mya.ṅan bsal.ba'i spriṅs.yig' ('Śokavinodana'). After quoting it in his 'sÑon.'gro'i zin.bris', fol. 4b, Padma dkar.po states: 'When even the solid mountains crumble to dust and the great and deep ocean becomes dry, why should the body of embodied beings, which has but little strength, not die? As is stated in the same work ('Śokavinodana'):

Where the earth is consumed by fire,
The mountains become dust,
And even the water of the ocean dries up—
What can one say of these embodied beings?'

21. This verse is also quoted in the 'sÑon.'gro'i zin.bris', fol. 4b.

22. Padma dkar.po in his 'sÑon.'gro'i zin.bris', fol. 3b, expresses this idea in the following way: 'Everything composite is transitory because that which has come about by causes and conditions perishes without waiting for two consecutive moments. As has been stated by the teacher Vīra (i.e. Aśvaghosa):

Thus death is in front
Of everything that has been born.'

23. The same in the 'sÑon.'gro'i zin.bris', fol. 3a, where the following verse by Mi.la.ras.pa is added:

'This life is passing like the shadow of the setting sun,
The farther the sun has gone, the longer the shadow has grown:
I have not seen liberation won by running away.'

The 'rDzogs chen kun.bzaṅ bla.ma', fol. 26b, makes use of this simile and states: 'It is uncertain when and where I shall die because from the moment we have been born we approach closer and closer to death, life instead of increasing decreases more and more, and the Lord of Death without waiting a single moment draws nearer like the shadow of the setting sun.'

24. In his 'sÑon.'gro'i zin.bris', fol. 3b–4a, Padma dkar.po gives several quotations illustrating the uncertainty: 'From Mi.la.ras.pa:

> You young men and girls assembled here
> Do not think that death will saunter to you;
> Death comes like lightning.

From Asaṅga:

> While so far there has been no danger of dying,
> Yet death is always lurking. You who are lazy must get ready for it.
> Mark my words,
> The time will come when in the hour of death you fight against it with your hands before your breast.
> Be blessed in being mindful of death.

From Śāntideva in his 'Bodhicaryāvatāra':

> He who thinks: I shall not die now,
> And lives happily is not wise.

From Candragomin in his 'Śiṣyalekha':

> I shall do this tomorrow, this a little later,
> And this at some future time—when a man thinks in this way,
> The Lord of Death with his club in his hands, looking askance
> With red, angry and scornful eyes, is smiling to himself.'

25. So also in the 'rDzogs chen kun.bzaṅ bla.ma', fol. 37a seq., with further details.

26. Also quoted in the 'rDzogs chen kun.bzaṅ bla.ma', fol. 27a. Before citing this verse, Padma dkar.po in his 'sÑon.'gro'i zin.bris', fol. 4a, states: 'The life of embodied beings, abiding in constant danger, is not to be trusted, because even if it does not now pass away like a bubble in the wind, it has not the power to stay on.'

27. In his 'sÑon.'gro'i zin.bris', fol. 3b, Padma dkar.po declares: 'Among the multitude of embodied beings, there is no guarantee that this one will die earlier and that one later. Death strikes like lightning a person who does not expect it.' See also note 24.

28. *go.ba.* This is used of understanding reality by hearing and pondering about it (*thos bsam*). It is essentially discursive. Out of it there results an understanding which is something like an experience

(*ñams.myoṅ*). After this comes comprehensive understanding as a direct esthetic contact with Reality through an indefinable empathy and intuition (*rtogs*). See, for instance, 'Phyag.chen zin.bris', fol. 7a; 'Phyag.rgya chen.po rnal.'byor bži'i bśad.pa ṅes.don lta.ba'i mig', fol. 7a; 'Phyag.rgya chen.po'i man.ṅag.gi bśad.sbyar rgyal.ba'i gan.mdzod', fol. 21b seq.

29. *rtogs.pa*. See the preceding note.

30. A more detailed discussion is found in the 'rDzogs chen kun.bzaṅ bla.ma', fol. 30a seq.: 'When an upāsaka (lay disciple) asked his kalyāṇamitra (spiritual friend) Pu.to.ba about the most important topic in epitomizing the Dharma, Pu.to.ba answered: "Concentrated attention to transitoriness. When you pay the closest attention to transitoriness by death, above all you give yourself a push on entering the Dharma, which creates a favourable condition for persevering in the practice of good, and lastly you acquire an intimate understanding of the sameness of all constituents of reality. Further, you give an impetus to the shattering of the fetters of this life, which creates a favourable condition for becoming detached from the multiplicities of Saṃsāra, and lastly you are on the verge of setting out on the way to Nirvāṇa. Further, you help the birth of confidence, which creates a favourable condition for energetic striving, and lastly you are very close to the birth of wisdom. Further, when by having paid the closest attention to this transitoriness all this has come into existence in the stream of your life and thought, you have a strong urge to strive after the Dharma, which creates a favourable condition for its realization, and then you complete the Dharma experience. Finally, when all this has come about by having paid the closest attention to transitoriness, you are impelled to strive energetically, which creates a favourable condition for applied energetic striving, and you then do so irreversibly." '

5
THE VICIOUS STATE OF SAṂSĀRA

IT IS PLAIN hedonism[1] if you think what does it matter that the transitory dies, or why should I not make the most of it when I have obtained the most perfect wealth of sensuous and sensual enjoyments among either gods or men,[2] regardless of whether I shall not be born again or have just been reborn. As a remedy the development of concentrated attention to the vicious state of Saṃsāra will be dealt with in this chapter. The following summary covers the whole field of misery:

> Three headings define the vicious state of Saṃsāra:
> The misery of conditioned existence,
> The misery of change and
> The misery of misery[3] (21a).

Should we try to illustrate this triad of misery by similes, that of conditioned existence would be like an unripe fruit; that of change would resemble a meal of rice gruel mixed with poison; and the misery of misery would be like the growth of mould on fruit. Or again, the first is a general feeling of indifference, the second a feeling of pleasure and the third of displeasure.

In stating the primary characteristics of this triad, you must know that the misery of conditioned existence is being affected by misery through having ascribed to ourselves the five psychosomatic constituents organized into a living organism.[4] However, ordinary beings do not feel this as misery, just as someone who is attacked by plague does not feel the slightest pain or heat in his body. But saintly people, such as those who have entered the path to liberation,[5] experience this misery of conditioned existence as such, just as someone who has just recovered from an attack of plague is sensitive to the slightest pain or heat in his body. Or, another simile might be given: A hair on the palm of the hand gives neither a pleasurable nor a displeasurable feeling, but should it enter the eye it causes unpleasantness and pain. So also the misery of conditioned existence, although it is present in ordinary beings, is not felt as misery by them, but is experienced as such only by saintly people. Therefore it is said in the 'mDzod.kyi ṭī.kā' ('Abhidharmakośaṭīkā'):[6]

> A single hair on the palm of the hand,
> If it enters the eye,

Causes unpleasantness and pain.
The fools who are like the palm of the hand (21b)
Do not feel the hair, the misery of conditioned existence,
But saintly people who are like the eye
Experience it as misery.

The second type, that of change, is so called because whatever pleasure there is in Saṃsāra will all come to an end and turn into misery or pain. Therefore it is stated in the 'sÑin.rje padma dkar.po'i mdo' ('Mahākaruṇāpuṇḍarīkasūtra'):

The realm of the gods is the cause for the origination of misery; so also is the realm of men.

Hence, even if a human being should have become a universal monarch, finally his happiness will turn into misery. As is written in the 'bŚes.sbriṅ' ('Suhṛllekha', 69):

Even having become a universal monarch,
In the course of the cycles of aeons he also becomes a servant.

But this is not all. Even if a human being has obtained the body and wealth of the sensuous and sensual enjoyments of Indra, king of gods, he has to die in the end and, by being transformed, he falls from his high place. As has been written:[7]

Even having become the praiseworthy Indra,
By the power of his Karma he falls to the earth again.

Finally, having become free from all sensual desires, like Brahmā, king of gods,[8] and others like him, and having obtained the blissful state of meditative absorption, he falls down again from this lofty height. As has been written:[9]

Even having obtained the desireless bliss of Brahmāhood,
He has again to suffer unending pain
Of having become fuel in the Avīci hell.

The third type, misery of misery, is the manifestation of great wretchedness in addition to the fact that the ascription of the five psychosomatic constituents organized into a living organism is in itself misery. There are two types of it, those (A) of evil and (B) of happy existences (22a).

(A) You must know that the evil existences are the three worlds of denizens of hell, spirits and animals. Each of these three classes of beings is to be known in a fourfold manner: (1) classification, (2) situation, (3) experience of misery and (4) duration of life.

(1) Classification of hells, means that there are eight hot and eight cold ones, totalling sixteen, to which are added the occasional (*ñi.tshe.ba.* Skt. *prādeśika*) and neighbouring hells (*ñe.'khor.ba* Skt. *utsada*), so that there are eighteen in all.

(2) The hot hells are below this Jambudvīpa,[10] because from here many go there on the shortest way. Further, lowest live the denizens of the mNar.med (Avīci) hell; above them, one on top of the other, are the Rab.tu tsha.ba (Pratāpana), Tsha.ba (Tapana), Ṅu.'bod chen.po (Mahāraurava), Ṅu.'bod (Raurava), bsDus.'joms (Saṃghāta), Thig.nag (Kālasūtra), and Yaṅ.sos (Saṃjīva) hells. As is stated in the 'Chos.mṅon.pa.mdzod' ('Abhidharmakośa' III, 58):

> Below here, twenty thousand miles away, is the Avīci hell.
> Above it there are seven other hells.

(3) The kind of misery experienced by beings in these hells is found in the etymology of the names and in their general description.

The first (i) is Yaṅ.sos (Saṃjīva, Reviving Hell). It is so called, because, when its denizens, tied one to the other, have been killed by piercing and beating each other, a cold wind rises and revives them. This lasts until their time in this hell is ended.[11]

(ii) Thig.nag (Kālasūtra, Black Thread Hell) bears this name, because its inhabitants are cut up with flaming saws or axes where a black thread has marked their bodies.[12] As has been written:[13]

> Some are carved into pieces with saws, and others
> Are cut up with excruciatingly sharp-edged axes.

(iii) bsDus.'joms (Saṃghāta, Crushing Hell) derives its name from its denizens being pressed and crushed together between mountains or iron plates (22b). In the first case twin mountains which are like the head of a sheep, come together and crush them. After that the mountains separate and by a cold wind that has risen the bodies of these beings are restored to their former life. Again they are crushed and revived and in this way the torture goes on until their time is exhausted. As is written in the 'sLob.sbriṅ' ('Śiṣyalekha'):

> Two terrifying, huge, mountain-like ram's horns,
> Come together, break and crush them to powder.

Others are pressed between iron plates and four streams of blood pour forth.

> Some are pressed like sesame seed and others
> Are crushed to dust like fine flour.[14]

(iv) Ṅu.'bod (Raurava, Howling Hell) is so named, because the inhabitants there utter terrifying cries.[15]

(v) Ṅu.'bod chen.po (Mahāraurava, Loud Howling Hell) is so called, because those who dwell therein utter still louder cries than in the other hells.[16]

(vi) Tsha.ba (Tapana, Heating Hell) means that the denizens are tormented by fire and heat. Molten bronze, poured into their mouths, burns away their intestines and they are pierced through from the anus to the crown of the head with thorny one-spiked weapons.[17]

(vii) Rab.tu tsha.ba (Pratāpana, Intense Heating Hell) is so called, because beings there are tormented in a very special way. When they have been burnt with molten metal so that no skin is left and while fire flames from the nine openings of the body, they are pierced through with three-spiked weapons from the anus and the soles of the feet to the head and shoulders.[18]

Some are boiled in a
Burning stream of molten bronze,
Others are impaled
On red-hot thorny iron stakes.[19]

(viii) The torture of the denizens of the mNar.med (Avīci) hell consists in being thrust into huge iron kettles filled with molten (32a) bronze or copper from vast cauldrons and then being boiled over an unbearably hot fire.[20] As has been written:[21]

Some are cast into iron kettles
Head down like the ingredients of rice soup.

Because of the uninterrupted pain this hell is called mNar.med (Avīci).[22]

(4) The span of life of those in these hells is:[22a]

In the six, beginning with Saṃjīva,
One day-and-night is equal to the life of the gods of the world of sensuous and sensual desires.
Therefore their span of life
Is to be measured by that of the gods of the world of sensuality.

Since the life of the Cāturmahārājikas is one day in that of the denizens of the Yaṅ.sos (Saṃjīva) hell, and since thirty such days form one month and twelve months one year, the inhabitants of this hell live five hundred such years. In human time this is one hundred and sixty-two thousand times ten million years.[23]

Similarly the life of the denizens of Thig.nag (Kālasūtra) is one thousand years, which is the span of the Trāyastriṃśa gods; in human time this is twelve times one hundred thousand ten million years and ninety-six thousand times ten million years.

The inhabitants of bsDus.'joms (Saṃghāta) live two thousand years, like the Yāma gods. This is ten million times ten million years and three hundred and sixty-eight thousand times ten million years.

The life of those in Ṅu.'bod (Raurava) is four thousand years, that of the Tuṣita gods. This is eight million times ten million years and two million times ten million years and nine hundred and forty-four thousand times ten million years.

In Ṅu.'bod chen.po (Mahāraurava) it is eight thousand years, that of the Nirmāṇarati gods (23b). This is six hundred and sixty times ten million years and three million times ten million years and five hundred and fifty-two thousand times ten million years.

The inhabitants of Tsha.ba (Tapana) live for sixteen thousand years, like the Paranirmitavaśavartin gods. This is five hundred ten million times ten million years and three hundred million times ten million years and eight million times ten million years and four hundred thousand times ten million years and sixteen thousand times ten million years.

The life of those in the Rab.tu tsha.ba (Pratāpana) is half an *antaḥkalpa*.

That of the denizens of the mNar.med (Avīci) hell is one *antaḥkalpa*.

Therefore also it is said:[24]

> In Pratāpana half an *antaḥkalpa*; in Avīci one *antaḥkalpa*.

The ñe.'khor (*utsada*, neighbouring) hells[25] are situated at the four cardinal points of the eight main ones.

First there is Me.ma.mur (Kukūla), a fire pit of live coals where you sink up to your knees. When beings go there to find some place where they might stay, they lose their skin, flesh and blood off their legs. When they pull out their feet, all this is restored. This is the first additional torture.[26]

Next to it is the Ro.myags (Kuṇapa), where in a dirty swamp of watery putrefaction live worms with white bodies and black heads, called mTshun.pa ('Pointed-beak'). They pierce beings to the bones. This is the second additional torture.

Then comes sPu.gri gtams.pa'i lam.po che (Kṣuramārga, the great road of razor blades); Ral.gri lo.ma'i nags.tshal (Asipattravana, a forest of leaves like knives) with brindled dogs (*khyi bsre.po*, *śyāmaśabala*) living in it; and lCags.kyi śal.ma.li (a forest with leaves like iron spikes). In it are birds with iron beaks (*khva lcags.kyi mchu.can*, *ayastuṇḍa*). Beings who go there suffer painful wounds. This is the third additional torture.

Finally there is the river Rab.med (Vaitaraṇī), full of ashes and boiling water. When beings go there, wardens with sharp weapons stand on the shore and prevent them from leaving the river. This is the fourth (24a) additional torture.

Thus there are sixteen additional hells (a group of four at each cardinal point) to each of the eight main ones. Hence:

At their four cardinal points
There are Kukūla, Kuṇapa, Kṣuramārga and the River.[27]

Are these hellish demons who preserve the appearance of human beings and the guardians of such as the ravens with iron beaks (khva lcags.kyi mchu.can) sentient beings? The Vaibhāṣikas say, and the Sautrāntikas deny, that they are, while the Yogācāras as well as Mar.pa and Mi.la.ras.pa in their Father-Son-Instruction declare that because of evil deeds committed by the victims, there arises in their minds the appearance of such hellish beings.[28] In the same way we read in the 'sPyod.'jug' ('Bodhicaryāvatāra' V, 7–8):

The weapons of the inhabitants of the hells—
By whom and for what purpose have they been made?
Who made the earth of glowing iron?
Whence has this mass of flames sprung forth?
The Buddha has declared that
These and similar phenomena are the creation of an evil mind.

The eight cold hells are Chu.bur.can (Arbuda), Chu.bur rdol. pa.can (Nirarbuda), Swo.tham.tham.pa (Aṭaṭa), A.chu zer.ba (Hahava), Kyi.hud zer.ba (Huhuva), Utpal ltar gas.pa (Utpala), Padma ltar gas.pa (Padma), and Padma chen.po ltar gas.pa (Mahāpadma). As is stated:[29]

There is another set of eight hells, which are cold, Arbuda and the others.
They are found below this Jambudvīpa, on top of the great hells.[30]

The type of misery which the inhabitants experience there is found in the etymology of their names and in the general description given below.

The first two hells obtained their names from changes that appear on the bodies of the inhabitants, because owing to unbearable coldness blisters rise on their bodies and then burst.

The next three hells were named from the cries of beings pained by the unbearable cold there.

Of the last three hells, one has the colour of green bark and is split into five or six openings, like a blue lotus (*utpala*); another is shaded from blue to red and has ten or more openings, like a red lotus (*padma*); and the third is of deep red and split into more than one hundred openings, like a great lotus (*mahāpadma*). These three hells also got their names from changes appearing on the bodies of the beings therein.

What is the span of life in these hells? The answer has been given by the Exalted One in a simile:[31]

> Bhikṣus, if in this country of Magadha there were a sesame store holding eighty bushels and crammed full and if once every hundred years someone takes out of it one single grain, Bhikṣus, in this way the whole sesame store holding eighty bushels in this country of Magadha will be emptied during the life of the denizens of the Arbuda hell. Bhikṣus, twenty Arbudas make one Nirarbuda, and so on until you come to twenty Padmas making one Mahāpadma.

The Teacher dbYig.gñen (Vasubandhu) condensed this passage as follows:

> When every hundred years out of a sesame store
> One sesame grain is taken and this store is emptied,
> The time elapsed is the span of life in the Arbuda hell.
> That in the other hells is twenty times greater.

Therefore the span of life in Chu.bur.can (Arbuda) is the time taken to empty one full sesame store, in Chu.bur rdol.pa.can (Nirarbuda) twenty stores, in Swo.tham.tham.pą (Aṭaṭa) four hundred, in A.chu zer.ba (Hahava) eight thousand, in Kyi.hud zer.ba (Huhuva) one hundred and sixty thousand, in Utpal ltar gas.pa (Utpala) three million two hundred thousand (25a), in Padma ltar gas.pa (Padma) sixty-four million, and in Padma chen.po ltar gas.pa (Mahāpadma) one thousand two hundred and forty million sesame stores.

The ñi.tshe (*prādeśika*, occasional) hells[32] are caused by an individual deed or by the acts of two or more people. There are many varieties of them and their location is indefinite. They are found in rivers, mountains and fearful deserts; some are under the earth and others in the countries of men, as was recorded by Venerable Maudgalyāyanīputra, while those in the deserts were seen by

Venerable dGe.'dun.'tsho (Sangharakṣita). The span of life in there is also uncertain.

This ends my record of the misery of the denizens of hell.

The classification of spirits is twofold: (i) Yama, their king, and (ii) the spirits sent out by him.

Where do they live? Yama dwells five hundred miles below this Jambudvīpa. The spirits sent out by him have no fixed abode such as deserts or similar places.[33]

The classification of the spirits sent out by Yama is triple: those whose vision is distorted (i) as to the outer, (ii) as to the inner appearance of food and drink and (iii) as to both.

What type of misery do these various spirits experience? Some experience something like the splendour of the gods. However, those whose vision is distorted with regard to the appearance of food and drink see it as dark blood; others having the illusion that they are prevented from eating and drinking deprive themselves of the opportunity. Those whose vision is distorted from within are thereby unable to eat or drink, although they are not prevented by others from so doing. As has been written:[34] (25b)

> Some whose mouth is like the eye of a needle
> And whose belly is the size of a mountain, although tormented by hunger,
> Are unable to find
> Even a particle of food on a dung heap.

There are two groups of those whose vision is thus entirely distorted, Fire-garlands and Filth-eaters. The former are consumed by fire as soon as they have eaten or drunk anything, while the latter cut and consume their own flesh and drink a mixture of dust and urine. This was observed in a fearful desert by Gro.bžin.skyes rna.ba bye.ba.ri.[35]

As to their span of life, one month of human beings is one day-and-night for spirits. Thus the latter live five hundred years. As has been stated:[36]

> Spirits
> Live five hundred years; one day to them being one month with human beings.

The classification of animals is fourfold: polypods, quadrupeds, bipeds and apods.

They reside in water, on dry earth and in the jungle. Their main home, however, is the great ocean.[37]

What kind of misery do they experience? They suffer that of servitude, slaughter and devouring each other.

The first occurs to those who have come under the power of man.

> Others, powerless and assaulted with hands and feet,
> Whips and iron goads, are slaves.[38]

The second to game animals:

> Some are killed for the sake of pearls, wool, bones,
> Blood, meat and skin.[39]

And the third to those who live mainly in the great ocean (26a).

> They eat what falls as food into their mouths.

The span of life of animals is uncertain, at the most it is one *antaḥkalpa.*

> The life of animals is one *kalpa* at the most.[40]

This ends my description of the misery of evil existences.

(B) The misery of happy existences is threefold: that of human beings, Asuras and gods.

The misery of human existence is eightfold, as is recorded in the 'mṄal.'jug.gi mdo' ('Garbhāvakrāntisūtra'):

> Thus (1) birth, (2) old age, (3) illness and (4) death are each misery; as is (5) to be separated from those who are dear, and (6) to meet those who are not dear, to us, (7) not to obtain what we covet is misery and (8) the difficulty of guarding our possessions.

(1) 'Birth' here means that, although it is the root of everything and is said to occur in four places,[41] generally it refers to issue from a womb. The misery of first entering the womb from the intermediate state is as follows.

All beings in the intermediate state between death and rebirth are endowed with miraculous powers; they walk through the air and with their divine eyes can see even from afar their future place of birth. However, as a result of their Karma there come to them in their sphere of life in the intermediate state, four bewildering experiences: the rising of a storm, the falling of heavy rain, the darkening of the sky and terrifying noises as if made by many people. Then according to their good or evil Karma ten erroneous thoughts arise. They think that they enter a heavenly palace (26b), ascend to the second storey of a house, mount a throne, go into a grass-thatched hut, enter a house made of leaves, or slip in between the grass; that they enter a jungle, or glide into the crevices of a wall or between straw. Thus thinking, even from afar they see their future father and mother cohabit and there they go. However, if great merit has been accumulated (during their previous life), as beings holding a high place of birth they will see heavenly palaces, two-storied houses and similar mansions to which they will hurry. If only mediocre merit has been accumulated, as beings holding a mediocre place of birth they will see grass-thatched huts and other hovels where they will rush. But if no merit has been accumulated, as beings holding a bad place of birth they will see crevices in a wall and slip in there. When they have gone to these places and when they are about to be conceived and born as a male they develop attachment for their mother and antipathy to their father. If they are to be conceived and born as a female they develop attachment for their father and antipathy to their mother.[42] The consciousness principle of beings in the intermediate state, coloured as the case may be by attachment or antipathy, mingles with the secretions of the father and mother.[43] From then on a being is said to stay thirty-eight weeks in the womb. Some, however, say that it is eight, nine or ten months, others that the time is not definite and that a being may remain in the womb for sixty years.

During the first week in the mother's womb a being is boiled and fried as in a warm vessel while the bodily sense organs and the consciousness principle (27a) experience unbearable pain. In this state the embryo is called 'of oval shape' (*mer.mer.po*, Skt. *kalala*) and it looks like rice water or sweetened curd.

In the second week, there rises from the mother's womb the so-called 'all-touching' (*kun.tu reg.pa*) wind, and by its 'touch' the four elements[44] manifest themselves. At this stage the embryo is called 'of oblong shape' (*nur.nur.po*, Skt. *arbuda*) and resembles thick cream or coagulated fat.

In the third week, there rises the so-called 'activating' (*mdzad.ka*) wind, and by its 'touch' the four elements manifest themselves strongly. At this stage the embryo is called 'a lump' (*ltar.ltar.po*, Skt. *peśī*) and is like an iron ladle or an ant.

In the seventh week there rises the so-called 'clasping' (*'khyil.bar byed.pa*) wind, and by its 'touch' the hands and feet are produced. At this stage a pain is felt which makes the embryo think that it is pulled up by a strong wind and spread out with a stick by someone.

In the eleventh week, there rises the so-called 'openings appearing' (*bu.ga snaṅ.ba*) wind from the mother's womb, and by its 'touch' the nine openings of the body are produced. At this time pain is felt as if an open wound was probed with a finger.

This misery of staying in a womb may be illustrated in another way. When a mother keeps an unbalanced diet by giving preference to cold food, the embryo suffers the pain of a naked person being thrown upon ice. In the same way there is pain when the food is either too hot or too sour. When too much is taken it is as if you are crushed between rocks (27b); when too little, it is as if you were suspended and rocked in mid-air. By walking hastily, jumping or slipping down, pain is felt as if you were rolling down the slope of a hill. When a mother indulges too often in sexual intercourse during her pregnancy, the embryo feels as if it were beaten with thorns.[45]

In the thirty-seventh week, while still in the uterus, the consciousness of the foetus, grieved by the state of dirtiness, stench, darkness and imprisonment, conceives the idea of escaping.

In the thirty-eighth week, there arises in the mother's womb the so-called 'flower gathering' (*me.tog sdud.pa*) wind. This turns the foetus around and pushes it near the mouth of the womb. It feels pain as if being damaged by iron machines.

Thus, having been boiled and fried in the womb's heat as in a hot vessel for a very long time, the foetus is 'touched' and shaken up by twenty-eight different winds. Having grown and been nurtured by the nutritive essence of the mother's blood, the oval shaped 'being' develops a normal body. As is said in the 'mṄal.'jug.gi mdo' ('Garbhāvakrāntisūtra'):

> First from the oval spot (*kalala*)
> Originates the fleshy oblong lump (*arbuda*).
> From this the larger mass (*peśī*) grows.
> This larger mass then becomes solid.
> When it has done so
> The head and the four extremities grow.
> When the bones have assembled the body is formed.
> All this is due to the driving power of Karma.

Finally there arises the so-called 'face looking down' (*kha thur.du lta.ba*) wind. It turns the head of the foetus downward and the child reaches the outer world with indrawn hands. This pain is as if being drawn through a net of iron wires (28a).

Some children are born dead and others die with their mother in the birth act. Further,[46] when in the process of birth the child is put on the ground it feels the pain of being laid on a rough coat. At a later stage it suffers the agony of being scraped on the edge of a wall and of its skin being peeled (when it is washed the first time, as the skin is so sensitive). For a long time the newly-born stays in misery and suffers much pain, heat, darkness and unpleasantness. If you were offered three gold coins to remain two days and nights in an unclean closed pit, you would not accept, however much you might want the money, and yet the misery of being in a womb is worse than that. So also is written in the 'sLob.sbriṅ' ('Śiṣyalekha'):

> Enwrapped by unbearable stench,
> Staying in utter darkness,
> Put to hell-like suffering by the womb,
> The body contracted:—so one has to live in great pain.

If we are convinced of such misery we should be haunted by the fear of entering a womb, if only once.

(2) The misery of old age is also immeasurable. There are ten varieties caused by complete changes in (i) stature, (ii) hair, (iii) skin, (iv) complexion, (v) efficiency, (vi) healthy appearance, (vii) stock of merits, (viii) health, (ix) mind and (x) the approach of the end of life.

(i) Deterioration of stature means that the body having once been strong and firm, changes and becomes crooked (28b) and bent, needing support from a stick.

(ii) The hair deteriorates when from shiny jet-black like a bee, it turns white and the head becomes bald.

(iii) It is the same with the skin which formerly was smooth and soft like Banaras cotton or Chinese silk, and now changes and becomes thick, lined and a very bag of wrinkles, just like a battered bangle.

(iv) likewise the complexion which once was bright and pure like a lotus bloom that has just opened, changes and becomes bluish and pale as a faded flower.

(v) Deterioration of efficiency means that power and alacrity weakens and become exhausted. Since all bodily strength is gone, we can no longer work hard; with mental strength exhausted there is but little joy for work; and since the power of the senses is gone they cannot grasp things properly or they fasten on an object other than the one wanted.

(vi) Deterioration of healthy appearance means that while we were once valued and respected by others, we are now scorned, by people lower than ourselves. No longer dear even to worthless people, we are threatened by children and derided by our children's children.

(vii) Deterioration of our stock of merits means that the former wealth of sensuous enjoyments and all the food and drink we have enjoyed lose their attraction; the body does not feel warm and the tongue does not taste what is savoury. In particular we want to eat what is not available, and it is most difficult to obtain and to provide what is needed.

(viii) Deterioration of health means that the misery of being stricken with that greatest of all diseases, old age, attracts all other complaints as well.

(ix) Deterioration of mind (29a) means that we immediately forget what we have said or done and that we are incoherent and mistaken.

(x) To have passed the peak of life and to approach death means that breath becomes short and the voice wheezing; our power of thought fades more and more and death approaches. As is said in the ''Phags.pa rGya.che rol.pa' ('Lalitavistara', p. 174):

> Old age makes the beautiful ugly;
> It robs one of healthy appearance and diminishes efficiency.
> It steals pleasures and brings about misery;
> It causes death and steals brightness as well.

(3) The misery of illness, though immeasurable, may be described in seven ways: (i) being afflicted by a virulent disease; (ii) being treated roughly (by the physician); (iii) having to depend on strong medicines; (iv) being restricted from eating and drinking what we want; (v) being forced to follow the doctor's advice; (vi) our necessaries being exhausted; and (vii) the fear of death. As is stated in the ''Phags.pa rGya.che rol.pa' ('Lalitavistara', p. 175):

> By the misery of the existence of many hundred diseases and of the misery of contracting them,
> All beings are persecuted as deer by the hunter.

(4) The misery of dying is also immeasurable. In the 'rGyal.po.la gdams.pa'i mdo' ('Rājāvavādaka') we read:

> Oh Mahārāja, in this way a man is afflicted by the pointed stake of the Lord of Death; he is deprived of food, without refuge, protector or friend; stricken by disease, his mouth is thirsty; his countenance changes; he cannot stir either hands or feet; he is useless for work; dirties his body with spittle, snot, urine and vomiting and wheezes; the doctors give him up; he sleeps in his bed for the last time, sinks down (29b) into the stream of transmigration and is frightened by the messengers of Yama; his breathing stops and his mouth and nostrils open wide; he has given up this world and goes to the next; he dies and enters deep

darkness; he falls into a deep abyss and is carried away by a great ocean; he is chased by the wind of Karma and goes where there is no firm ground; he has to distribute his property and, although he may cry: 'Oh my mother! my father! my children!', there is, oh Mahārāja, at that time no other refuge, protector or friend than the Dharma.

(5) Misery of being separated from those who are dear to our heart, means that our father, mother, children and children's children may die and there is infinite misery of mourning, distress, lamentation, weeping and other expressions of sadness.

(6) Misery of meeting those who are not dear to us, means that when we have hateful enemies there is misery of quarrelling, while that of strife and of getting a beating is very great.

(7, 8) The last two types are easy to understand (and need not be discussed here).

Among the Asuras there is, in addition to the misery of the gods, that of pride, envy and quarrelling. As is said:[47]

Because among the Asuras there is by nature envy
For the splendour of the gods, there is great sadness.

The gods of the sphere of sensuality experience the misery of quarrelling with the Asuras, remain unsatisfied by sensual enjoyments, are humiliated, killed, violated, slaughtered and banished. They suffer death and transformation and fall into lower forms of life. As is stated:[48]

When a god is to die there are five omens: his dress becomes soiled (30a); his garlands of flowers fade; perspiration breaks forth from his arm-pits; an evil smell rises from his body and he is dissatisfied with his seat.

This type of misery does not exist in the Rūpaloka (world of pure form) and Ārūpyaloka (world of formlessness), where there is neither independence from death, transformation, nor a permanent home, so that the misery of another existence in a bad and lower sphere is experienced. Even such happy lives and paradise-like states as those just mentioned turn into miserable ones with the exhaustion of the Karma which has brought about that happiness.

Therefore this sphere of Saṃsāra is by nature great misery and like a house in flames. As is recorded in the 'mÑal.'jug.gi mdo' ('Garbhāvakrāntisūtra'):

Alas! since this ocean of transmigratory existence is aflame, burns and blazes, not a single individual is unaffected by it.

> This blazing fire is that of attachment, antipathy and bewilderment, of birth, old age and death, of mourning, lamentation, distress and affliction. It is always burning and ablaze, not a single individual escapes from it.

Thus, he who knows the vicious state of Saṃsāra turns his mind away from the pleasures of this world. As is stated in the 'Yab.sras mjal.ba'i mdo' ('Pitāputrasamāgamanasūtra'):

> An attitude of aversion is born
> When you see the vicious state of Saṃsāra;
> When you behold the prison of the three world-spheres
> You renounce it with assiduity.

And the Teacher kLu.sgrub (Nāgārjuna) affirms:[49]

> Since Saṃsāra is such that either among Asuras,
> In hells (30b) or among spirits and animals
> There is no happy birth, know that birth is indeed
> The vessel of much harm.

The fifth chapter, dealing with the vicious state of Saṃsāra,
from the Jewel Ornament of Liberation or
The Wish-Fulfilling Gem of the
Noble Doctrine.

NOTES TO CHAPTER 5

1. Lit.: attachment to the sensual pleasures in this world. See also Chapter 4, note 3.

2. 'God' is a term for the more happy existences in the three world spheres, namely the lower heavens of the world of sensuality and the higher forms of existence in Rūpadhātu and Ārūpyadhātu.

3. This triple division of misery is already met with in the Pāli Canon. See 'Saṃyuttanikāya' IV, 259; V, 56; 'Dīghanikāya' III, 216. Padma dkar.po, in his 'sŇon.'gro'i zin.bris', fol. 6b, defines the three types very concisely: 'The misery of misery means that among men there is the misery of birth, old age and death, and among gods of death, transformation and descending into lower forms of existence. The misery of change is the transitoriness of all heavenly pleasures. That of conditioned existence are the five psycho-somatic constituents which we ascribe to ourselves.' A more detailed account

of the three types is also found in the 'rDzogs chen kun.bzaṅ bla.ma', fol. 56a.

4. *ñe.bar len.pa'i phuṅ.po*, Skt. *upādānaskandha*. According to 'Visuddhimagga' XIV, 214, we ascribe the five constituents of our psychosomatic existence to ourselves and consider them to be our real nature under the influence of the emotional elements of attachment, antipathy and bewilderment (*upādānakkhandā sāsava-upādāniyabhāvena*). *upādāna* is according to 'Aṭṭhasālinī' II, 50 (cp. V, 99), a firm grasping (*dāḷhagāhaṃ gaṇhantī ti attho*). According to Sthiramati in his commentary on Vasubandhu's 'Triṃśikā', p. 19. it is the residue of those habit-forming thoughts which divide the real into the opposites of a spiritual principle (*ātman*) and non-spiritual elements (*dharma*, such as *rūpa* and all that is believed to be material) (*ātmādivikalpavāsanā rūpādidharmavikalpavāsanā*).

5. *rgyun.du žugs.pa*, Skt. *srota-āpanna*. In Hīnayāna he is a man who having had a glimpse of reality has developed the habit of seeing everywhere isolated transitory entities (*dharma*); in Mahāyāna he is a man who has realized that there is neither annihilation nor any new origination. See 'Madhyamakavṛtti', p. 11.

6. This verse is also quoted in the 'sÑon.'gro'i zin.bris', fol. 6b. The Sanskrit version is found in 'Madhyamakavṛtti', p. 476. See also 'Bhāṣya' ad 'Abhidharmakośa' VI, 3 (pp. 126 seq.).

7. 'Suhṛllekha', 69. Also quoted in the 'sÑon.'gro'i zin.bris', fol. 6b. Indra is the ruler over the Trāyastriṃśa gods.

8. Brahmā is a god in the Rūpadhātu.

9. 'Suhṛllekha', 74. Also quoted in 'sÑon.'gro'i zin.bris', fol. 6b; and in 'rDzogs chen kun.bzaṅ bla.ma', fol. 67b.

10. Jambudvīpa is India in the narrower sense of the word. In the wider sense it denotes the whole world.

11. Life in the hells has always stimulated the phantasy of the Tibetans. Though basically the same, the description of their landscape and tortures is more elaborate in the 'rDzogs chen kun.bzaṅ bla.ma', fol. 43a.

12. Cp. 'rDzogs chen kun.bzaṅ bla.ma', fol. 43b.

13. 'Suhṛllekha', 78.

14. ibid. See also 'rDzogs chen kun.bzaṅ bla.ma', fol. 44a.

15. Cp. 'rDzogs chen kun.bzaṅ bla.ma', fol. 44a.

16. Cp. ibid., fol. 44b.

17. Cp. ibid., fol. 44b.

18. Cp. ibid.

19. 'Suhṛllekha', 79.

20. Cp. 'rDzogs chen kun.bzaṅ bla.ma', fol. 45a.

21. 'Suhṛllekha', 82.

22. The explanation given by sGam.po.pa is the first interpretation of this term in 'Bhāṣya' ad 'Abhidharmakośa' III, 58 (p. 148).

22a. 'Abhidharmakośa' III, 82.

23. The same duration is given in 'rDzogs chen kun.bzaṅ bla.ma', fol. 43b seq.

24. 'Abhidharmakośa' III, 83ab.

25. sGam.po.pa follows here the account given in 'Abhidharmakośa' III, 59a–c. A slightly different account is given in 'rDzogs chen kun.bzaṅ bla.ma', fol. 45b.

26. Cp. 'Abhidharmakośa' and the 'Bhāṣya', pp. 151 seq.

27. 'Abhidharmakośa' III, 59a–c.

28. The 'Bhāṣya' ad 'Abhidharmakośa' III, 59 (p. 152), only knows the first two alternatives. sGam.po.pa, it will be remembered, was a disciple of Mi.la.ras.pa and therefore quotes the opinion of his teacher.

29. 'Abhidharmakośa' III, 59cd.

30. See 'Bhāṣya' ad 'Abhidharmakośa' III, 59cd (p. 154).

31. 'Suttanipāta', p. 126; 'Saṃyuttanikāya' I, 152; 'Aṅguttaranikāya' V, 173; 'Bhāṣya' ad 'Abhidharmakośa' III, 84 (p. 176).

32. Cp. 'Bhāṣya' ad 'Abhidharmakośa' III, 59cd, (p. 155). See also 'rDzogs chen kun.bzaṅ bla.ma', fol. 48a, where a more detailed account is given about the location.

33. Cp. 'Bhāṣya' ad 'Abhidharmakośa' III, 59cd, (p. 156). The 'rDzogs chen kun.bzaṅ bla.ma', fol. 50b, classifies spirits into those who live deep down in this world and those who roam through the air. Several legends are related about them.

34. 'Suhṛllekha', 92. Before quoting this verse, Padma dkar.po in his 'sÑon.'gro'i zin.bris', fol. 6a, gives a vivid description of spirits: 'Spirits are those whose body is a blazing fire and whose belly though without bowels is as large as a mountain range. They are unable to move away from their place, their mouths are as small as the eye of a needle, their skin is rough and they have bristling hair. Some look like the burnt stump of a tree, others like a birch rod. They know nothing of food and drink; they eat vomit which turns into boiling water and burns them. In the 'sLob.sbriṅ' ('Śiṣyalekha') is written:

> Among spirits, in summer time
> Even the moon is hot and in winter even the sun is cold.
> Trees grow fruitless and by their
> Very look rivers dry up.'

The same idea is also found in the 'rDzogs chen kun.bzaṅ bla.ma', fol. 51a.

35. His story is told in the 'rDzogs chen kun.bzaṅ bla.ma', fol. 51b seq.: 'When Gro.bžin.skyes.rna.ba.bye.ba.ri had come to the realm of spirits he found four of them sitting in a palace near the throne of a beautiful woman, adorned with precious ornaments. When the lady offered him food she said: "If these spirits should ask you for food do not give them anything." While Gro.bžin.skyes was eating the spirits came to beg for some. When he gave it to them, it turned into chaff for the first spirit and into an iron ball for the second, while the third began to eat her own flesh and the fourth drank dark blood. When the hostess returned she said: "Did I not tell you not to give any food to these spirits? Do you think you are more compassionate than I?" Then Gro.bžin.skyes asked her why they had become spirits, and she told him: "This is my husband, that is my son, this is my daughter-in-law and that is my female servant." When he further asked how it had happened that they had been born among spirits, she explained: "I was a Brahmin woman in our village. When I had prepared dainty food on a lunar festival, the Venerable Mahākātyāyana came for alms which I, having grown confident, gave him. Thinking that my husband would be pleased if he were given the chance to express his joy, I gave alms to Lord Buddha's disciple, the Venerable Mahākātyāyana, and when I told my husband to be happy, he got angry and shouted: 'Did you give the first offering of alms to this shaven beggar, without having given anything to the Brahmans and without first having entertained our relatives? Why not put chaff into the mouth of this shaven beggar?' When he then spoke to my son, the latter also got angry and said: 'Why should this shaven beggar not eat iron balls?' When in the evening my relatives sent dainty food to me, my daughter-in-law ate it all and gave me the bad food. When I asked her whether she had not eaten the dainty and given me the bad food, she lied and said: 'Before eating your food why should I not devour my own flesh?' In the same way, when I sent dainty food to my relatives, my female servant ate it all herself and declared: 'I would drink dark blood rather than steal your food.' Thinking that I would like to see where these people were reborn on account of their evil deeds the fruit of which they have to experience, I was born a powerful spirit. Otherwise I would have become a deity among the Trāyastriṃśa gods because I gave alms to a noble follower of the Buddha. When you go to my village visit my daughter who lives by prostitution and tell her that you have seen her father and mother and that her profession is a

bad one, and that she should give up this evil way of life. If she does not believe you tell her that in her father's house there are four iron vessels full of gold, a golden stick and a round vessel for pouring offerings. She should give them as alms to the Venerable Mahākātyāyana in our name, so that our Karma becomes less." '

36. 'Abhidharmakośa' III, 83b–d.

37. See 'Bhāṣya' ad 'Abhidharmakośa' III, 59cd (pp. 155 seq.) 'sÑon.'gro'i zin.bris', fol. 6b. 'rDzogs chen kun.bzaṅ bla.ma', fol. 54a.

38. 'Suhṛllekha', 90.

39. ibid.

40. 'Abhidharmakośa' III, 83b–d. The discrepancy between *antaḥkalpa* and *kalpa* is also found in the 'Bhāṣya', p. 175.

41. They are egg, womb, sweat and apparition. See 'Abhidharmakośa' III, 8cd and 'Bhāṣya' (pp. 27 seq.), for a more detailed description.

42. See 'Bhāṣya' ad 'Abhidharmakośa' III, 15ab (p. 50).

43. This conception is as old as 'Majjhimanikāya' II, 156, where it is stated that fecundation takes place only when the Gandharva, the organizing principle in the state between death and reincarnation, is present at the time of the fertile period of the mother and father.

44. The four elements are 'earth', 'water', 'fire' and 'wind', symbolizing solidity, cohesion, temperature and mobility. See 'Abhidharmakośa' I, 12, 13, and 'Bhāṣya' (pp. 21 seq.). For a detailed discussion see my 'Philosophy and Psychology in the Abhidharma', pp. 223 seq.

45. A similar account is also found in the 'rDzogs chen kun.bzaṅ bla.ma', fol. 58a seq.

46. Similarly, 'rDzogs chen kun.bzaṅ bla.ma', fol. 58b.

47. 'Suhṛllekha', 102.

48. See also 'Bhāṣya' ad 'Abhidharmakośa' III, 44ab (p. 136).

49. 'Suhṛllekha', 103.

6

KARMA AND ITS RESULT

IF YOU THINK about the driving force from which the misery just depicted has taken its origin, you will realize that it has sprung from sullied actions (Karma).[1] As is stated in the 'mDo.sde las brgya.pa' ('Karmaśatakasūtra'):

> Actions are of various kinds; by them
> The various walks of life have been created.

In the 'sÑiṅ.rje padma dkar.po' ('Mahākaruṇāpuṇḍarīkasūtra'):

> The world is made and produced by Karma; beings are the result of and have originated from it as motive; they are divided into groups and status by it.

And in the 'Chos.mṅon.pa.mdzod' ('Abhidharmakośa' IV, 1):

> The variety of the world is born from Karma.

If you then ask what it is, the answer is motivation and motivatedness.[2] As is explained in the 'Chos.mṅon.pa kun.las btus.pa' ('Abhidharmasamuccaya', p. 53):

> What is Karma? It is motivation and motivatedness.

In the 'mÑon.pa.mdzod' ('Abhidharmakośa' IV, 1):

> Karma is motivation and what has come about thereby.

And in the 'rTsa.śe' ('Mūlamadhyamakakārikā' XVII, 2):

> The Exalted Seer has declared:
> Karma is motivation and motivatedness.

If you further ask what these are, the reply is that motivation is mental activity,[3] and what has been set up by it is motivatedness, the latter being known as bodily and vocal activities. This is also stated in the 'mÑon.pa.mdzod' ('Abhidharmakośa' IV, 2):

> Motivation is mind's activity;
> What is set up by it are bodily and (31a) vocal activities.

In the discussion of such activity and of the result produced by it, the following will serve as a guide:

> Six headings outline Karma and its results:
> Classification, primary characteristics,
> Ascription, strict result,
> Small causes with big results and inevitableness.

Classification is threefold: the cause and effect of non-meritorious, meritorious, and subliminal actions.[4]

In discussing the primary characteristics of each class, the cause and effect of non-meritorious actions will first be dealt with.

Although, generally speaking, there are many such actions, all of them come under the heading of the ten unhealthy[5] types of which there are three by way of the body such as murder and other violent acts; four by way of speech such as lies and other untrue utterances; and three by way of mind such as covetousness and other forms of greed. In each group there are again three sections: classification of the act, the result, and the most outstanding action.

1. Under murder there are three subdivisions: those done through (i) cupidity, (ii) malevolence and (iii) deludedness. Of these the first is committed for the sake of meat, skin and other parts of an animal; for sport or money; or to protect ourselves and our friends. The second is perpetrated because of antipathy to those who have a grudge against us or who have become our enemies; while the third takes place when performing sacrifices.[6]

In the result which such actions bear there are also three types to be distinguished: (i) maturation of the act;[7] (ii) natural outflow of the existing condition;[8] and (iii) the general result.[9] Maturation of the act means that the individual will be reborn in hell (31b). The natural outflow of the existing condition means that even if the evil-doer is reborn as a human being, his life will be short and he will suffer from many diseases; while the general result is that he will be born in a country in which many calamities happen, and in a place of little prosperity.[10]

The most outstanding action means that of all types of murder parricide or the slaying of an Arhant is the most heinous crime.[11]

2. Theft also has three subdivisions: (i) by force, (ii) in secret and (iii) by deceit. The first is to commit robbery with violence and without giving notice of our intentions; the second is to break into houses and steal without somebody noticing it; while the third is to deceive by measures, coins and other mercantile practices.[12]

The result of such actions is also of three types: maturation means that the evil-doer is reborn among spirits; natural outflow of the existing condition means that even if he is born as a human being, he will be deprived of the objects of enjoyment; while the general result is that he will be reborn in a place where there is much cold and hail.[13]

The most outstanding action means that of all types of theft that of the property of a Guru or of the Triple Gem is the most heinous crime.

3. Sexual misdemeanour also has three subdivisions: against those who are guarded (i) by the family, (ii) by a master and (iii) by religion and custom.[14] The first is sexual misdemeanour with our mother, sister or other female relative; the second is with a woman who has been married by the ruler or any one else; while the third is of five varieties: even if she be our own wife, sexual relation with her is considered to be improper if it is practised (a) at an improper part of the body, (b) in a place or (c) at a time that is improper, (d) too often and (e) in general. Of these the first (a) is to have sexual intercourse by way of the mouth or the anus. (b) Improper place (32a) is near the retinue of a Guru, a monastery, a funeral monument (*stūpa*), or where many people have gathered. (c) Improper time means to have sexual intercourse with a woman who has taken a vow, is pregnant or nursing a child, or in daylight. (d) Improper frequency is more than five successive times. (e) General improperness means to coerce a woman to sexual intercourse by beating. It also means to have intercourse with a male or in a eunuch's mouth or anus.

Of the three results of such actions, maturation means that the culprit is reborn among spirits; natural outflow of the existing condition means that even if the evil-doer is born as a human being, he will be one who gets a hostile wife; while the general result is that he will be born in a place with much dust.[15]

The most outstanding action means that of all types of sexual misdemeanour to have intercourse with our mother or with an Arhatī is the most heinous crime.

4. Telling lies has three subdivisions: (i) destructive, (ii) big and (iii) small. The first is to lie about the qualities and faculties of a sublime person without knowing and possessing them; the second is a lie which harms us and others; while the third hurts no one.

Of the three results, maturation means that the individual is reborn as an animal; natural outflow of the existing condition means that even if the liar is born as a human being, he will become a great slanderer; while the general result is that he is born with halitosis.[16]

The outstanding act means that slander of the Tathāgata and telling lies to a Guru are the most heinous of all crimes.

5. In calumny by slander there are three subdivisions: (i) severe, (ii) prejudicial and (iii) clandestine. The first is to smear two friends in their presence and thereby to divide them against each other; the second (32b) is to separate them by prejudicing the one against the other; while the third is to disunite friends by creating discord clandestinely.

Of the three results of such action, maturation means that the individual will be reborn in hell; natural outflow of the existing condition that even if the slanderer is born as a human being, he will be deprived of friends; while the general result is that he is born in a place which is not level.[17]

The most outstanding action means that of all types of calumny slander which split the Sangha by insulting it is the most heinous crime.[18]

6. Words that hurt are divided into three subdivisions: (i) public or (ii) clandestine speaking and (iii) transmitting words that hurt. The first is to divulge various faults publicly to outsiders; the second is to reveal them to the public by mixing with untrustworthy or worthless people; while the third is to speak of them in the presence of friends and others of those concerned.

Of the three results maturation means that the individual is reborn in hell; natural outflow of the existing condition that even if the evil-doer is born as a human being, he will in his next incarnation have to hear many unpleasant things; while the general result is that he will be born among wicked people in a place which is dry and hot.[19]

The most outstanding action means that to speak hurting words to father, mother and other kindred people is the most heinous crime.

7. Idle talk also has three subdivisions: (i) wrong, (ii) worldly and (iii) idle talk though it is true. The first is to utter the mumble-jumble of the Tirthikas; the second is useless chatter; while the third is to instruct in the Dharma someone who is not willing or not a proper person for instruction.

Of the three results of such action, maturation means that the individual is reborn as an animal (33a); natural outflow of the existing condition that even if the evil-doer is born as a human being, he will become a person whose words are not credited; while the general result is that he is born in a place where the seasons of summer and winter are thrown into confusion.[20]

The most outstanding action means that of all types of idle talk, to confuse those who are eager to learn the Dharma is the most heinous crime.

8. Covetousness also has three subdivisions: (i) as to what is our own, (ii) what belongs to others and (iii) what does not belong to either. The first is to want the best for our own life, family, form and appearance, qualities, and wealth. It is the thought: there is none like me. The second is to covet the merits of others. It is the thought: why should his not be mine? The third is to hanker after the treasures

under the earth which are not for us nor for others. It is the thought: why should they not be under my control?[21]

Of the three results of such activity, maturation means that the individual is reborn among spirits; natural outflow of the existing condition that even if the evil-doer is born as a human being, he becomes a person who is exceedingly greedy; while the general result is that he is born in a place which yields poor crops.[22]

The most outstanding action means that the desire to rob those who have renounced everything of the little they have is of all types of covetousness the most heinous crime.

9. Wickedness also has three subdivisions: (i) being born from antipathy, (ii) envy and (iii) spite. The first is the intention to kill another person out of antipathy, as if he were our enemy; the second is the intention (33b) to slay him through fear that as my rival he might get the better of me; while the third is the intention to murder a man out of malice, because some time ago he has done me some harm.

Of the three results of such activity, maturation means that the individual will be reborn in hell; natural outflow of the existing condition that even if he is born as a human being, he will be a spiteful man; while the general result is that he will be born in a place where food is bitter and coarse.[23]

The most outstanding action means that of all types of wickedness the perpetration of capital offences is the most heinous crime.[24]

10. Erroneous views also have three subdivisions: (i) those concerning the relation between a deed and its result, (ii) the Truths and (iii) the Jewels. The first is the non-acceptance of the fact that good or evil actions are the cause of good or bad results respectively; the second is the view that from the acceptance of the Truth of the Path[25] the Truth of Disappearance[26] does not follow; while the third is to hold the Three Jewels as untrue and to slander them.[27]

Of the three results of such activity, maturation means that the individual is reborn as an animal; natural outflow of the existing condition that even if he is born as a human being, he will be completely dull; while the general result is that he is born in a place where there are no crops at all.[28]

The most outstanding action means that of all types of erroneous views rationalism[29] is the most heinous crime.

So far the result of the maturation of an act has been explained in its general nature. In particular, however, it may be listed according to the topics of determination by way of (i) emotional imbalance, (ii) frequency of performance and (iii) objective.

(i) When we commit evil deeds through malevolence we are reborn in hell (34a), when through cupidity we become spirits and when through deludedness we are born as animals. This is stated in the 'Rin.chen 'phreṅ.ba' ('Ratnāvalī'):

> As a rule, through cupidity one becomes a spirit;
> Through malevolence one is born in hell;
> Through deludedness one becomes an animal.

(ii) By constantly committing evil deeds we are reborn in hell, by doing many we become spirits and when we only do a few we are reborn as an animal.

(iii) When we commit evil deeds against beings of high status we are reborn in hell, when against those of medium status we become spirits and when against those of low status, animals.

In this way the relation between cause and effect of non-meritorious actions has been described. In the 'Rin.chen 'phreṅ.ba' ('Ratnāvalī') it is summed up as:

> Deeds caused by cupidity, malevolence and deludedness
> Are unwholesome;
> Unwholesome deeds produce all misery
> And also all evil existences.

The relation of cause and effect of meritorious deeds is subsumed under the ten healthy acts, that is, the abjuration of the ten unhealthy ones. This means that, when we lead a life in accordance with such positive acts, we preserve the lives of others, make lavish gifts and lead a chaste life;[30] we speak the truth and reconcile enemies; we speak meaningful words quietly and sincerely, have few desires and are contented; we develop benevolence and compassion attentively, and enter Reality.[31]

Of the three results of such activity, maturation means (34b) that we are reborn among the gods and men of the world of sensuality;[32] natural outflow of the existing condition that by having abjured murder and having preserved another being's life we attain a long life; while the general result is that we are born in places with good and strong properties. The same also holds good for the other wholesome actions.

In this way the relation between cause and effect of meritorious actions has been described. The 'Rin.chen 'phreṅ.ba' ('Ratnāvalī') sums it up as follows:

> Deeds done in the absence of cupidity, malevolence and deludedness

Are healthy;
Healthy deeds produce happiness in all existences
And in all births.

The relation between the cause and effect of subliminal actions is simple. Meditations as cause (*samāpattidhyāna*) lead to certain meditational results (*upapattidhyāna*).[33] The causes (*samāpattidhyāna*) consist of eight preliminary stages (*sāmantaka*),[34] eight types of dhyāna[35] and the modification of the first type of dhyāna (*dhyānāntara*).[36] The results (*upapattidhyāna*) are the seventeen classes of gods in the Rūpadhātu[37] and the four infinities of the Ārūpyadhātu.[38] For each cause-and-effect relation the practice of the ten wholesome deeds is the general condition.

We are born as a Brahmakāyika god by having concentrated first on the unobstructed path of the preliminary stage (*sāmantaka*) being the earliest moment in meditation (*anāgamya*) of the first discursive dhyāna.[39] The resulting absorption (*samādhi*) is endowed with the four basic factors of deliberation (*vitarka*), which is the first step in meditation leading to a steadily moving reflection (*vicāra*) and culminating in joy (*prīti*) and pleasure (*sukha*),[40] and leads to the first perfecting dhyāna.[41]

By concentrating attentively on that aspect or modification of the first dhyāna which is free from deliberation (*dhyānāntara*) we become Mahābrahmā.[42] We become a Parīttābha, or god of the second dhyāna, by doing the same on the path of the preliminary stage of the second discursive dhyāna and then moving on to the resulting absorption (*samādhi*) endowed with joyful and pleasant feelings in which deliberation and reflection are absent (35a).

In each case attentive concentration on the preliminary stage (*sāmantaka*) is presupposed, so that the resulting absorption (*samādhi*), endowed with the pleasure of the third perfecting dhyāna in which joy has been left behind, leads to rebirth as a Parīttaśubha, a god of the third dhyāna.

Similarly the absorption (*samādhi*) of the fourth dhyāna in which all four basic factors have been eliminated results in rebirth as an Anabhraka. And so on.

Infinity of Space (*nam.mkha' mtha'.yas skye.mched*, Skt. *ākāśānantyāyatana*) is realized by detachment from the four dhyānas, and by attentive concentration on it we become a god of the Sphere of Infinity of Space. Detachment from this leads to Infinity of Consciousness (*rnam.śes mtha'.yas skye.mched*, Skt. *vijñānānantyāyatana*) in the Sphere of which we become a god by similar attentive concentration. The two further Spheres which follow and in which we can also become gods are those of ordinary Nothingness (*ci.yaṅ.med.pa'i skye.mched,* Skt. *ākiṃcanyāyatana*) and Neither Sensation nor Non-Sensation (*'du.śes.med 'du.śes.med.min skye.mched,* Skt. *naivasaṃjñānā-saṃjñāyatana*).

What sort of way, you may ask, is 'detached from this and that'? It is a mind-born path on a low level because it leads to, but is not yet, desirelessness.

If you further ask whether the Sphere of Infinity of Space is so called because it has as its frame of reference the space perceived, the answer is No. The first three Infinities have received their respective names through an act of deliberation at the time of their realization (*samāpatti*), but later when this realization has been overcome there is no thought with which to make a judgment.[43]

The last stage bears its name owing to a feeble sensation (35b); there is there no clear sensation, but neither is there no sensation.[44]

In conclusion it may be stated that all the eight fundamental dhyānas are states of concentration in a healthy attitude.[45]

Thus the relation between the cause and effect of subliminal actions has been described. In the 'Rin.chen 'phreṅ.ba' ('Ratnāvalī') we read:

> Through dhyānas, boundlessness, and formlessness
> The bliss of Brahmā and others is experienced.[46]

Therefore the creator of things and events in Saṃsāra is this triad of sullied actions.

Ascription, the third heading, means that Karma operates by itself in the results produced by it. It ripens into the psychosomatic constituents of him who commits the deed, but nowhere else. As is stated in the 'mṄon.pa kun.las btus.pa' ('Abhidharmasamuccaya', p. 61):

> What is ascription of Karma? It is the experience of the fruition of the Karma one has done oneself. Being dissimilar to others it is called one's own.

If this were not the case, Karma done would be exhaustible and the evil consequences of meeting with the result of what we have not done would have to be faced. As is said in a Sūtra:

> The deeds committed by Devadatta do not mature in the ground, nor in water, nor anywhere else, but solely in the psychosomatic constituents and the operational fields of him who owns them. Where else can they mature?

The fourth topic is the strict result of Karma. This means that infallibly a good or a bad result of a good or bad deed is experienced; by storing up good Karma good results are experienced; by storing up bad Karma bad results.[47] As is stated in the 'mŃon.pa kun.las btus.pa' ('Abhidharmasamuccaya', p. 61):

> What is strict result? It is the experience of the result of what one has done, because good or bad Karma transmits its elements respectively.

In the 'Dran.pa ñer.bžag chun.ba' (36a):

> Through good one attains good;
> From evil originates misery.
> Thus the result of good and evil
> Karma has been pointed out.

And in the 'Ńes.pas žus.pa'i mdo' ('Surataparipṛcchāsūtra'):

> Out of pungent seeds pungent fruits are born;
> Out of sweet seeds sweet fruits.
> By this example the wise should know
> The bitter result of evil deeds and
> The sweet result of good ones.

The fifth topic is the great result out of a small deed. With respect to evil deeds this means that, as has been explained above, they will be experienced in hell for as many aeons as there are thought-instants. In the 'Byaṅ.chub.sems.dpa'i spyod.pa.la 'jug.pa' ('Bodhicaryāvatāra' I, 34) you will read:

> The Buddha said: He who towards such a royal patron
> Harbours an evil attitude,
> Will stay in hell
> For so many aeons as he has shown this evil attitude.

It is also said that we will have to experience the misery of five hundred rebirths for each evil word we have uttered. This is stated in the 'Tshoms' ('Udānavarga' XXVIII, 24):

> The doing of even a little evil deed
> Becomes in the next world a terrifying
> And noise-making misery,
> Just like poison that has entered the marrow.

And similarly even a little wholesome deed gives a great result. As is affirmed in the 'Tshoms' ('Udānavarga' XXVIII, 25):

> Even little merits done
> Attract great happiness in the next world.

They become great benefactors,
Just like the ripening of excellent grain.

The sixth topic (36b) is the inevitableness of Karma. This means that except when a counter-action to a particular Karma to be experienced is done and will be experienced, the result is never lost or spent without maturing. Even those who for a long time have been lulled into security, will feel the result of whatever deed they have committed, as soon as in some way or other the occasion arises. Therefore, when we are terrified by the misery of Saṃsāra and begin to believe in the concatenation of Karma and its results, we are but men of mediocre intelligence, as is stated in this verse:[48]

He who turns his back on the pleasures of the world
And abstains from evil deeds,
But provides only for his own peace,
Is called a mediocre man.

As an example the story of the seven wives of King Kri.kri may be referred to.

In the 'mDo.sde las brgya.pa' ('Karmaśatakasūtra') you can read:

The deeds of beings
Are not exhausted even in hundreds of aeons;
Having become accumulated, when the proper time arrives
They will mature into their fruits.[49]

And in the 'Dran.pa ñer.bžag chuṅ.ba':

Fire may become cold;
The wind may be caught with a leash;
Sun and moon may fall down on the earth;
But the result of Karma is infallible.

The sixth chapter, dealing with Karma and Its Results,
from the Jewel Ornament of Liberation or
The Wish-Fulfilling Gem of the
Noble Doctrine.

NOTES TO CHAPTER 6

1. *zag.bcas.pa'i las*, Skt. *sāsrava karman.* The idea that our life is sullied by certain elements (*āsrava*) which assist it to go on in an unsatisfactory way, runs right through all strata of Buddhism. There

are four such elements which have the effect of keeping man on a low level of spirituality and make him unable to grasp the nature of good and evil actions and their respective results. They are: 'sensuality' (*kāma*), 'naïve realism' (*bhava*), 'opinionatedness' (*dṛṣṭi*), in particular the non-acceptance of the law that exists between action and its result, and 'ignorance' (*avidyā*). Their influence can be stopped by insight (*darśana*) into the nature of things and by attentive concentration (*bhāvanā*) to that which has been perceived.

2. *sems.pa*, Skt. *cetanā*; *bsam.pa*, Skt. *cetayitvā*. 'Motivation' means more than the urge to do something. It includes the goal which differs according to whether it is inspired by ignorance, thus leading to entanglement in worldly preoccupations, or whether it is the result of 'discriminating awareness' (*prajñā*) which leads to a realization of Reality. In either case man is both driven in a certain direction and drawn toward something. Thus emphasis directs the dynamics of life. In Buddhist conception, *cetanā* is never random activity.

3. *yid.kyi las*, Skt. *manaskarman*. It is that particular force which forms our attitude (*sems*, Skt. *citta*) and allows the other psychic function-events to work in a predetermined way, be this healthy, unhealthy or indifferent. See also 'Vijñaptimātratāsiddhi', p. 52.

4. A meritorious (*bsod.nams*, Skt. *puṇya*) action leads to a happy existence in the world of sensual desires, whether of gods or men. An action which is non-meritorious (*bsod.nams ma.yin.pa*, Skt. *apuṇya*) leads to unhappy existences such as hells, spirits and animals. Subliminal actions (*mi.g'yo.ba*, Skt. *āniñjya*) lead to the happy experiences of meditative absorption in the Rūpadhātu and Ārūpyadhātu. See also 'Vijñaptimātratāsiddhi', pp. 474, 494.

5. *mi.dge.ba*, Skt. *akuśala*. As the opposite to *dge.ba*, Skt. *kuśala* 'wholesome', it suggests unhealthiness, for only mental health, seeing things as they are, is conducive to spiritual development.

6. Cp. 'Bhāṣya' ad 'Abhidharmakośa' IV, 68d (pp. 144 seq.). 'rDzogs chen kun.bzaṅ bla.ma', fol. 72b.

7. *rnam.par smin.pa'i 'bras.bu*, Skt. *vipākaphala*. This refers to a result which does not come about immediately, but in the slow ripening of an evil or good deed, the good quality, however, being held back by the influence of defiling and disturbing elements (*kuśala-sāsrava*). See 'Bhāṣya' ad 'Abhidharmakośa' II, 57ab (p. 290). As is pointed out by Padma dkar.po in his 'sÑon.'gro'i zin.bris', fol. 5a, an action may be 'a powerful one which matures now and will be experienced during the present life (of an individual), during his next existence or after many lives in a variety and number of effects'.

The 'rDzogs chen kun.bzaṅ bla.ma', fol. 80b, explains this as follows: 'Result of the maturation of the act means that, if any of the ten unwholesome deeds has been done under the influence of malevolence giving rise to such activity, rebirth will take place in the hells; if under that of cupidity, among spirits; and if under deludedness, among animals. Having been reborn in these evil existences, the individual has to suffer their respective miseries. Further, when Karma has been accumulated by the motives which give rise to activity, such as cupidity, malevolence and deludedness, and when these have been operating strongly for a long time, rebirth takes place in the hells; if of medium strength and duration, among spirits and if of little strength and duration, among animals.'

8. *rgyu mthun.pa'i 'bras.bu*, Skt. *niṣyandaphala*. Lit.: 'a result similar to its cause'. This result belongs to the same level as the cause, as for instance the world of sensuality in which the cause was operating. It also has the same ethical value as the cause (*kliṣṭa*). See 'Bhāṣya' ad 'Abhidharmakośa' II, 57c (p. 291). An exhaustive description is given in the 'rDzogs chen kun.bzaṅ bla.ma', fol. 80b seqq.: 'Although an individual may have escaped from evil existences in accordance with the ripening of his Karma and may enjoy having attained a human body as a working basis, there is also in lower existences a variety of misery corresponding to the actions as cause (81a). This correspondence is by activity (*byed.pa rgyu.mthun*) and experience (*myoṅ.ba rgyu.mthun*). The first means to be born in a corresponding sphere of activity, as, for instance, if a man has formerly taken life he will now delight in killing, or if a man has been taking what was not given to him he will also now delight in stealing. Thus, some people from early youth onward kill worms and flies as soon as they see them and delight in so doing because this corresponds to what they did before. In the same way, under the influence of Karma accumulated through former existences, some people from early youth take pleasure in killing, while others feel inclined to wholesome deeds. Since this is the outcome of or in correspondence with their former activity, all that has been done before is reflected in this bodily existence and where we shall be reborn depends on our present action. But this is not all. Even among animals, falcons and wolves like to kill and cats to steal, which is what they were wont to do before.

'Each of the ten unwholesome deeds has two sides. The result of having taken life in former existences is that the present life is short and full of diseases. Some children die as soon as they are born and this is (81b) because they took life in former existences. For many existences to come they will die as soon as they are born. Similarly, some people are from early youth afflicted by many diseases from which they are never free until death in old age. Since this is the maturation of Karma which consisted in killing and fighting, without giving a thought to the matter, it is necessary to confess and feel ashamed of what we have done and to strive to counteract evil Karma by doing good and renouncing evil.

'By taking what has not been given to us we become poor in wealth and even if there is little of it we are usually like enemies who rob and steal. On the other hand, there are even now poor people who, instead of making exertions as big as a mountain, delight in accumulating merits, be they small as a spark of fire. If as a result of non-liberality in former existences we have no power or ability to find riches and wealth, the greatest exertion will be of no avail; and even if by robbery we have gained so much that it is difficult to increase it, it is a fact that all others who have done so have died in poverty. On the other hand, there are many people who do not make the slightest exertion and who look upon trading, banking and their gains thereby as futile. If this is due to former liberality, they are not deprived of wealth in their life (82a). Therefore it is necessary to spend liberally so that wealth may come. Knowing that what is done in youth comes to maturity in old age in this world, we must be prepared that everything will ripen in the immediate future. Therefore, as regards to wealth we must know that every attempt at fraudulent trading and thieving leads to cupidity and malpractice. For many aeons such a being will not escape from being born among spirits, and even in this life, stricken by inescapable Karma, he will become poor and wretched, or if he should possess some little wealth, he will not have the power to enjoy it. Due to his avarice he will think that his gains are little or nothing and his wealth will become the cause of evil. Though there is wealth it is useless and like a treasure guarded by spirits. Therefore those who seem to be rich, on closer inspection, are worse off than the poor, because all that is the cause of happiness in this life and hereafter, such as food, dress, medicines and comforts, are of no use. From now on laying the foundation of an existence among spirits they will reap the reward of economy.

'Sexual misconduct results in the marriage partner being ugly, easy-going and more like an enemy (82b). Although the couple are almost always quarrelling and spiteful, each thinks that it is the other who has a bad temper. Since this is in correspondence with former acts of sexual misdemeanour, instead of stirring up hatred around us, we must realize what is the result of former bad actions and be very tolerant. As is stated by rJe Dam.pa Rin.po.che:

Married life is transitory like a fair,
Do not quarrel in spitefulness, oh Diṅ.ri.ba.

'Further,

As a result of telling lies
We ourselves hear many abuses
And others often deceive us.

'Therefore, when now we are wrongly accused or abused, knowing that this is the result of having formerly told lies, without feeling hatred toward the speaker and without spiteful retaliation, we should think that thereby much of our bad Karma disappears and try to be glad about it. As was said by Rig.'dzin 'jigs.med gliṅ.pa:

To be wronged by an enemy is spiritual gain,
To be wrongly accused is the whip of admonition to good.
Since this is a teacher for losing attachment and hatred,
Look at it in such a way that you cannot but be grateful.

'As a result of calumny and tale-bearing we get disobedient servants and meet aggressive people (83a). The pupils of a Guru, the personal attendants of a master, and the hired workmen in a household are mostly at variance with us. Without listening to anything we say, they oppose it. Even if they are asked to do something easy, the workmen will turn a deaf ear until we repeat it twice or thrice; then having become angry they answer back harshly and work slowly in their own time. When they have finished, they will not say so, but will always show a bad temper. Since this is the result of former tale-bearing by the master, we must feel ashamed of any bad work and strive to solve the disagreement between us and others.

'A man who speaks words that hurt, will always hear unpleasant things said to him, and whatever he says will give cause for quarrel. Moreover, words that hurt are worse than evil deeds, as a proverb says:

Though words may not have arrows and swords, they tear a man's heart to pieces.

'Accidentally to bring about hatred in another man's heart and to speak only one bad word to a countryman has the result that for many successive existences we will not be liberated from evil existences. Once the Brahman Seṅ.skya called 'Od.sruṅ, a disciple of the Buddha (83b), "you horse-head, you bull-head", and was reborn as an eighteen-headed sea-monster for a whole aeon; when he was finally liberated he is said to have been reborn in hell. Further, a certain Bhikṣuṇī called another a bitch, and for five hundred existences she herself became one. Many such incidents could be related. Therefore we should train ourselves to speak gentle words and, in particular, since we do not know whether the person we address is a spiritual person or a Bodhisattva, we should use pure language to all and speak words of virtue and praise. To abuse or curse a Bodhisattva is said to be a more serious crime than to kill all beings in the three world spheres:

> Greater than killing all beings in the three worlds
> Is the crime of abusing Bodhisattvas.
> Make a confession of the senseless evil you have accumulated.

'The result of idle talk is that if a mild and sincere speaking man talks vehemently, others will not believe him and are frightened as if he were said to have many diseases.

'As a result of covetousness, our wishes will not be fulfilled and we will get just what we do not want.

'Through wickedness, we become frightened and terrified and incur many dangers (84a).

'Through erroneous views, we remain entangled in evil views and our mind gets hardened by fraudulence.'

9. *dbaṅ.gi 'bras.bu*, Skt. *adhipatiphala*. This refers to the environment into which a being is born as the result of the collective acts of sentient beings. 'Bhāṣya' ad 'Abhidharmakośa' II, 56b (p. 288). 'rDzogs chen kun.bzaṅ bla.ma', fol. 84a. The same work, fol. 84ab, adds the *skyes.bu byed.pa'i 'bras.bu*, Skt. *puruṣakāraphala*. This result is the inherent potential of an act: 'Any work that has been done will multiply and increase. It will continue in endless misery through one and successive births and having built up one evil deed upon another it will roam through endless cycles.'

10. 'Bhāṣya' ad 'Abhidharmakośa' IV, 85ab (pp. 186 seq.).

11. ibid., IV, 103ab (p. 213). 'rDzogs chen kun.bzaṅ bla.ma', fol. 72b.

12. 'Bhāṣya' ad 'Abhidharmakośa' IV, 73cd (pp. 155 seq.). 'rDzogs chen kun.bzaṅ bla.ma', fol. 75a.

13. 'Bhāṣya' ad 'Abhidharmakośa' IV, 85ab (pp. 186 seq.).

14. ibid., IV, 74ab (pp. 157–8). 'rDzogs chen kun.bzaṅ bla.ma', fol. 76b.

15. 'Bhāṣya' ad 'Abhidharmakośa' IV, 85ab (p. 186).

16. ibid., 'rDzogs chen kun.bzaṅ bla.ma', fol. 77a.

17. 'Bhāṣya' ad 'Abhidharmakośa' IV, 85ab (p. 187). 'rDzogs chen kun.bzaṅ bla.ma', fol. 77b.

18. 'Abhidharmakośa' IV, 105ab.

19. 'Bhāṣya' ad 'Abhidharmakośa' IV, 85ab (p. 187). 'rDzogs chen kun.bzaṅ bla.ma', fol. 78a.

20. 'Bhāṣya' ad 'Abhidharmakośa' IV, 85ab (p. 187).

21. This accounts for the aversion the Tibetans have for mining.

22. 'Bhāṣya' ad 'Abhidharmakośa' IV, 85ab (p. 186).

23. ibid., p. 187. 'rDzogs chen kun.bzaṅ bla.ma', fol. 79a.

24. *mtshams.med*, Skt. *ānantarya*. Such actions find immediate retribution in hell. See 'Bhāṣya' ad 'Abhidharmakośa' IV, 96 (p. 204). The five actions belonging to this class are: murder of mother, father and an Arhant, bloodshed and dividing the Sangha. 'rDzogs chen kun.bzaṅ bla.ma', fol. 72b.

25. *lam.gyi bden.pa*, Skt. *mārgasatya*.

26. *'gog.pa'i bden.pa*, Skt. *nirodhasatya*.

27. Cp. 'Abhidharmakośa' IV, 78bc; 79c.

28. 'Bhāṣya' ad 'Abhidharmakośa' IV, 85ab (p. 187).

29. 'Rationalism' is meant in the sense of naïve realism and the inability to see that 'facts' are not isolated events but form part of a larger whole.

30. *tshaṅs.par spyod.pa.la gnas.pa*, Skt. *brahmacaryāvāsa*.

31. *yaṅ.dag.pa'i don.la 'jug.pa*, Skt. *bhūtārthapraveśa*. Reality is not something unattainable, but may be experienced in all its vividness when we succeed in divesting our mind of the habits which induce us into all kinds of silly beliefs about reality.

32. 'Bhāṣya' ad 'Abhidharmakośa' IV, 108cd (p. 222).

33. *sñoms.'jug.gi bsam.gtan*, Skt. *samāpattidhyāna*, *skye.ba'i bsam.gtan*, Skt. *upapattidhyāna*. The former is the cause or concentration (for want of a better term), the latter is the effect or attainment of a particular stage of meditation as outlined by its cause. 'Bhāṣya' ad 'Abhidharmakośa' VIII, 1 (p. 128). On these topics of meditation see my 'Philosophy and Psychology in the Abhidharma,' pp. 147 seqq.

34. *ñer.bsños*, Skt. *sāmantaka*. 'Abhidharmakośa' VIII, 22a and 'Bhāṣya' (p. 178).

35. *dṅos.gźi*, Skt. *maula*, *dravya*. 'Bhāṣya' ad 'Abhidharmakośa' VIII, 6 (p. 145). They are the four stages belonging to Rūpadhātu and the four of Ārūpyadhātu.

36. *bsam.gtan khyad.par.can*, Skt. *dhyānāntara*. 'Abhidharmakośa' VIII, 22d.

37. They are: First Dhyāna: Brahmakāyika, Brahmapurohita, Mahābrahmā;
Second Dhyāna: Parīttābha, Apramāṇābha, Ābhāsvara;

Third Dhyāna: Parīttaśubha, Apramāṇaśubha, Śubhakṛtsna;
Fourth Dhyāna: Anabhraka, Puṇyaprasava, Bṛhatphala, Avṛha, Atapa, Sudṛśa, Sudarśana, Akaniṣṭha.

See 'Bhāṣya' ad 'Abhidharmakośa' III, 2 (p. 2).

38. To this sphere belong the *ākāśānantyāyatana*, *vijñānānantyāyatana*, *ākiṃcanyāyatana*, and *naivasaṃjñānāsaṃjñāyatana*. 'Bhāṣya' ad 'Abhidharmakośa' III, 3b (p. 5).

39. *'phen.byed bsam.gtan.*

40. *rtog.pa*, Skt. *vitarka*; *dpyod.pa*, Skt. *vicāra*; *dga'.ba*, Skt. *prīti*, *bde.ba*, Skt. *sukha*. The first two factors are 'intellectual', the latter two 'emotional'. *vitarka* is the first step of concentrative attention; *vicāra* is the steadily moving reflection; *prīti* is joyfulness and *sukha* is the feeling of pleasantness. The gradual disappearance of each preceding factor is equal to an increased emotive appreciation and a lessening of the judgemental character of analysis and discourse.

41. *rdzogs.byed bsam.gtan.*

42. 'Abhidharmakośa' VIII, 23b.

43. 'Abhidharmakośa' VIII, 4cd. 'Bhāṣya' ad VIII, 3d; 4ac (p. 143).

44. 'Bhāṣya' ad 'Abhidharmakośa' VIII, 4cd (p. 144).

45. Cp. ibid., VIII, 1 (p. 128).

46. The *dhyānas* have been explained in the text; for the *ārūpyas* see note 38. The four *apramāṇas* or immeasurable divine states of mind are benevolence (*maitrī*), compassion (*karuṇā*), joy over the good done by others (*muditā*) and equanimity (*upekṣā*).

47. As to the difference between Karma 'done' and 'accumulated', 'stored up', see 'Bhāṣya' ad 'Abhidharmakośa' IV, 119 (p. 242) and IV, 120.

48. 'Bodhipathapradīpa', 4.

49. See also 'Madhyamakavṛtti', p. 324.

7
BENEVOLENCE AND COMPASSION

THE DEVELOPMENT of Benevolence and Compassion as a remedy against attachment to self-complacency[1] will be discussed in this chapter. Self-complacency is to be understood in the sense of desiring to attain Nirvāṇa for ourselves and not working for the benefit of others, because we have no affection for sentient beings. Those who do so are the followers of the Hīnayāna form of Buddhism. Therefore it is said:

> 'For our own interest
> The interests of others, though they be many,
> Have to be sacrificed,'
> When in this way we are concerned with our own interests
> They naturally grow supreme.

However, when Benevolence and Compassion are born in us, out of affection for sentient beings we cannot bear the idea of (37a) attaining liberation for ourselves alone. Therefore Benevolence and Compassion must be developed. The Teacher 'Jam.dpal grags.pa (Mañjuśrīkīrti) also affirmed:

> A follower of Mahāyāna must not be without Benevolence and Compassion for a single moment.

And,

> The interests of others are safeguarded by Benevolence and Compassion, not by hatred.

First we shall discuss the meaning of Benevolence:

> Boundless Benevolence is dealt with
> Under the six heads of
> Classification, frame of reference, causal characteristic,
> Method of practice, measure of perfection, and merits.

Classification is threefold: (i) Benevolence with reference to sentient beings; (ii) to the nature of the whole of reality; and (iii) without reference to any particular object. As is stated in the ''Phags.pa bLo.gros mi.zad.pa'i mdo' ('Akṣayamatiparipṛcchāsūtra'):

> Benevolence with reference to sentient beings is found in Bodhisattvas who have just formed an enlightened attitude; with reference to the nature of the whole of reality in Bodhi-

sattvas who live practising good; and without reference to any particular object in Bodhisattvas who have realized and accepted the fact that all entities of reality have no origin.[2]

In this book, I shall discuss only the first type of Benevolence because of its practical importance, and you have to bear in mind that its frame of reference is the totality of sentient beings.[3]

The causal characteristic, is the desire that all beings may find happiness.

The method of practice, is pondering over the benefits that stem from sentient beings, because the root of Benevolence lies in the memory of benefits received. In this life here on earth the greatest benefactor is our mother, because she (i) provides us with a body, (ii) suffers for our sake, (iii) gives us life and (iv) shows us the world. As is recorded in the ''Phags.pa brGyad.stoṅ.pa' ('Aṣṭasāhasrikā-prajñāpāramitā'):

> Why is this so? Our mother (37b) raises us; undergoes hardships for our sake; gives us life; and shows us the world.

(i) This is the benefit of providing us with a body. It did not start fully grown, complete with muscles and of a pleasant complexion. In our mother's womb from its stages of an oval spot (*mer.mer*, Skt. *kalala*) and oblong lump (*nur.nur*, Skt. *arbuda*) it has been built up in a special and gradual way by the nutritive essences of her flesh and blood. It has grown bigger by the nourishing properties of her food; and it has been produced by the endurance of all kinds of acts we feel shy about, of indispositions, and of pain. Even after birth, by nursing us from a tiny little infant to a big, strong person she contributes to the forming of our body.

(ii) The benefit of going through hardships for our sake means that she not only dressed and adorned us, but gave us her inheritance, keeping nothing of her own, not even a crumb, giving us all her food and drink, so that when we set out for foreign parts we should not suffer from hunger and thirst, giving us clothes to keep out the cold and money to prevent our pining in poverty. Unlike people who, because they do not want a thing, give it to a child, she allows herself a minimum of food, drink and clothing. A mother does not do things for the sake of happiness in this life, nor refrains from action for the sake of enjoyment in the hereafter, she just nurses and protects her baby. When for instance she has done evil and unwholesome things, such as fishing and butchering, she brings him up on what she earns in that way: or, when her circumstances (38a) are unpleasant, after going to market or to work in the fields, day and night with the coarse soil as her shoes, wearing the stars as her cap, riding her legs as a horse, using the woollen threads of her torn frock as a whip, offering her legs to the dogs (to bite and bark at) and her face to men (to gaze at), she gives whatever she has gained by her efforts to her child.

She loves the helpless unknown baby more than her own benefactors, than her father, mother and teacher; she looks on her baby with eyes of love, wraps him in gentle warmth, dandles him on her ten fingers, calls him with words of kindness: 'Oh my joy, my lovely one, lu, lu, how you delight Mummy.'

(iii) The benefit of giving us life, means that we have not come into the world knowing how to use our hands and our mouth and how to perform difficult tasks with all our strength. While we were feeble like a worm, of no importance and silly, our mother did not throw us away but served us, took us on her lap, protected us from fire and water, held us back from precipices, removed what might harm us, and made religious offerings for our well-being. Out of fear that we might die or fall ill, she did things nobody else would think of or could be enumerated, such as casting dice, consulting astrologers, observing omens, reading the lines in our hands, and so on, thus giving life to her child.

(iv) The benefit of showing us the world, means that we did not come here, knowing and understanding everything merely by seeing it and having keen senses. When we cried for friendly company, when we could not use our hands and feet and knew nothing, she taught us how to eat, dress, walk and speak. Having taught us all sorts of crafts by saying Yes or No (38b), she made the uneven even for us and the unusual usual.

But this does not exhaust what a mother is always doing and has always done since beginningless Saṃsāra. As is said in the ''Khor.ba thog.ma.med.pa'i mdo':

> If one individual were to transform all the earth, stones, trees and groves in this world into single juniper kernels, another might well be able to finish counting them. But no one can count what his mother has done for him.

And in the 'bŚes.sbriṅ' ('Suhṛllekha', 68):

> If a man were to count the times a mother has come to him by grains of soil not larger than juniper kernels,
> The earth would not be able to produce a like quantity.

In this way the benefit of a mother's every single action is to be counted.

Thus, since a mother's kindness is immeasurable, we should ponder about what makes her heart full of happiness and bliss, and this is not all. Since all beings have been our mother (from time out of mind), they have all benefited by what a mother has done. Should you ask what is the limit of sentient beings, the answer is that they encompass the bounds of heaven. As is stated in the 'bZaṅ.po spyod.pa'i smon.lam.gyi mdo' ('Bhadracaryāpraṇidhānamahārāja-paribandha'):

What is the end of the sky
Is also that of all beings.

Therefore we should develop concentrated attention to the growth of a worthy mind, desiring all sentient beings to profit and to feel happy.

Such an attitude leads to real Benevolence. In the 'mDo.sde.rgyan' ('Mahāyāna-sūtrālaṅkāra' XIII, 20) also is declared:

A Bodhisattva is towards all beings
As to a child (39a).
With great Benevolence out of his innermost heart
He always desires to procure their happiness.

When through the power of Benevolence out of our eyes tears spring forth or when on our body the hair rises in delight, then there is great Benevolence. When the latter is enjoyed by all sentient beings, then it is immeasurable.

The measure of perfection, means that when we only desire the happiness of all sentient beings instead of ourselves, then there is perfection of Benevolence.

The merits accruing from having practised it cannot be measured. As is stated in the 'Zla.ba sgron.ma'i mdo' ('Candrapradīpasūtra'):

Whatever immeasurable offerings there may be and however varied,
Filling millions and millions of universes—
Offering them to the most sublime being (the Buddha)
Does not equal the merits of Benevolence.

The merits accruing from having practised Benevolence only for a little while also cannot be measured. As is written in the 'Rin.chen 'phreṅ.ba' ('Ratnāvalī'):

Even if one were to give out food
Cooked in three hundred pots, daily thrice a day,
This would not equal the merits
Of one moment of Benevolence.

When we practise Benevolence and until we reach enlightenment, we possess eight qualities. This is stated in the 'Rin.chen 'phreṅ.ba' ('Ratnāvalī'):

Beloved by gods and men,
And also protected by them,
Peace of mind and many other blessings of this kind,
Not being harmed by poison or by weapons,
Attaining our aim without exertion,
And being reborn in the Brahma world—
Even if we should not attain final liberation,
At least we obtain these eight qualities through Benevolence.

However, the practice of Benevolence is good for preserving ourselves and for protecting others as may be seen respectively from the stories of the Great Bram.ze sbyin.pa (Brahmadatta) and of King Byams.pa'i stobs (Maitrībala).

When Benevolence has been perfected then there is no difficulty in practising Compassion.

Compassion is our next theme (39b).

Boundless Compassion is dealt with
Under the six heads of
Classification, frame of reference, causal characteristic,
Method of practice, measure of perfection and merits.

Classification is threefold: (i) Compassion with reference to sentient beings, (ii) the nature of the whole of reality, and (iii) without reference to any particular object.

The first means that Compassion arises by seeing the misery of sentient beings in evil lives; the second that when we have practised the Four Truths[4] and thereby understood the relation between cause and effect our mind turns away from the concepts of permanence and solidity.[5] Here Compassion arises by thinking that other beings live in bewilderment, ignorant of the relation between cause and effect and clinging thereby to permanence and solidity. The third means that by having understood thoroughly the Śūnyatā of all entities through immediate experience[6] Compassion arises in particular for sentient beings who cling to the idea of material reality. As has been said:

A Bodhisattva who has become perfected
Through the power of practising Compassion
Is particularly merciful
To sentient beings who are obsessed by the demon of material reality.

Of the three types of Compassion mentioned in this book, the first is recommended for practical purposes.

The frame of reference, is the totality of sentient beings.

The causal characteristic, is the desire to liberate beings from misery and its cause.

The method of its practise is our capacity for feeling deep compassion for our mother (the root of our being) if she is beaten, burnt or boiled alive, or if in very cold weather blisters appear on her body, break and begin to ooze. So also, since all sentient beings who are now in hell have in fact been our mother, how should we not feel compassion for them when they are struck to the core by such misery? Compassion should be practised in the desire to free them both from it and its cause.

(40a) Again we feel deep compassion when our mother is pained by thirst or hunger, suffers from disease and fever and is disheartened by fear and anxiety. So also, since all sentient beings who are now born as spirits have been our mother, how should we not feel compassion for them, when they are struck by such misery? Compassion should be practised in the desire to liberate them from it.

Similarly we feel deep compassion when our mother has become old and feeble, is enslaved by others since she is powerless, or when she is beaten, perhaps to death. So also, since all sentient beings who have been born as animals have been our mother, why should we not feel compassion for them, when they suffer such misery? Compassion should be practised in the desire to free them from it.

Again we feel the same way if our mother suffers great distress through finding herself on the brink of a precipice and about to fall into a very deep abyss out of which she could never climb. So also why should we not feel compassion over this great abyss of the bad existences of gods, men and demons, from which it is difficult for us to escape once we have fallen in, and in which we suffer through not having a spiritual friend at hand and so not knowing how to abjure evil. Compassion should be practised in the desire to liberate beings from this misery.

Measure of perfection, means that when we have broken the fetters that hold us to deem ourselves better than others and when the wordless desire to liberate all sentient beings from misery has risen (40b), perfection of Compassion is present.

The merits that accrue from having practised Compassion cannot be measured. As is stated in the 'sPyan.ras.gzigs.kyi rtogs.pa brjod. pa':

> When there is one virtue present it is as if all the qualities of the Buddhas are in the palm of one's hand. Which virtue? Great Compassion.

In the 'Chos yaṅ.dag.par sdud.pa'i mdo' ('Dharmasaṅgītisūtra'):

> Exalted One, so it is. When there is the precious wheel of the universal monarch there are also all his troops. Exalted One, so, where there is a Bodhisattva's Great Compassion, there are all the other Buddha qualities also.[7]

And in the 'De.bžin.gśegs.pa'i gsaṅ.ba'i mdo' ('Tathāgatācintya-guhyanirdeśa'):

> Guhyapati (Lord of the Mystic Teaching), the spiritual awareness of the Omniscient One has grown out of the root of Compassion.

In this way, desiring that beings may attain happiness by Benevolence and be freed from misery by Compassion, we are unable to reserve the happiness of tranquillity for ourselves alone. Thus a remedy is found against self-complacency by the joyful realization that Buddhahood may be attained. When someone in whom Benevolence and Compassion are born, praises others as greater than himself, he becomes filled with excellence. This may be seen from the example of the Great Bram.ze.sbyin (Brahmadatta) and is taught in the following verse:

> He who seriously wants to dispel
> All the misery of others,
> Is an excellent man,
> Because in the stream of his own being he has understood the nature of misery.[8]

The seventh chapter, dealing with Benevolence and Compassion, from the Jewel Ornament of Liberation or The Wish-Fulfilling Gem of the Noble Doctrine.

NOTES TO CHAPTER 7

1. See Chapter 4, p. 41.

2. *mi.skye.ba'i chos.la bzod.pa*, Skt. *anutpattikadharmakṣānti*. It is a type of knowledge by experience after prolonged meditation and belongs to the eighth level of spirituality. See 'Vijñaptimātratāsiddhi', pp. 546 seq., 'Daśabhūmika', p. 47. 'Mahāyāna-sūtrālaṅkāra' XIX, 36.

3. sGam.po.pa's work is a manual introducing the student into the practical aspect of Buddhist discipline. He therefore points to the immediately given. The other types of Benevolence and Compassion can be realized only after the Path has been traversed, they are never meant for beginners who would be unable to grasp their significance.

4. The Truth of misery; the Truth of the origination of misery; the Truth of the annihilation of misery and the Truth of the Path leading to the annihilation of misery.

5. 'Permanence' is the naïve belief that there is an unchanging, well-defined principle which will last for ever, a belief which is contradictory to the immediate experience of our senses. 'Solidity' is the belief in the material existence of things and ideas. Buddhism is concerned with epistemology in all theories of cognition, it deals with percepts but not with the beliefs about them. Although it considers percepts to be mental, mentality is not absolute, but an emergent quality.

6. *mñam.par gžag.pa*, Skt. *samāhita*. It is synonymous with *nirvikalpakajñāna* 'knowledge by experience into which no concepts enter'.

7. Great Compassion is a quality of the Buddhas, it is free from attachment, unlike ordinary compassion which is often nothing more than sentimentality. The nature of Great Compassion has also been discussed in the 'Bhāṣya' ad 'Abhidharmakośa' VII, 33 (pp. 77–9).

8. 'Bodhipathapradīpa', 5.

8

TAKING REFUGE[1]

THE REMEDY against ignorance about the means to attain Buddhahood[2] (41a) will be discussed in this and the following chapters.

Twelve heads indicate
What produces an enlightened attitude:
Working basis, essence,[3] classification,
Frame of reference, motive, locality,
Technique, usefulness, the deplorableness of its loss,
The way of incurring it, the means of its recovery and the training.[4]

The working basis or the individuals who develop an enlightened attitude are those who belong to the Mahāyāna family, who have taken refuge in the Three Jewels, and who observe one or the other set of rules to be followed by the seven groups mentioned in the Prātimokṣa.[5] Therefore from the time that persons have taken refuge in the Three Jewels they are the working basis for developing an aspiration for enlightenment, because only those who thus aspire[6] can persevere in the work of winning it.[7] Should you ask why this is so, the answer is that the 'Byaṅ.chub.sems.dpa'i sa' ('Bodhisattvabhūmi', p. 12) states that aspiration must precede perseverance in the work; in the 'Byaṅ.chub.lam.sgron' ('Bodhipathapradīpa', 9) it has been said that the taking refuge necessarily comes before the aspiration for enlightenment and that the Prātimokṣa is necessary as the basis for perseverance in winning it ('Bodhipathapradīpa', 19). In the 'Chos.mṅon.pa.mdzod' ('Abhidharmakośa' IV, 30) it has been declared that the taking refuge must precede the acceptance of the Prātimokṣa; and in the 'Byaṅ.chub.sems.dpa'i sa' ('Bodhisattvabhumi', pp. 2, 11) that except for the Mahāyāna family no enlightened attitude can be developed. Therefore all these prerequisites must unite.

The first is that, generally speaking, it must be the Mahāyāna family, and in particular, the Awakened family. This has been explained in detail above.[8]

In connection with the second prerequisite, the taking refuge, it may be asked whether we should take refuge in such asylums as the powerful deities Brahmā, Viṣṇu, Mahādeva and others (41b), or in the mighty Nāgas who live in the mountains, rocks, lakes, trees and other places of our country. The answer is that since they all are unable to protect us they provide no refuge. As has been said in a Sūtra:

The world takes refuge in mountains,
Forests and shrines,
Groves and stones,
And deities of trees:
But these are no proper asylum.[9]

Should we then take refuge in father or mother, in friends and other persons who are dear to us and who rejoice at our well-being? The answer again is that they are unable to protect us. As is stated in the ''Jam.dpal rnam.par rol.pa'i mdo' ('Mañjuśrīvikrīḍitasūtra'):

Father or mother are no refuge for you,
Neither are friends nor relatives;
Having forsaken you
They depart just as they like.

You may now ask why they all are unable to protect us. The reply is that a protector must himself be free from fear and not suffer from misery. But all those who have been mentioned are frightened and subject to misery. Therefore, since only the Buddha is perfectly free from misery, while the Dharma provides the only attainment of Buddhahood and the Sangha alone can help with the Dharma, we must take refuge in them. So also it has been said:

Take now your refuge in the Buddha,
The Dharma and all the Sangha,
Who eradicate fear in the frightened
And who protect the unprotected.

And since they have the power to protect, there is no doubt that they will do so when we come to them for refuge. As is stated in the 'mDo.sde mya.ṅan 'das chen' ('Mahāparinirvāṇasūtra'):

He who takes refuge in the Three Jewels
Will gain fearlessness (42a).

In explaining the taking refuge in the Three Jewels the following will serve as a guide:

There are nine topics in taking refuge:
Classification, working basis, object, time,
Intention, method, function,
Training and benefits.

Classification is twofold: (i) taking refuge in an ordinary and (ii) in a particular way.[10]

The working basis or the individual is twofold: (i) ordinary persons who are frightened by the misery of Saṃsāra and hold the Three Jewels to be gods, and (ii) particular people who belong to the Mahāyāna family and have obtained the pure body of either gods or men.

The object is of two kinds:

(i) The ordinary object is the Jewel of the Buddha or The Buddha, the Exalted One, endowed with the excellences of renunciation, knowledge and spiritual greatness; the Jewel of the Dharma in its double aspect as taught in the twelve divisions of verbal teaching and as understood, in other words the Truths of the Path and of Cessation; and the Jewel of the Sangha in its twin aspect of the community of ordinary beings or the assembly of more than four fully ordained Bhikṣus and the Noble Sangha or the eight worthy individuals such as he who is in the stream running towards enlightenment and others.[11]

(ii) The special object means: (a) the objects in front of us, (b) those intuitively understood and (c) the ultimately real.

Of these, (a) those in front of us are the Buddha in the image of the Tathāgata, the Dharma as the Mahāyāna scriptures, and the Sangha or the assembly of Bodhisattvas. (b) Those intuitively understood are the Buddha as the possessor of the Three Kāyas[12] (42b), the Dharma as the sublime experiences of tranquillity and Nirvāṇa, and the Sangha or the Bodhisattvas living on a high level of spirituality.[13] (c) The ultimately real is the Buddha alone as refuge. So also in the 'Theg.pa chen.po rgyud.bla.ma' ('Mahāyānottaratantraśāstra' I, 21cd):

> In the ultimate sense, the refuge for the world is Buddha(hood) alone.

Why is the Buddha able to be the ultimate refuge?

> Because the Sage possesses the Dharmakāya and because the devotees find their fulfilment in Him.[14]

The Sage (or Buddha) is without beginning and end, is purified and desireless. He is the ultimate refuge because He possesses the Dharmakāya and the devotees of the three paths[15] also find their fulfilment in Him by obtaining the final pure Dharmakāya.[16]

However, you may ask whether the Dharma and the Sangha are

not the ultimate refuge. The answer is contained in the 'rGyud.bla. ma' ('Uttaratantra' I, 20):

> The two kinds of the Dharma and the assembly of the saintly
> Are not the ultimate refuge.

But why are they not? The Dharma that is taught is only a collection of words and letters and has to be discarded like a raft when we have reached the other shore. The Dharma that is understood has two aspects, the Truth of the Path and the Truth of the Cessation of Misery. The former is a product and not eternal, hence is deceptive and no refuge, while the latter has no real existence being compared by the Śrāvakas to the extinction of a lamp.[17] The Sangha itself also has taken refuge in the Buddha, because it was afraid of Saṃsāra and (43a) so is no ultimate refuge. Therefore also it is stated in the 'rGyud.bla.ma' ('Uttaratantra' I, 20):

> Because it has to be discarded and is deceptive,
> Because it does not exist and is afraid—
> The two kinds of the Dharma and the assembly of the saintly
> Are not the ultimate excellent refuge.

And the Teacher Thogs.med (Asanga) declared:[18]

> The unfailing, eternal, lasting, real refuges are one and the same, namely, the Tathāgatas, Arhants and Samyaksambuddhas.

However, if you were to object that this is contradictory to the above-mentioned triad of refuges, you should remember that the three refuges are only the means to attract those who are to be educated.[19] As is declared in the 'Thar.pa chen.po mdo':

> In brief, refuge is only one, the means is threefold.

The question why the one has been split up into three according to the means, is answered in the 'Theg.pa chen.po rgyud.bla.ma' ('Mahāyānottaratantraśāstra' I, 19):

> With respect to the qualities of The Teacher, the Doctrine and the Discipline according to
> Three courses, three actors and
> Three types of interest
> Three refuges have been set up.

In other words, the three types of refuge have been declared with respect to the three kinds of qualities (found in The Buddha, his Doctrine, and his Discipline), the three courses and types of active individuals (of Bodhisattvas, Pratyekabuddhas, and Śrāvakas) and of interest.

In order to reveal the qualities of The Teacher, the Buddha is the refuge for those who are working to become Bodhisattvas and who are interested in the excellent career of a Buddha. They say: 'I take refuge in The Buddha, the most sublime being among men.'

In order to reveal the qualities of the Doctrine, the Dharma is the refuge for those who wish to be Pratyekabuddhas and who are interested in the good work of the Dharma. They say: 'I take refuge in the Dharma, the most excellent refuge for those who are desireless' (43b).

In order to reveal the qualities of the Discipline, the Sangha is the refuge for those who follow the Śrāvaka way of life and are interested in the work of the Sangha. They say: 'I take refuge in the Sangha, the most excellent refuge for devotees.'

Thus, in a threefold manner, the Exalted One has taught conventionally these three types of refuge for six types of people in order to establish all sentient beings gradually on the five paths to enlightenment, one succeeding the other.[20]

Time is of two kinds: (i) ordinary and (ii) particular.

(i) The first means: from now on as long as I live I take refuge.

(ii) The second: from now on until I have attained enlightenment I take refuge.

Intention also is of two kinds:

(i) ordinary means that I take refuge because I cannot bear my individual misery;

(ii) particular that I take it because I cannot bear the misery of others.

Method is twofold as well:

(i) The ordinary one is as follows:

First the disciple formally requests the teacher to set up images of the Three Jewels and to worship them. If this is not possible he visualizes them in the sky and mentally worships them. The disciple then repeats after him: 'May all the Buddhas and Bodhisattvas be gracious to me. May the teacher be gracious to me. I, so and so, from now on until I have attained enlightenment take refuge in the Buddha, the most sublime being among men. I take refuge in the Dharma, the most excellent refuge for those who are desireless (44a). I take refuge in the Sangha, the most excellent refuge of devotees.' This is to be repeated with conviction three times.

(ii) The special method consists of (a) a preparatory stage, (b) the actual ceremony, and (c) the conclusion.

(a) In the first stage a maṇḍala is prepared with flowers and offered to someone who may act as a spiritual friend and who is then requested to initiate. Thereafter the spiritual friend, having accepted the disciple as a man belonging to the Mahāyāna family and as a worthy vessel for instruction, during the first night consecrates the images of the Three Jewels, worships them and explains to the disciple the merits of taking refuge and the deplorableness of not doing so.

(b) On the second night the actual initiating ceremony is held. First we personify the objects of refuge in front of us[21] as really being the Three Jewels, make obeisance and worship them; then we repeat after the teacher the words: 'May all the Buddhas and Bodhisattvas be gracious to me. May the teacher be gracious to me. I, so and so, from now on until I have attained enlightenment, take refuge in the Buddha, the Exalted One, the most sublime being among men. I take refuge in tranquillity and Nirvāṇa, the most excellent places of refuge for those who are desireless. I take refuge in the Bodhisattvas who do not relapse into worldliness, the most excellent refuge of devotees.' This to be repeated three times.

Thereafter in front of the intuitively understood objects of refuge, visualizing them as if actually there, we make obeisance and worship them, thinking that whatever we do, the Buddhas and Bodhisattvas will be aware of it. We again repeat thrice the formula of taking refuge.

After that (44b) we take refuge in the ultimately real object of refuge by making obeisance and worshipping with a pure motive[22] and, since all entities are from the very beginning without an individuality of their own[23] and can nowhere be found as concrete entities, we also see the Buddha, the Dharma and the Sangha in this way. This is the unfailing, eternal, lasting refuge.[24] As is expressed in the 'Ma.dros.pas žus.pa'i mdo' ('Anavataptanāgarājaparipṛcchā-sūtra'):

> What is taking refuge with a mind free from the hustle and bustle of the world? By knowing all entities to be non-existent, to see them as incapable of being given form and primary characteristics, of being taken as entities in themselves, but to see them as being perfect Buddhahood, is taking refuge in the Buddha. To see all entities follow the way of the Dharmadhātu, is taking refuge in the Dharma. To see the conditioned and unconditioned as not to be split up into a duality, is taking refuge in the Sangha.

(c) During the third night comes the conclusion: the thanksgiving to the Three Jewels.

About the function the 'mDo.sde.rgyan' ('Mahāyāna-sūtrālaṅkāra' IX, 8) says:

(Because it protects) against all distress,
Evil existences, frustration,
Realistic-materialistic philosophy[25] and the Hīnayāna,
It is the real refuge.

This means: by the ordinary way of taking refuge we are protected against all sorts of distress, the three evil existences,[26] frustration, and the views presented in realistic-materialistic philosophies. By the special way of taking refuge we are protected against all that comes from the Hīnayāna.

Training is subdivided into (i) three general and (ii) three special kinds and (iii) three common to the other two.

(i) The first of these (45a) consists of (a) constantly exerting ourselves to venerate the Three Jewels, even by making offerings of our food; (b) of not forsaking the Three Jewels even for the sake of our life or on account of bribery; and (c) of taking refuge again and again by remembering the qualities of the Three Jewels.

(ii) The three special kinds mean: (a) when we have taken refuge in the Buddha we do not go to other gods. As is said in the 'mDo mya.ṅan.'das chen' ('Mahāparinirvāṇasūtra'):

He who has taken refuge in the Buddhas
Relies on the really wholesome
And need not go for refuge
To other gods.

(b) Having taken refuge in the Dharma we do not hurt other beings. As is said in a Sūtra:

He who has taken refuge in the noble Dharma
Does not think of hurting and destroying.

(c) Having taken refuge in the Sangha we do not rely on realists.[27] As is stated in a Sūtra:

He who has taken refuge in the Sangha
Does not rely on realists.

(iii) The three kinds common to the other two are to rejoice (a) even at a clay figure of the Tathāgata as the representative of the Buddha Jewel; (b) at a letter from the scriptures and books of the Noble Doctrine as the Dharma Jewel; and (c) at a patch from the yellow robes of spiritual friends as representative of the Sangha Jewel.[28]

There accrue eight benefits from taking refuge: (i) As a follower of Buddhism we become an enlightened being, (ii) we become the foundation of all disciplines, (iii) all evil we have done formerly fades away, (iv) we are not hindered by obstacles raised either by men or demons (45b), (v) we achieve everything upon which we set our minds, (vi) we acquire great merits which are the cause for further spiritual development, (vii) we do not fall into evil existences and (viii) we quickly attain perfect Buddhahood.

The third prerequisite is the discipline called Prātimokṣa.[29] It consists of four groups or eight working bases.[30] In this book (which deals with the practical side of winning enlightenment) all these working bases are to be adopted except the Upavasatha.[31] They are the Bhikṣu, the Bhikṣuṇī, the Śikṣamāna,[32] the Śramaṇera,[33] the Śramaṇerikā,[34] the Upāsaka[35] and the Upāsikā.[36] As is explained in the 'Byaṅ.chub.sems.dpa'i sa' ('Bodhisattvabhūmi'):

> The seven sections who have taken up the discipline called Prātimokṣa are the Bhikṣu, the Bhiksuṇī, the Śikṣamāna, the Śramaṇera, the Śramaṇerikā, and, being householders, the Upāsaka and the Upāsikā. The last two groups are again subdivided into householders proper and Prāvrajikas.[37]

If you ask whether this discipline is necessary for the perseverance in winning enlightenment the reply is yes and may be known by (i) simile, (ii) scriptural authority and (iii) reason.

(i) The simile is as follows. No dung, dirt or uncleanliness is allowed about the throne of a universal monarch, but the room is swept clean and decorated with beautiful jewels and other precious things. In the same way, the place where the king, Enlightened Attitude (*byaṅ.chub.kyi sems*, Skt. *bodhicitta*), is to rest cannot be found in an attitude infected by the evils of body, speech and mind and defiled by the impurities of evil inclinations (46a). It must be free from these evils and beautifully adorned by ethics due to discipline.[38]

(ii) Scriptural authority is the chapter on the Formation of an Enlightened Attitude in the 'mDo.sde.rgyan' ('Mahāyāna-sūtrālaṅkāra'). There (IV, 4) we read:

> The basis is discipline in ethics.

Further, fasting is a small discipline lasting only one day; but the seven sections of the Prātimokṣa are great because they are not like the former.[39] They are called the basis for the formation of an enlightened attitude. In the 'Byaṅ.chub.lam.sgron' ('Bodhipathapradīpa', 20) it is stated:

He who always keeps
One or the other of the seven disciplines,
Is endowed with the Bodhisattva-discipline.
Not so others.

In this way it has been made clear that one or other of the seven disciplines are the basis.

(iii) The reason is that the discipline called Prātimokṣa is the renunciation of doing harm to others.[40] The Bodhisattva-discipline is benefiting others and this cannot be done without abjuring harm.

If people say that the Bodhisattva-discipline does not necessarily arise from the Prātimokṣa because the latter cannot, while the former can, be found amongst the impotent, eunuchs,[41] gods and other beings,[42] and that it cannot serve as a foundation for the continuance of the discipline, because unlike the Bodhisattva variety it is abandoned at death,[43] the refutation is that there are three types of Prātimokṣa discipline according to the intention with which it is observed. If one or the other of the seven sections is taken up (i) out of a desire to attain the pleasures of the three world-spheres, it is called a discipline with vested interest,[44] (ii) if to get rid of our own misery, it is escapism[45] as practised by Śrāvakas, and (iii) if to attain Great Enlightenment, it is the ethics of the Bodhisattva-discipline. The two former are no foundation for that discipline, because they cannot be practised by the impotent, eunuchs, gods and other beings, are abandoned at death and cannot be revived once they have been destroyed.[46] The ethics of the Bodhisattva-discipline, however, are found among such beings; they are not abandoned at death and can be revived once they have been destroyed; they are therefore the basis of the beginning as well as for the continuance of an enlightened attitude. Consequently it is stated in the commentary to the 'mDo. sde.rgyan' ('Mahāyāna-sūtrālaṅkāra' IV, 4):

> What is the basis of this attitude? It is the discipline in Bodhisattva ethics.

It has further been asserted that while this discipline is necessary as a basis for the formation of an enlightened attitude, it is optional for its continuance:

> Just as discipline born from meditative concentration[47] is necessary for the beginning of unsullied discipline[48] and optional for its continuance.

The method of taking the discipline called the Bodhisattva Prātimokṣa cannot be reversed. We have first to undergo the training of a Śrāvaka and then, when we have grasped the discipline with the particular intention (which a Bodhisattva has) and when it has become lasting with us, it develops into the Bodhisattva-discipline. This means giving up a low-level, but not a renouncing, attitude.

Thus a man who belongs to the Mahāyāna family, who has taken refuge in the Three Jewels, and who observes one of the disciplines of the seven sections of the Prātimokṣa, becomes (47a) the working basis for the formation of an enlightened attitude.

The eighth chapter, dealing with the Refuge, from the
Jewel Ornament of Liberation or the
Wish-Fulfilling Gem of the
Noble Doctrine.

NOTES TO CHAPTER 8

1. With this chapter the special section of that which is necessary for attaining Enlightenment or Buddhahood begins. The preceding chapters are known as the ordinary (*thun.moṅ*, Skt. *sādhāraṇa*) procedure which is open to everybody. The extraordinary (*thun.moṅ ma.yin.pa*, Skt. *asādhāraṇa*) one which has found its fullest elaboration in Mahāyāna, needs all that is in man. Naturally this does not mean that the extraordinary procedure makes the ordinary one unnecessary. The latter is the preparatory stage of the Sahajayoga which leads to the realization of Mahāmudrā as living Buddhahood. As Padma dkar.po in his 'Phyag.rgya.chen.po'i man.ṅag.gi bśad.sbyar rgyal.ba'i gan.mdzod', fol. 70b seq., points out, all those topics mentioned in the preceding chapters such as the contemplation of the difficulty of being born and the importance of being human, the attention to what misery in this world means and to the immediacy of death, are indispensable for spiritual development.

2. See Chapter 4, p. 41.

3. This topic and the following ones are discussed in Chapter 9.

4. This is dealt with in Chapter 10.

5. See pp. 106 seq.

6. *smon.pa'i sems*, Skt. *praṇidhicitta*. Lit.: 'an attitude which is devotedly attentive'.

7. *'jug.pa'i sems*, Skt. *prasthānacitta*. Lit.: 'an attitude which is on its way toward enlightenment'. This and the preceding term have

been explained in the Pañjikā to 'Bodhicaryāvatāra' I, 15. Further details are given in Chapter 11.

8. See Chapter 2.

9. Cp. 'Dhammapada', 188–92; 'Udānavarga' XXVII, 28–30; 'Bhāṣya' ad 'Abhidharmakośa' IV, 32 (p. 80).

10. The ordinary, and the particular, way refer to the associations connected with the Three Jewels. They have been dealt with below, pp. 103 seq. A different account, due to the tradition followed, is given in the 'rDzogs chen kun.bzaṅ bla.ma', fol. 125b seq.

11. The eight individuals are he who (i) has entered the stream by which he will proceed toward Nirvāṇa (*srota-āpanna*), and (ii) is enjoying the fruit of having entered the stream (*srota-āpatti-phalastha*), (iii) will only once return to this world (*sakṛdāgāmin*) and (iv) is enjoying the fruit thereof; (v) he who will not relapse into worldliness (*anāgāmin*) and (vi) who is enjoying the fruit of not relapsing therein; (vii) the Arhant and (viii) he who enjoys the fruit of having attained Arhantship. See 'Abhidharmakośa' VI, 29–31, and 'Bhāṣya' (pp. 194 seq.).

12. i.e. Nirmāṇakāya, Sambhogakāya and Dharmakāya.

13. i.e. those who live on the three last of the ten stages of spirituality. They have been discussed in detail in Chapters 18 and 19.

14. 'Mahāyānottaratantra' I, 21cd.

15. The three paths are those of the Śrāvakas (*Śrāvakayāna*), the Pratyekabuddhas (*Pratyekabuddhayāna*) and the Bodhisattvas (*Bodhisattvayāna*). The two former belong to the Hīnayāna form of Buddhism, the latter to the Mahāyāna. See Chapter 1. 'Gaṇḍavyūhasūtra', p. 197.

16. This is taken from the commentary on 'Mahāyānottaratantra'. I, 21.

17. That Nirvāṇa is non-existence, is the view of the Sautrāntikas. See 'Mūlamadhyamakavṛtti', p. 527; Commentary on 'Mahāyānottaratantra' I, 20; 'Bhāṣya' ad 'Abhidharmakośa' II, 55 (pp. 285 seq.) and my 'Philosophy and Psychology in the Abhidharma', pp. 291 seq.

18. Commentary on 'Mahāyānottaratantra' I, 21.

19. Until the realization of enlightenment sentient beings are in need of education (*vinaya*); at the same time, however, because of the innateness of Buddha-nature (see above Chapter 1), education is also a process of maturation (*vipāka*) and the Buddha's work is to bring beings to spiritual maturity by his instructions.

20. This whole passage is taken from the commentary on 'Mahāyānottaratantra' I, 19. The Five Paths are discussed in Chapters 18 and 19.

21. See above, p. 101.

22. *'khor gsum rnam.par dag.pa*, Skt. *trimaṇḍalapariśuddhi*. The meaning is that the receiver of any gift or worship, the act of giving or worshipping and the person who makes a gift or worships must all be in a state of disinterestedness. There must not be any preconceived ideas as to what may be the result of our action. As is stated in the commentary on 'Mahāyāna-sūtrālaṅkāra' XVII, 5: *jñānaṃ nirvikalpaṃ pūjakapūjyapūjānulambhataḥ* 'Knowledge without preconceived ideas with respect to the man who worships, to him who is worshipped, and to the act of worshipping'. Cp. also 'Mahāyāna-sūtrālaṅkāra' XII, 11; 'Vijñaptimātratāsiddhi', p. 629.

23. *bdag.med*, Skt. *anātman*.

24. See note 18.

25. *satkāya-dṛṣṭi*, the view that there is an abiding personality. See also 'Vijñaptimātratāsiddhi', pp. 16, 348.

26. i.e. the hells and the worlds of spirits and animals. See above, Chapter IV.

27. *mu.steg.pa*, Skt. *tīrthika*. This term refers to all non-Buddhist schools, in particular to the adherents of the Vaiśeṣika school. The Buddhists, or at least the followers of the Mādhyamika system, rejected all ontological arguments. In this way they are unique in the whole of Indian thought which has never been able to free itself from ontology. Buddhism, being psychological and epistemological, always scorned and rejected the views of those who attempted to establish ontological proofs.

28. Even today in Buddhist countries pieces of cloth worn by Lamas are highly cherished by laymen and often stitched on to their clothes.

29. See also 'Abhidharmakośa' IV, 13cd and seq., as well as the 'Bhāṣya'.

30. 'Abhidharmakośa' IV, 14a.

31. The Upavāsastha is a person who observes a one-day fast. See 'Abhidharmakośa' IV, 28–30, and 'Bhāṣya' (pp. 65 seqq.). An explanation of this term is given in the same work, on p. 66: 'Living like the Arhants, close (*upa*) to the Arhants.'

32. The Śikṣamānā is a woman who observes the rules valid for the Śramaṇerikā, without being herself a Śramaṇerikā. See the note to 'Bhāṣya' ad 'Abhidharmakośa' IV, 14a (pp. 43 seq.).

33. The Śramaṇera is a male novice.

34. The Śramanerikā is a female novice.

35. The Upāsaka is a male lay devotee.

36. The Upāsikā is a female lay devotee.

37. The Prāvrajika is a man who without being either a novice or a Bhikṣu ceases to act as a householder.

38. *sdom.pa'i tshul.khrims*, Skt. *saṃvaraśīla*. Cp. 'Abhidharmakośa' IV, 16ab.

39. Cp. 'Abhidharmakośa' IV, 27ab, and 'Bhāṣya' (p. 62).

40. The same etymological explanation of Prātimokṣa is given in the 'Bhāṣya' ad 'Abhidharmakośa' IV, 16cd (p. 48).

41. *za.ma*, Skt. *ṣaṇḍha*; *ma.niṅ*, Skt. *paṇḍaka*. Various sexually deficient people are mentioned in Yaśomitra's 'Abhidharmakośa Bhāṣya' II, 1.

42. They are the inhabitants of the mythical continent Uttarakuru. See 'Bhāṣya' ad 'Abhidharmakośa' IV, 43 (pp. 103 seq.).

43. 'Abhidharmakośa' IV, 38.

44. *smon.gyi tshul.khrims*.

45. *ṅes.par 'byuṅ.ba'i tshul.khrims*.

46. 'Bhāṣya' ad 'Abhidharmakośa' IV, 39 (p. 99).

47. *bsam.gtan.gyi sdom.pa*, Skt. *dhyānasaṃvara*. See 'Abhidharmakośa' IV, 17b, and 'Bhāṣya' (p. 50).

48. *zag.pa.med.pa'i sdom.pa*, Skt. *anāsravasaṃvara*. See 'Abhidharmakośa IV, 17c, and 'Bhāṣya' (p. 50); 'Abhidharmakośa' IV, 26, and 'Bhāṣya' (p. 59).

9
THE ACQUISITION OF AN ENLIGHTENED ATTITUDE

THE ESSENCE of the formation of an enlightened attitude is the desire for perfect enlightenment in order to be able to work for the benefit of others. As is expressed in the 'mÑon.rtogs.rgyan' ('Abhisamayālaṅkāra' I, 18ab):

> The formation of an enlightened attitude
> Is the desire for perfect enlightenment for the benefit of others.

Classification is threefold: (i) by simile, (ii) demarcation and (iii) primary characteristics.

(i) The first, that by similes ranging from the level of an ordinary being to that of a Buddha, has been given by saintly Byams.pa (Maitreya) in his 'mÑon.rtogs.rgyan' ('Abhisamayālaṅkāra' I, 19–20):[1]

> Earth, gold, moon, fire,
> Treasure, jewel-mine, ocean,
> Diamond, mountain, medicine, spiritual friend,
> Wish-Fulfilling Gem, sun, song,
> King, treasury, highway,
> Carriage, reservoir,
> Echo, river and cloud—
> These are the twenty-two similes.

They range from the earnest desire for ultimate reality to the realization of the Dharmakāya, and in their relation to the Five Paths they mean as follows:

When the formation of an enlightened attitude is accompanied by an earnest desire it is like the earth, forming a solid basis for all positive qualities; when by a general intention it is like gold, not changing until enlightenment has been attained; and when by a strong inclination it is like the waxing moon, increasing all wholesome qualities. These three varieties are on a novice's level since they correspond respectively to the smaller, mediocre and greater 'Preparatory Path' (*tshogs.lam*, Skt. *sambhāramārga*).

When the formation of an enlightened attitude is accompanied by an earnest application it is like fire, consuming as fuel the veils which hide the three kinds of omniscience[2] (47b). This is the 'Path of Application' (*sbyor.lam*, Skt. *prayogamārga*).

When the formation of an enlightened attitude is accompanied by the perfection of liberality[3] it is like a great treasure, satisfying all sentient beings; when by the perfection of ethics and manners[4] it is like a jewel mine, forming a solid basis for precious virtues; when by the perfection of patience[5] it is like a great ocean, not being disturbed by all the undesired things that sink to its bottom; when by the perfection of strenuousness[6] it is like a diamond, too hard to be destroyed; when by the perfection of meditative concentration[7] it is like the king of mountains, not shaken by the assault of the sense objects; when by the perfection of discriminating awareness born from wisdom[8] it is like medicine, appeasing the diseases due to the veils of conflicting emotions and of primitive beliefs about reality; when by the perfection of beneficial expediency[9] it is like a spiritual friend, never forsaking the welfare of sentient beings; when by the perfection of aspiration[10] it is like the Wish-Fulfilling Gem, bearing fruit according to aspiration; when by the perfection of strength[11] it is like the sun, maturing those who are to be educated; when by the perfection of transcending awareness born from wisdom[12] it is like the resounding of the Dharma, showing those properties which make beings who are to be educated, desirous for them. These ten varieties in their above order, fall under the ten levels of spirituality, beginning with that called 'The Joyous One'.[13] They have their operational field in the 'Path of Insight' (*mthoṅ.lam*, Skt. *darśanamārga*) and the 'Path of Concentrated Attention' (*sgom.lam*, Skt. *bhāvanāmārga*).

When the formation of an enlightened attitude is accompanied by higher understanding[14] it is like a great king, making the welfare of sentient beings a reality by his unrestricted power; when by merits and spiritual awareness it is like a treasury, being the storehouse of these virtues in abundance; when by qualities conducive to enlightenment[15] it is like a highroad, because it is traversed by all saintly people, one following the other; (48a) when by Tranquillity and Insight[16] it is like a carriage, running smoothly without deviating to either Saṃsāra or Nirvāṇa; and when by acceptance and rejection[17] it is like a reservoir, not becoming exhausted by holding or discharging what has and has not been heard. These types make up the special path of the Bodhisattvas.

When the formation of an enlightened attitude is accompanied by the 'grove of the Dharma'[18] it is like an echo to which those who are to be educated and want liberation delight to listen; when by a path which may be followed in one direction only it is like the current of a river, always helpful to sentient beings; and when by the Dharmakāya it is like a cloud on which the good of sentient beings depends, because it illustrates the stages of The Buddha's life from His stay in the Tusita heaven onwards. These three types belong to the Buddha level of spirituality.

Thus the twenty-two similes range from the novice's level to the Buddha level.

(ii) Classification by demarcation is fourfold: (a) accompanied by interest, (b) strong intention, (c) maturation and (d) the removal of the two veils which are conflicting emotions and primitive beliefs about reality. The first of these is the level of interested behaviour;[19] the second extends from the first to the seventh level of spirituality; the third from the eighth to the tenth; and the fourth is the Buddha level. As is stated in the 'mDo.sde.rgyan' ('Mahāyāna-sūtrālaṅkāra' IV, 2):

> The formation of an enlightened attitude
> Is held to be accompanied at various levels
> By interest, strong intention
> And maturation as well as by the removal of the veils.

(iii) Classification by primary characteristics is twofold: (48b) (a) the ultimately and (b) the relatively real enlightened attitude.[20] As is said in the 'dGoṅs.pa ṅes.par 'grol.pa'i mdo' ('Sandhinirmocana-sūtra'):

> There are two types of an enlightened attitude: the ultimately and relatively real.

(a) What is the ultimately real enlightened attitude? It is Śūnyata endowed with the essence of Compassion, radiant, unshakable and impossible to formulate by concepts or speech. As is stated in the Sūtra just mentioned:

> This ultimately real enlightened attitude is beyond this world, cannot be formulated by concept or speech, is extremely radiant, the image of the Ultimate, immaculate, unshakable, and very bright like the steady glow of a lamp on a calm night.

(b) And what is the relatively real enlightened attitude? The same Sūtra says:

> It is the vow to deliver all sentient beings from Saṃsāra through compassion.

While the ultimately real enlightened attitude springs from the ultimate nature of all things, the relatively real one is said in the 'mDo.sde.rgyan' ('Mahāyāna-sūtrālaṅkāra' IV, 7) to arise from an intimation and its acceptance.

Should you ask from which level of spirituality the ultimately real enlightened attitude rises, the answer is from the first, called 'The Joyous One'. This is stated in the commentary of 'mDo.sde.rgyan' ('Mahāyāna-sūtrālaṅkāra' IV, 8):

> The formation of the ultimately real enlightened attitude starts on the first level of spirituality called 'The Joyous One'.

The classification of this relatively real enlightened attitude is twofold: (1) aspiration for and (2) perseverance in winning enlightenment. This is expressed in the 'sPyod.'jug' ('Bodhicaryāvatāra' I, 15):

> An enlightened attitude, in brief,
> Is known to be of two types:
> One where there is aspiration
> And another where one actually strives to win enlightenment.

(49a) There are many different views as to the definition of the particular features of these two types of attitude, in which we aspire for and actually strive to win enlightenment.

The Teacher Ži.ba.lha (Śāntideva), a disciple of the school of the Teacher kLu.sgrub (Nāgārjuna), which began with saintly 'Jam.dpal (Mañjuśrī), states that aspiration is similar to the wish to go, being the intention to attain perfect Buddhahood, while perseverance in the work of winning it is like the actual going being the effort to realize Buddhahood. As is recorded in the 'sPyod.'jug' ('Bodhicaryāvatāra' I, 16):

> Just as one knows the difference
> Between the desire to go and the actual going,
> So also the wise know the difference
> Between the two attitudes in their above order.

The Venerable gSer.gliṅ.pa (Dharmakīrti), a disciple of the school of the Teacher Thogs.med (Asanga), which was founded by saintly Byams.pa (Maitreya), states that aspiration is taking the vow to reach the final goal, thinking that I will attain perfect Buddhahood for the benefit of all sentient beings, and that perseverance in this work is taking the vow to realize the cause, thinking that I will train myself in the six perfections[21] as the cause of Buddhahood.

This is borne out by the 'Chos.mṅon.pa kun.las btus.pa' ('Abhidharmasamuccaya'):

> The formation of an enlightened attitude is twofold: an ordinary and a particular one. The former is the idea that I shall become an unsurpassably enlightened being; while the latter is the idea that I shall perfect myself in the perfections beginning with

liberality and ending with discriminating awareness born from wisdom.

This ends my discussion of the formation of an enlightened attitude by simile, demarcation and primary characteristics.

The frame of reference in forming an enlightened attitude is (i) enlightenment and (ii) the welfare of sentient beings (49b). So it is said in the 'Byaṅ.chub.sems.dpa'i sa' ('Bodhisattvabhūmi'):

> Therefore the formation of an enlightened attitude has as its frame of reference enlightenment and all sentient beings.

(i) Enlightenment as the frame of reference means seeking spiritual awareness in the Mahāyāna. This is also stated in the chapter of the Formation of an Enlightened Attitude in the 'mDo.sde.rgyan' ('Mahāyāna-sūtrālaṅkāra' IV, 3):

> Its frame of reference is the quest for awareness.

(ii) Sentient beings as the frame of reference does not mean one, two or a few individuals, but all beings as limitless in number as the infinity of celestial space. The formation of an enlightened attitude relieves them from the miseries caused by their being subject to Karma and emotional instability. As is said in the 'bZaṅ.spyod smon. lam' ('Bhadracaryāpraṇidhāna' 46):

> Only when the limits of space are reached,
> Only when the end of sentient beings is reached,
> Only when Karma and emotional instability are exhausted,
> Will my vow have found its fulfilment and end.

The motive for adopting an enlightened attitude is given in the 'Chos bcu.pa'i mdo' ('Daśadharmakasūtra'):

> Such an attitude is formed by four motives: (i) seeing the profitableness of it, (ii) having confidence in the Tathāgata, (iii) seeing the misery of sentient beings and (iv) being urged on by spiritual friends.

In the 'Byaṅ.chub.sems.dpa'i sa' ('Bodhisattvabhūmi'):

> (i) The most perfect family[22] is the first motive for the formation of a Bodhisattva attitude; (ii) to be taken hold of by the Buddhas, Bodhisattvas and spiritual friends is the second (50a); (iii) compassion for sentient beings is the third; and (iv) fearlessness as to the misery of Saṃsāra and that of an austere life, however lasting, varied, severe and interminable, is the fourth.

And in the 'mDo.sde.rgyan' ('Mahāyāna-sūtrālaṅkāra' IV, 7):

> By the power of friends, of the motive force, of the root,

And of hearing, by the practice of the wholesome,
The formation of an enlightened attitude as hinted at by others
Is said to be frail or firm.

That is to say: The formation of an enlightened attitude as 'hinted at by others' and 'deriving from an intimation and its subsequent acceptance' mean that others have revealed it to us. It is relatively real and springs from the advice of spiritual friends. 'By the power of the motive force' means that it originates in the power of the family (which can be smaller or greater according to the strength of the motive). 'By the power of the root of what is good and wholesome' means that it comes from the good doctrine spread by the respective family. 'By the power of hearing' means that it arises by constantly hearing this or that exposition of the Dharma. 'By the practice of the wholesome' means that it arises by constantly hearing, holding and keeping to the teachings in this life. And further, while it is 'frail' when it originates by the power of friends, it is 'firm' when due to the power of the motive force and the other factors.[23]

(ii) The motive for the formation of the ultimately real enlightened attitude is given in the following words:[24]

When the Perfectly Enlightened One is honoured,
When merits and spiritual awareness have been acquired,
When there is non-discursive knowledge of the Dharma,
The attitude is held to be the ultimately real one.

(50b) In other words it arises from the particular ways in which the scriptures are expounded, defended and understood.

The locality or place where we vow to form an enlightened attitude is to be determined by whether there (i) is, or (ii) is not a spiritual teacher.

(ia) If the journey to a spiritual teacher is not dangerous for our life or chastity, we must visit him, however distant he may be, and there vow to form an enlightened attitude. The primary characteristics of such a teacher[25] are that he must be well versed in the method of imparting the discipline; that he has learned the discipline and does not stray from it; moreover he must understand the inner meaning of ritual gestures and chants (in which each movement is a symbol and each word a prayer in itself); and that he must guard his disciple with tenderness, without, however, getting involved in trifles. So it is stated in the 'Byaṅ.chub.lam.sgron' ('Bodhipathapradīpa', 22–3):

Endowed with the proper characteristics,
Having obtained discipline from a good teacher

Learned in the method of dealing with and
Retaining whatever discipline he has got,
Patient and compassionate in imparting it—
By these qualities a good spiritual teacher is to be recognized.

And in the 'Byaṅ.chub.sems.dpa'i sa' ('Bodhisattvabhūmi'):

In order to express the vow to form an enlightened attitude one must be in harmony with the Dharma, disciplined, learned and able to grasp and understand what is meant by the mantras.

(ib) If our life or chastity would be in danger by going to such a spiritual teacher, then he is not for us. Instead we can acquire the necessary attitude of aspiration for or perseverance in the actual work of winning enlightenment by repeating thrice before an image of the Tathāgata the formula which refers to either attitude. So it is said in the 'Byaṅ.chub.sems.dpa'i sa' ('Bodhisattvabhūmi'):

When there is no such individual endowed with these qualities, a Bodhisattva (51a) shall make the vow that he will take upon himself the discipline in ethics and manners as is proper for a Bodhisattva in front of a Buddha image.

(ii) When neither a spiritual teacher nor an image of the Buddha is available, we may obtain the discipline by imagining the Buddhas and Bodhisattvas as present in the sky and then repeating the formula three times. This is stated in the 'bsLab.pa kun.las btus.pa' ('Śikṣāsamuccaya', p. 12):

If there is no such spiritual friend, by having imagined the Buddhas and Bodhisattvas as present in the ten directions, one takes upon oneself the discipline by one's own strength.

To judge by the instructions handed down by learned spiritual teachers there are many different techniques for acquiring an enlightened attitude. This book, however, will only discuss those of (i) the Teacher Ži.ba.lha (Śāntideva), a disciple of the school of the Teacher kLu.sgrub (Nāgārjuna), which started with saintly 'Jam.dpal (Mañjuśrī), and (ii) of the Teacher gSer.gliṅ.pa (Dharmakīrti), a disciple of the school of the Teacher Thogs.med (Asanga), which was founded by saintly Byams.pa (Maitreya).

(i) According to the Teacher Ži.ba.lha (Śāntideva) there are three stages: (A) the preparatory, (B) the actual ceremony and (C) the conclusion.

(A) The preparatory stage has six subdivisions: (I) worship, (II) confession of the evil we have done, (III) delight in the good deeds others have done, (IV) the incentive to turn the Wheel of the Dharma, (V) the request not to pass into Nirvāṇa, and (VI) the transmutation of the good and wholesome.

(I) Worship involves (i) the object worshipped and (ii) the means used.

(i) The object can be manifest or not because worship of the Buddhas is of equal value whether they are present or not. This is stated in the 'mDo.sde.rgyan' ('Mahāyāna-sūtrālaṅkāra' XVII, 1):

> To worship the Buddhas by offering them robes and other things,
> Whether they are present or not,
> With a lucid mind
> Brings the accumulation of merits and spiritual awareness.

(ii) The means are twofold: worship (1) with what, and (2) with what cannot, be surpassed. Of these the former is also twofold: worship (a) with something trifling and (b) by which something is achieved.

(1) The first (a) consists of folding our hands, singing songs of praise, arranging the ceremonial utensils in proper order, donating new ones and giving up our body.

(b) Worship by which something is achieved means to concentrate on the Devakāyamahāmudrā[26] and to offer the thought forms from meditative absorptions of Bodhisattvas.

(2) Worship with what cannot be surpassed (a) has and (b) has no frame of reference.

(a) The first is concentrated attention to the nature of an enlightened attitude. As has been said:

> Having bestowed concentrated attention on the meaning of an enlightened attitude, the wise
> Worship the Buddha and His spiritual sons.
> This is real worship.

(b) Worship with no frame of reference is concentrated attention to the meaning of non-individuality.[27] This is the best form. As the 'lHa'i bu blo.gros rab.gnas.kyis žus.pa'i mdo' ('Susthitamatidevaputraparipṛcchāsūtra') states:

> A Bodhisattva who, desirous for enlightenment,
> For aeons as innumerable as the sand of the Ganges
> Has offered flowers, incense, food and drink
> And thereby worshipped the Buddha, the supreme among human beings
> After having heard the Doctrine which says

That nobody finds anywhere a Self or a Soul (52a)
Or an individuality,
Obtains the satisfaction which sees that all entities are without origin in their primordial light,
And worships the supreme among human beings with real adoration.

And in the 'Seṅ.ge.sgra chen.gyi mdo':

Not producing ideas and forms and entering non-duality through neither accepting nor rejecting anything is Tathāgata worship. Friends, since the Body of the Tathāgata[28] has the primary characteristic of not being an entity, it is difficult for him who clings to the idea that it must be one, to worship it.

This concludes my discussion of the modes of worship.

II. Confession of the evil we have done, means that, generally speaking, good and evil depend on the emergence of a subjective frame of mind,[29] which is the Lord, while body and speech are the servants. As is said in the 'Rin.chen 'phreṅ.ba' ('Ratnāvalī'):

Since the subjective frame of mind precedes everything,
It is known as the Lord.

Therefore, after the subjective frame of mind in which the emotionally disturbing elements of cupidity, malevolence and deludedness are inherent, has become effective, the five heinous and the five similar crimes are committed, the ten unwholesome actions are indulged in, the discipline is violated and the vows are broken by us. Or we instigate others to do so and rejoice thereat, and this is called the evil and unwholesome. But this is not all. To hear, ponder over and give concentrated attention to the Noble Doctrine with such a frame of mind, also is unwholesome. The result is the origination of misery. This is stated in the 'Rin.chen 'phreṅ.ba' ('Ratnāvalī'):

The deeds caused by cupidity, malevolence and deludedness
Are unwholesome;
Unwholesome deeds (52b) produce all misery
And evil existences.

And in the 'sPyod.'jug' ('Bodhicaryāvatāra' II, 63):

Day and night I should
Only think about this matter:
How can I escape from this
Misery that has been brought about by the unwholesome.

Therefore it is necessary that we confess the evil we have done. But is confession a sure way to become purified? Yes, it is. As is stated in the 'mDo mya.ṅan.'das chen' ('Mahāparinirvāṇasūtra'):

> When one has done evil for which out of contrition one then atones, it is like muddy water becoming clear by the touch of the Water-Jewel or like the moon shining forth brilliantly when she has emerged from the clouds.

And,

> Therefore one becomes purified to the extent one feels contrite for evil done and confesses it completely.

How is confession made good, you may ask, and the reply is by four powers. So it is declared in the 'Chos.bži bstan.pa'i mdo' ('Caturdharmanirdeśa'):

> Maitreya, when a Bodhisattva Mahāsattva possesses four powers, the evil done and accumulated becomes defeated. They are the power (A) to effect an atonement; (B) to practise good as an antidote to evil; (C) to desist from evil; and (D) the power of reliance.

(A) Power to atone for the evil done involves a feeling of deep contriteness and then confession before the Buddha and his celestial company. How is such feeling of contriteness to be brought about? There are three ways: (i) by realizing the utter futility of doing (53a) evil, (ii) by appreciating the terribleness of its effects and (iii) by understanding the necessity to become free of it as soon as possible.

(i) The first means that the evil which I have committed was done at times to subdue an enemy, at others to protect a friend, to preserve the body or to accumulate wealth. But when I die and change my existence for the next world, neither my enemies, friends, possessions, body nor wealth will accompany me, only the shadows of my evil deeds will follow and become my hangman wherever I am reborn. As is stated in the 'Khyim.bdag dPa'.sbyin.gyis žus.pa'i mdo' ('Vīradatta-Gṛhapati-paripṛcchāsūtra'):

> Father, mother, brothers, sisters, children, one's wife,
> Servants, wealth and the crowd of relatives
> Will not follow behind the dead.
> Ones deeds however will do so.

And,

> When the time of the great misery has come,
> My children and my wife do not become a refuge.

Alone I must suffer in misery,
As they do not share my fate.

And in the 'sPyod.'jug' ('Bodhicaryāvatāra' II, 35):

Not knowing
That I would have to go from here, leaving everything behind,
I did many evil deeds
For the sake of friends and enemies.
Friends, enemies, I myself,
Thus everything, become nothing.

Therefore, although evil has been done for the sake of friends, enemies, my body and my pleasures, yet these four will not stay with me for ever. Thinking that evil will be very troublesome, while the gain from it is very small, we should develop a feeling of deep contrition (53b).

(ii) If we were to believe that, because evil is a trifling matter, no harm will come to us, we should think better and develop a feeling of contrition by realizing the terribleness of its result. This nightmare is threefold: the horror of evil hanging over us (a) at the time when death approaches, (b) when dying and (c) after death.

(a) Evil-doers, when death approaches, already feel excruciating pain as if their vital parts were pierced and other misery. As has been said:[30]

While I am lying on my death-bed here,
Although I am surrounded by my relatives,
Alone I have to bear
The pain that kills my life.

(b) When dying we feel how dreadful are the effects of evil. This means that the black and ugly messenger of Yama throws a leash round our necks and drags us to hell. We are then tormented by fiends who brandish sticks, swords and other sharp weapons, and much tribulation and suffering is caused. As is stated:[31]

When caught by the messenger of Yama,
What use are friends and relatives?
At that time merits alone are a refuge,
But these I did not acquire.

And in the 'sLob.sbriṅ' ('Śiṣyalekha'):

Having riveted the fetter of time round our neck, Yama's
Fierce messengers will drag us along and beat us.

If you think that you will not be afraid of Yama's messenger, remember these words:[32]

A man who is being led to the place
Where his limbs will be cut off, trembles,
His mouth becomes dry and his eyes and ears
Turn wide and pale.
How then can one describe the horror
When one is caught by Yama's messenger
Whose frightening looks make one's flesh creep,
And when one is afflicted by a terrible disease (54a).

(c) The terrible results of evil mean that when we have fallen into hell, we will experience the unbearable pain of being boiled and burnt. And so it has been said about this awful horror:[33]

Although the hells may be described, seen, heard about, remembered, read about and pictured,
When the great terror has come and unbearable
Misery is experienced, what can one say then?

Therefore, since the results of evil are so awful, we must create a feeling of contrition.

(iii) It is folly to think that confession can be postponed. We must confess as soon as possible. Why? Death may come before you have been purified of evil. As has been said:[34]

I may die
Before my evil has been atoned for;
Quickly help me
That I may be fully delivered from it.

Should someone say that he will not die while the evil is still unatoned for, he should be reminded that death is uncertain,[35] because the Lord of Death does not care whether the evil I have done has been atoned for or not, and steals life at the first opportunity. As has been stated:[36]

This Lord of Death who is not to be trusted,
Does not wait for my having done or not my duty.
Because of all the varying states of disease and health,
Time, being fortuitous, must not be trusted.

Therefore, without trusting life and our span of it in particular, we must confess as soon as possible, since we may die before the evil has been atoned for. And so when we have the chance of feeling contrite we must develop that feeling. When for these three reasons we have done so we must confess the evil we have committed in the presence of the ordinary or special objects of our worship. This purification through atonement (54b) is like asking something of a creditor to whom we still owe money.

Even such a villain as Angulīmāla who had burdened himself with the evil of having murdered nine hundred and ninety-nine men, by the power of making atonement, was purified from it and obtained the fruit of Arhantship. As has been written:[37]

> He who formerly has been without scruples,
> But later becomes scrupulous,
> Becomes radiant like the moon freed from clouds:
> Just as it happened with Nanda, Angulīmāla, Ajātaśatru and Udayana.

(B) The power of practising good as an antidote to evil, means to engage in the good and wholesome. By such means the obscuring and sullying influences[38] are stopped, as has been explained in the 'mṄon.pa kun.las btus.pa' ('Abhidharmasamuccaya', p. 55):

> Counteracting Karma is to be viewed as stronger than adverse Karma, because the former changes the effect, even if it has been outlined by the latter.

In the 'De.bžin.gśegs.pa'i mdzod' ('Sarvatathāgataguhyamahāguhyakośākṣayanidhadīpamahāpratapasādhanatantrajñānāścaryadyuticakra'):

> By concentrated attention to Śūnyata,

In the 'rDo.rje.gcod.pa' ('Vajracchedikā'):

> By reciting the profound Sūtras,

In the 'Dam.tshig gsum bkod.pa'i rgyal.po' ('Trisamayavyūharāja') and 'dPuṅ.bzaṅ.gis žus.pa'i mdo' ('Subāhuparipṛcchātantra'):

> By uttering the mantras,

In the 'Me.tog brtsegs.pa'i gzuṅs' ('Puṣpakūṭanāmadhāraṇī'):

> By having worshipped the funeral monument of a Tathāgata,

In the 'De.bžin.gśegs.pa'i sku.gzugs.kyi le'u':

> By setting up a Buddha statue, by hearing, reading, copying the Dharma (55a) and other meritorious works evil is atoned for.

And in the ''Dul.ba.luṅ' ('Vinayāgamottaraviśeṣāgamapraśnavṛtti'):

> He who abolishes the working of evil
> By the good and wholesome

Shines in this world
Like the sun or moon coming out from clouds.

However, you might ask whether he who engages in good and wholesome deeds as an antidote against evil must do as many good deeds as he has committed evil ones. No, that is not so, for in the 'Mya.ṅan.'das chen.gyi mdo' ('Mahāpariṇirvāṇasūtra') it has been declared:

One single good deed overcomes many evil ones.

And,

Just as a huge mountain is split by a small Vajra, a minor fire burns grass and trees or a little poison kills many sentient beings, so also a small good deed overcomes great evil and so is really a powerful antidote.

And in the 'gSer.'od dam.pa'i mdo' ('Suvarṇaprabhāsottama-sūtra' IV, 38):

He who in thousands of aeons
Has done inexhaustible evil,
By confessing it once only
Becomes purified from it all.

This purification by the practice of good as an antidote against evil is like a man who, after falling into and escaping from a foul swamp, and then taking a bath, anoints himself with fragrant oils.

Although, long ago, the boy Udayana killed his mother, by using the power of practising good as an antidote, he was purified from evil and became a godlike person endowed with the fruit of having entered the stream running towards enlightenment.[39] As has been written:[40]

He who formerly has been without scruples,
But later becomes scrupulous
Becomes radiant like the moon free from clouds:
Just as it happened with Nanda, Angulīmāla, Ajātaśatru and Udayana (55b).

(C) The power to desist from evil is the discipline of ceasing to do it, because we are terrified by its results. As has been stated:

I ask the leaders of mankind
To forgive the evil I have done.
Since to commit evil is not good
I shall stop doing so henceforth.

In this way purification by the power of desisting from evil is like diverting the current of a dangerous river.

Formerly, although Nanda had burdened himself with evil by being infatuated with women, by using the power of desisting, he became purified from it and obtained the fruit of Arhantship. As has been written:[41]

He who formerly has been without scruples,
But later becomes scrupulous
Becomes radiant like the moon free from clouds:
Just as it happened with Nanda, Angulīmāla, Ajātaśatru and Udayana.

(D) The power of reliance means (i) taking refuge in the Three Jewels and (ii) forming an enlightened attitude.

(i) The purification from evil by taking refuge in the Three Jewels is pointed out in the 'Phag.mo'i rtogs.pa brjod.pa' ('Sūkarikāvadāna'):

He who takes refuge in the Buddha
Does not fall into evil existences.
After having vacated the human body
He acquires that of a god.

And in the 'Mya.ṅan.'das chen.gyi mdo' ('Mahāparinirvāṇasūtra'):

By taking refuge in the Three Jewels
Fearlessness is gained.

(ii) The purification from evil by forming an enlightened attitude is explained in the ''Phags.pa sDoṅ.po bkod.pa'i mdo' ('Gaṇḍavyūhasūtra', p. 494):

It is like the regions under this earth, because it abolishes all unwholesome conditions (56a). It is like the fire at the end of time, because it burns all evil.

And in the 'sPyod.'jug' ('Bodhicaryāvatāra' I, 13):

Why should the timid not rely on enlightenment
As a result of which they become free in a moment
From evil, however unexpiable it may seem,
Just as great terror subsides by relying on a hero.

Thus purification by the power of reliance is like a poor servant coming to his master, or poison being expelled by charms.[42]

Formerly, although King Ajātaśatru had burdened himself with the evil of parricide, he was purified by the power of reliance and became a Bodhisattva. As has been written:[43]

He who formerly has been without scruples,
But later becomes scrupulous
Becomes radiant like the moon free from clouds:
Just as it happened with Nanda, Angulīmāla, Ajātaśatru and Udayana.

While each power separately produces purification, what happens when all four work together? By such confession and atonement in this manner we dream of the signs that denote purification. As is stated in the 'sKul.byed.kyi gzuṅs' ('Cundadhāraṇī'):

> One becomes purified from evil when one dreams that one vomits bad food, drinks cream and milk, sees sun and moon, walks in the air, watches a blazing fire, buffaloes, powerful men clad in black[44] and an assembly of Bhikṣus and Bhikṣuṇīs, climbs milk-producing trees, elephants, bulls, mountains, lion-thrones and palaces, and listens to the Dharma (56b).
>
> This concludes my discussion of the confession of evil.

III. To delight in the good and wholesome is the attentive endeavour to rejoice in the merits acquired by all beings who do good in the past, present and future.

One's attention should therefore be concentrated on the constant delight of thinking that one is about to rejoice at all that is good and wholesome being rooted in goodness. It has been so rooted from the time when the innumerable countless and inconceivable Buddhas, who appeared in all the worlds, first acquired an excellent enlightened attitude, obtained the two acquisitions,[45] tore the two veils,[46] and until they found enlightenment. It has been so rooted ever since, after bringing their pupils to spiritual maturity, they entered the final Nirvāṇa while turning the Wheel of Dharma. It has been so rooted for the continuity of the Dharma, even after they have passed into Nirvāṇa; it has been so rooted in the saintly Pratyekabuddhas and Śrāvakas who have appeared in this world; and finally in ordinary human beings.

In the same way we shall rejoice at the good and wholesome in the present and the future. As has been said:

I delight in the enlightenment of the Protectors
And I rejoice at the spiritual levels attained by the Sons of the Buddha.

This concludes my exposition of delighting in the good and wholesome.

IV (57a). Urging them to turn the Wheel of Dharma means that even now the Buddhas in the ten regions of the world have still much to say before the Jewel of the Dharma is respected, or those who wish that it were are brought to perfection. The request to teach the Doctrine is made for their sake. As is stated:[47]

The Buddhas of all the regions in the world
I request with folded hands
That they may kindle the lamp of the Dharma
In order to dispel the darkness of misery in sentient beings.

V. The request not to pass into Nirvāṇa means that even now in this world with its ten regions there are many Buddhas who are about to enter Nirvāṇa in order to disprove the views of those who believe in permanence or to instil strenuousness into the lazy. It is for their sake that this request is made. As is said:[48]

The Buddhas who want to pass into Nirvāṇa
I request with folded hands
That for countless aeons they may stay on
So that sentient beings may not become blind.

This concludes my discussion of the urging them on and the requesting them not to enter Nirvāṇa.

VI. Transmutation of good means that all the good and wholesome that has been accomplished is dedicated to and becomes the cause of the abolition of misery of all sentient beings so that they find happiness, as is declared:[49]

All the good and wholesome I have done
And accumulated
May burn away the misery
Of all sentient beings.

Thus is merit transmuted. This concludes the preparatory stage.

B. The ceremony itself involves repeating the vow as is laid down in the 'bsLab.btus' ('Śikṣāsamuccaya', p. 13) where it is said that as the Venerable 'Jam.dpal (Mañjuśrī), when he was the king Nam. mkha' (Amba), went to the Buddha 'Brug.sgra.dbyaṅs (Meghanādaghoṣa) and obtained instruction in the formation of an enlightened attitude together with the Bodhisattva-discipline, so also I will receive both instructions together, and

From beginning to end
Of beginningless and endless Saṃsāra
I will live a life

Devoted to the benefits of beings.
In the presence of the Lord of the World
I form an enlightened attitude.

These or similar words must be repeated three times.

Or, he will receive instruction after having expressed his desire in concise words as laid down in the 'Byaṅ.chub spyod.'jug' ('Bodhicaryāvatāra' III, 23 seq.):

Just as the Sugatas of yore
Adhered to
An enlightened attitude
And the training of a Bodhisattva in this sequence,
So also for the benefit of sentient beings
I shall train myself, in the same sequence,
In the formation of an enlightened attitude
And the Bodhisattva training.

This is to be repeated thrice.

If you want to develop an enlightened attitude and a Bodhisattva discipline separately, you must recite the words which refer to either the one or the other training.

This concludes my exposition of the method of the ceremony.

C. In view of the great goal that lies before us we conclude by giving thanks while worshipping the Three Jewels and then concentrating on and being attentive to the development of great joy and happiness. As has been stated:

A judicious man,
In order further to develop such an attitude far and wide
Once he has adopted it,
Will praise it in this way.

Thus the preparatory stage, the actual ceremony and its conclusion have been explained according to the technique taught by Ži.ba.lha (Śāntideva) (58a).

(ii) In the technique of Lord gSer.gliṅ.pa (Dharmakīrti), a disciple of the school of the Teacher Thogs.med (Asanga), which was founded by saintly Byams.pa (Maitreya), there are two sections: (I) the formation of an attitude of aspiration and (II) the acceptance of the discipline which has to be followed while winning enlightenment.

I. The first section has three subdivisions: (A) the preparatory stage, (B) the actual ceremony and (C) its conclusion.

A. In the preparatory stage there are three further sections: (i) making the request, (ii) accumulating the necessary prerequisites and (iii) the special type of taking refuge.

(i) The first is as follows. The disciple who wants to develop an enlightened attitude has to approach a spiritual friend with the necessary qualifications and greet him by folding his hands. The spiritual friend, on the other hand, instructs the disciple so that he feels disgust for Saṃsāra, compassion for sentient beings, desires Buddhahood, has confidence in the Three Jewels and develops devotion to the spiritual teacher. Then the disciple repeats after the teacher the following words: 'May the teacher be gracious to me. Just as the former Tathāgatas, Arhants, Samyaksambuddhas, Exalted Ones and Bodhisattvas living on a high level of spirituality first developed an attitude directed towards unsurpassable perfect great enlightenment, so also I, so and so (by name), request the teacher to help me in developing such an attitude.' This he repeats three times.

(ii) Then according to our means we worship with the things at hand or in our mind's eye (58b). We receive the discipline of a Śramaṇera from the elder instructor, of a Bhikṣu from the Sangha and the two types of an enlightened attitude[50] from an accumulation of merits.

If we have great wealth, it is not enough to offer a few things, we must give lavishly; the Bodhisattvas of yore, who had much wealth, gave generously: having offered ten million palaces they formed an enlightened attitude. This is recorded in the 'bsKal.pa bzaṅ.po'i mdo' ('Bhadrakalpika'):

> The Sugata Grags.sbyin during the reign of king 'Dzam.gliṅ
> After having offered ten million palaces
> To the Tathāgata Zla.ba'i tog,
> For the first time developed an enlightened attitude.

When we have a modicum of riches, we can give accordingly. The Bodhisattvas of old who had little wealth still gave something. They developed an enlightened attitude after offering a blade of grass as a lamp. As has been recorded:

> The Sugata 'Od.phro during the reign of Groṅ.khyer brten.pa
> After having offered a lamp made of a single blade of grass
> To the Tathāgata mTha'.yas 'od,
> For the first time developed an enlightened attitude.

To have no wealth does not mean that we should not make an offering. It is enough to fold our hands reverently three times. The

Bodhisattvas of old who had no money also folded their hands thrice and then developed an enlightened attitude. As has been said:

The Sugata Yon.tan 'phreṅ.ldan
After having folded his hands thrice
Before the Tathāgata bGyid.ldan bžud (59a),
For the first time developed an enlightened attitude.

(iii) The special type of taking refuge is performed in the manner described above.[51]

B. During the actual ceremony the teacher instructs the disciple thus: You must deepen the feeling of compassion and implant it firmly in your heart, remembering that sentient beings are as limitless as celestial space and that as long as there are sentient beings they will be affected by conflicting emotions,[52] which will cause them to do evil, for which in turn they will suffer; that all sentient beings suffering misery are your parents and so your benefactors, and that, since they are drowning in the great ocean of Saṃsāra, are tormented by immeasurable tribulations and without a protector, toil along in difficulties and have to experience the dreadful effects of conflicting emotions, they should in time all be delivered from that misery and win happiness. Therefore think: since I cannot now work for their benefit, I will obtain enlightenment in order to do so. And you must realize that as a result they will be freed from evil, become perfect in virtue and be able to work for the benefit of all sentient beings.

The disciple then repeats after the teacher: 'May the Buddhas of the ten regions of the world and all the Bodhisattvas be gracious to me. May the teacher be gracious to me. I, so and so (by name) (59b), will practice, and rejoice in so doing, the good which grows from being liberal, ethical and concentrated, now and for evermore, thus emulating the Tathāgatas, Arhants, Samyaksambuddhas, Exalted Ones and the Bodhisattva Mahāsattvas living on a high level of spirituality, who in ancient times developed an attitude directed towards unsurpassable perfect great enlightenment. From now on until I have become the very quintessence of enlightenment[53] I will develop an attitude directed towards unsurpassable perfect great enlightenment so that the beings who have not yet crossed over may do so, who have not yet been delivered may be, who have not yet found their breath may find it and who have not yet passed into Nirvāṇa may do so.' Repeating these words he will act accordingly.

In this vow the expression 'the beings who have not yet crossed over' refers to the denizens of hell, spirits and animals, because they have not yet finished with the misery of evil existences which is like an ocean.

The words 'may cross over' mean that by following the path which leads to a life as a god or human being they are delivered from the misery of evil existences and attain the divine or human level.

'Who have not yet been delivered' refers to gods and men who are still bound by the iron fetters of emotional instability.

'May be delivered' means that by following the path which leads to what is evidently the best they are freed from the fetters of emotional instability and experience the joy of (60a) liberation.

'Who have not yet found their breath' is said with reference to the Śrāvakas and Pratyekabuddhas, because they have not yet found rest in the Mahāyāna.

'May find it' means that by developing an excellent enlightened attitude they recover their breath (and so their quiet faith) in the Mahāyāna way of life and realize a spiritual state that exists on the ten levels of spirituality.

'Who have not yet passed into Nirvāṇa' refers to the Bodhisattvas, because they have not yet attained the unconditioned Nirvāṇa.[54]

'May pass into it' means that by reaching the various levels of spirituality and the various paths they will enter Nirvāṇa and attain the rank of a Buddha.

'So that' has the meaning of intention indicating the vow to become a Buddha and to fulfil one's task.

C. The conclusion is to develop concentrated attention to the spreading of great joy and happiness out of consideration for the great goal that lies before us. This is called the Training. Such a formation of an enlightened attitude is named 'Bodhisattva' (quintessence of enlightenment); it is the desire for enlightenment for the sake of all sentient beings; it is the desire to deliver beings after the attainment of enlightenment; it has as its frame of reference enlightenment and sentient beings;[55] and involves indomitable courage and compassion for the benefit of beings.

This concludes the description of the technique developed in the formation of an enlightened attitude of aspiration.

II. In the acceptance of the discipline to be adhered to when you persevere in the actual work of winning enlightenment, there are also three stages: (A) the preparatory, (B) the actual performance and (C) the conclusion.

A. The preparatory stage is tenfold: (i) the request, (ii) the question about difficulties in general, (iii) the explanation of the unsavoury state of falling from the discipline, (iv) the deplorable situation of having fallen from it, (v) the usefulness of practising it, (vi) the accumulation of the prerequisites, (vii) the question about the unusual difficulties met with, (viii) the encouragement, (ix) developing a special intention, (60a) and (x) the short instruction in the training.

B. The actual performance is as follows. When the disciple has developed an attitude favourable to the discipline, the teacher asks him three times: 'Oh son of a good family, having this name, do you want to accept from me, a Bodhisattva bearing this name, the basic training and the ethics of all the Bodhisattvas of the past and the present in the ten regions of the world; that in which all the Bodhisattvas of the past did, of the future will, and of the present do train themselves together with all their ethical disciplines, their means of acquiring the good and wholesome and of working for the benefit of all sentient beings?' Thrice the disciple has to utter his assent.

C. The conclusion is sixfold: (i) the request for realizing omniscience, (ii) the profitableness of adopting a view of comprehensive understanding, (iii) fearlessness as to the rashness of the discipline, (iv) the understanding of the training in a condensed form, (v) mindfulness of favours bestowed and (vi) the transmutation of the good and wholesome.

This concludes the discussion of the acceptance of the discipline to be adhered to in order to persevere in the work of winning enlightenment.

This is the explanation of the technique adopted and taught by Lord gSer.gliṅ.pa (Dharmakīrti).

The usefulness of forming an enlightened attitude (61a) is of two types: (A) countable and (B) uncountable.

A. The first is twofold: the usefulness of forming an attitude (I) of aspiration and (II) of perseverance.

I. The first has eight qualities: (i) we enter the Mahāyāna fold, (ii) we become the foundation of all the training a Bodhisattva has to undergo, (iii) all evil is eradicated, (iv) the seed of unsurpassable enlightenment is planted, (v) immeasurable merits are acquired, (vi) all Buddhas are delighted with us, (vii) we become useful to all sentient beings and (viii) we quickly realize perfect Buddhahood. Now to explain these qualities in a more detailed way:

(i) A man who does not even begin to wish for enlightenment cannot, however excellent and perfect his behaviour may be, enter the fold of the Mahāyāna and so cannot attain perfect Buddhahood.

But he will do so once he has started to desire supreme enlightenment and has entered the Mahāyānic fold. As is stated in the 'Byaṅ.sa' ('Bodhisattvabhūmi'):

> Immediately after he has formed this attitude he enters upon a course of unsurpassable enlightenment.

(ii) A man who has no desire to attain Buddhahood which starts with what is called an attitude of aspiration can never practise the three types of ethics and manners[56] in the Bodhisattva training. But the mind of the man who desires to attain Buddhahood and in whom the three types arise and continue, is the foundation for such training. As is written in the 'Byaṅ.sa' ('Bodhisattvabhūmi'):

> This formation of an enlightened attitude is the foundation for the Bodhisattva training (61b).

(iii) The antidote against evil is the good and wholesome, the perfection of which from within is the enlightened attitude. This is the undeniable remedy and rule for exhausting all that is unfavourable and in opposition. As has been affirmed:

> Just like fire at the end of time, with this antidote
> He burns the greatest evil in a single moment.

(iv) When an enlightened attitude which is like a seed has been planted in the life of a sentient being, which is like a field watered with benevolence and compassion, the thirty-seven branches conducive to enlightenment[57] spread and by having ripened into the fruit of perfect Buddhahood bring about the happiness and welfare of sentient beings. Therefore, by the formation of this enlightened attitude the seed of Buddhahood is planted. As is stated in the 'Byaṅ.sa' ('Bodhisattvabhūmi'):

> This formation of an enlightened attitude is the root of unsurpassable perfect enlightenment.

(v) The attainment of immeasurable merits is described in the 'dPa'.sbyin.gyis žus.pa'i mdo' ('Vīradatta-Gṛhapati-paripṛcchā-sūtra'):

> If the merits that accrue from an enlightened attitude
> Were to become visible,
> They would fill the whole expanse of the sky
> And still more would be left over.[58]

(vi) The fact that all Buddhas are delighted with us is expressed in the 'dPa'.sbyin.gyis žus.pa'i mdo' ('Vīradatta-Gṛhapati-paripṛcchā-sūtra'):[59]

If a man were to fill completely
All the Buddha fields which are as numerous as the sand in the Ganges,
And were to make a gift of it to the Sugatas,
Yet worship would be better
When he but folded his hands
And directed his mind towards enlightenment.
Such worship knows no end (62a).

(vii) That we become useful to all sentient beings is stated in the ''Phags.pa sDoṅ.po bkod.pa'i mdo' ('Gaṇḍavyūhasūtra'), p. 494:

It is like a foundation because of its usefulness to all worlds.

(viii) That we quickly realize perfect Buddhahood is explained in the 'Byaṅ.sa' ('Bodhisattvabhūmi'):

When this attitude has been adopted, one does not cling to extremes, but quickly realizes perfect Buddhahood.

II. The usefulness of forming an enlightened attitude of perseverance in winning enlightenment also has ten qualities. In addition to the eight merits just described (ix) our interests are continuously safeguarded and (x) so also those of others.

(ix) After the formation of this attitude the whole situation has changed for all time, since, whether we dream, sleep or are careless, the proper merits are working. As is written in the 'sPyod.'jug' ('Bodhicaryāvatāra' I, 19):

After such an attitude has been adopted
Whether one sleeps or
Is careless, the power of merits
Works uninterruptedly
And becomes equal to the expanse of celestial space.

(x) That the interests of others are safeguarded means that the misery of sentient beings is abolished, happiness is realized and emotional instability is overcome. As is also stated in the 'sPyod.'jug' ('Bodhicaryāvatāra' I, 29–30):

He who gives satisfaction through happiness
And abolishes all the misery
Of those who are deprived of happiness
And are afflicted with many woes,
And who dispels the darkness of the spirit,
Where does one ever find a good man like Him?
Where does one find such a spiritual friend?
Where are such virtues found?

B. Uncountable (62b) means that all the qualities acquired from the time that an enlightened attitude is formed until Buddhahood is attained cannot be counted.

The deplorableness of having lost an enlightened attitude is threefold: By such loss (i) we enter evil existences, (ii) fail in working for the benefit of others and (iii) the attainment of spiritual levels is very remote.

(i) The first means that by not keeping our vow and ceasing to preserve an enlightened attitude we cheat sentient beings of their due and so are reborn in evil existences. As is stated in the 'sPyod.'jug' ('Bodhicaryāvatāra'):

> When one has taken the vow
> And does not fulfil it by one's deeds,
> One cheats all sentient beings:
> What will be one's own destiny?

(ii) To fail in working for the benefit of sentient beings is expressed in the words:

> When this happens
> One fails in working for the benefit of all beings.

(iii) That the attainment of spiritual levels is very remote is stated in this verse:

> When the power to fall
> And the power for enlightenment
> Become mixed in Saṃsāra
> The attainment of spiritual levels is very remote.

There are two ways of violating the formation of an enlightened attitude: violation of the attitude of (A) aspiration and (B) perseverance.

A. The first is brought by (i) excluding sentient beings from our thoughts,[60] (ii) adhering to four dark actions[61] and (iii) adopting an attitude opposed to enlightenment.

B. Violation of the attitude of perseverance is referred to in the 'Byaṅ.sa' ('Bodhisattvabhūmi'):

> When one is fully ensnared by four actions which are as disastrous as the four inexpiable offences, such behaviour is called a violation. When one is ensnared by them in a mediocre or minor way it is called only a disgrace.[62]

In the 'sDom.pa ñi.śu.pa' ('Saṃvaravimśaka'):

> This violation is worse than that of an attitude of aspiration.

And in the 'rNam.par gtan.la dbab.pa bsdu.ba':

> The causes for renouncing the Bodhisattva discipline are four. The former two (i.e. violation of the attitudes of aspiration and perseverance), the forsaking of the training and the adoption of wrong views. According to the Teacher Ži.ba.lha (Śāntideva) the discipline is also forsaken by adopting an attitude opposed to enlightenment.

To restore any one of these attitudes or disciplines after it has been forsaken or violated means that one must take it up again from the start. If, however, we are but mildly ensnared by the four dark actions which are as disastrous as the four inexpiable offences, confession will suffice. This is affirmed in the 'sDom.pa ñi.śu.pa' ('Saṃvaraviṃśaka'):

> The discipline has to be taken up from the start.
> If the transgression is of a mediocre or minor sort it will do to make a confession.
> When one discipline is violated so are all others.
> Do not fall into emotional instability, (preserve a pure) mind as I do.

The ninth chapter, dealing with the Formation of an Enlightened Attitude,
from the Jewel Ornament of Liberation or
The Wish-Fulfilling Gem of the
Noble Doctrine.

NOTES TO CHAPTER 9

1. The same list of similes is given in 'Mahāyāna-sūtrālaṅkāra' IV, 15–20. The explanation in the commentary to this passage, however, differs from sGam.po.pa's in certain respects. On the whole, sGam.po.pa's interpretation is logically more consistent than Asaṅga's.

2. The three types of omniscience are: (1) knowledge of the foundation or motive (*gži.śes*) which is the starting point for meditative processes that will eventually lead to the realization of the goal or enlightenment. (2) Intimately connected with this knowledge is that of the causal characteristic (*rnam.śes*) of 'mind' as the basis in the sense that mentality is an emergent quality and capable of manifest-

ing itself as anything about which we believe that it exists in space and time. (3) Finally, there is the knowledge of the path (*lam.śes*) which by making use of that of the causal characteristic of mind assists in traversing the path from its starting point (the foundation of all life) to the realization of the goal. This interpretation of the three types of omniscience corresponds to sGam.po.pa's discussion in his 'bsTan.chos.luṅ.giñi.'od' and runs through all works dealing with the Sahajayoga which was developed particularly by the bKa'-rgyud.pa school whose organizer was sGam.po.pa. Three types of omniscience are also mentioned in 'Abhisamayālaṅkāra' I, 1.

3. *sbyin.pa'i pha.rol. tu phyin.pa*, Skt. *dānapāramitā*. See Chapter 12.

4. *tshul.khrims*, Skt. *śīlapāramitā*. See Chapter 13.

5. *bzod.pa*, Skt. *kṣāntipāramitā*. See Chapter 14.

6. *brtson.'grus*, Skt. *vīryapāramitā*. See Chapter 15.

7. *bsam.gtan*, Skt. *dhyānapāramitā*. See Chapter 16.

8. *śes.rab*, Skt. *prajñāpāramitā*. See Chapter 17.

9. *thabs*, Skt. *upāya* (*kauśalya*). Here and in the following topics sGam.po.pa connects those qualities and processes which are necessary for the formation of an attitude directed toward enlightenment with certain perfections which, in a sense, are the outcome of the perfection of discriminating awareness or the application of discrimination in our life.

10. *smon.lam*, Skt. *praṇidhāna*. See 'Vijñaptimātratāsiddhi', p. 623.

11. *stobs*, Skt. *bala*. ibid., p. 624.

12. *ye.śes*, Skt. *jñāna*. ibid., p. 624. See also Chapter 20 for a more detailed discussion of the meaning of *jñāna*.

13. The ten stages of spirituality are discussed in Chapter 19.

14. *mṅon.śes*, Skt. *abhijñā*. See Chapter 4, note 19.

15. There are thirty-seven topics essential for realizing enlightenment (*byaṅ.chub.kyi phyogs daṅ mthun.pa'i chos*, Skt. *bodhipākṣika dharma*). They are:

4 Smṛtyupasthāna: inspection of what constitutes our physical existence (*kāya*), our emotional (*vedanā*) and intellectual life (*citta*), and that which we call the whole of reality (*dharma*);

4 Samyakprahāṇa: to put an end to existing evil and prevent it arising; bring good into existence and develop existing good;

4 Ṛddhipāda: strong interest (*chanda*), disposition (*citta*), strenuousness (*vīrya*) and investigation (*mīmāṃsā*);

5 Indriya: confidence (*śraddhā*), strenuousness (*vīrya*), inspection (*smṛti*), concentrative absorption (*samādhi*) and discrimination (*prajñā*);

5 Bala: The same as indriya (controlling powers) but now by virtue of increased practice 'unshakable powers';
7 Bodhyaṅga: analysis (*dharmapravicaya*), strenuousness (*vīrya*), enthusiasm (*prīti*), tension relaxation (*praśrabhdi*), inspection (*smṛti*), concentrative absorption (*samādhi*) and equanimity (*upekṣā*);
8 Āryamārgāṅga: right view (*samyagdṛṣṭi*), right purpose (*samyaksaṃkalpa*), right speech (*samyagvāc*), right action (*samyakkarmānta*), right livelihood (*samyagājīva*), right striving (*samyagvyāyāma*), right inspection (*samyaksmṛti*) and right meditative absorption (*samyaksamādhi*).

See also 'Bhāṣya' ad 'Abhidharmakośa' VI, 66 (pp. 281 seqq.); 'Mahāyāna-sūtrālaṅkāra' XVIII, 42–65, and commentary.

16. Tranquillity and Insight (*źi.gnas lhag.mthoṅ*, the printed text has erroneously *sñiṅ.rje lhag.mthoṅ*) are the starting point for the meditation according to the 'lHan.cig.skyes.sbyor' dealing with the realization of Mahāmudrā.

17. i.e. to accept all that is positive for spiritual development and to reject all that is opposed to it.

18. The text has *chos.kyi skyed.mos.tshal*, which corresponds to Skt. *dharma-udyāna*. 'Mahāyāna-sūtrālaṅkāra' reads *dharma-uddāna* 'a pithy saying on the basis of the Dharma'.

19. The same explanation is given in the 'rDzogs chen kun.bzaṅ bla.ma', fol. 160a. A further account is found in 'Vijñaptimātratāsiddhi', p. 731.

20. The same distinction in the 'rDzogs chen kun.bzaṅ bla.ma', fol. 160b.

21. They are: liberality, ethics and manners, patience, strenuousness, meditative concentration and discriminating awareness. See Chapters 12 to 17.

22. It is the Mahāyāna family and in particular the Awakened Family. See above, Chapter 1.

23. See commentary of 'Mahāyāna-sūtrālaṅkāra' IV, where the same explanation is given.

24. 'Mahāyāna-sūtrālaṅkāra' IV, 8.

25. The qualities which a teacher must have in order to be respected, are given in the 'rDzogs chen kun.bzaṅ bla.ma', fol. 97a seq.: 'Although in this degenerated age it is difficult to find a teacher who possesses all the qualities as laid down in the precious Tantras, it is essential that one on whom we can depend must possess the following qualities in full: outwardly he must follow the Prātimokṣa,

inwardly his attitude must be directed toward enlightenment, and spiritually he must know the mantras; he must have a lucid mind so that he does not err as to whom the three types of discipline may be imparted and to whom not; he must be deeply learned in the subject matter of Sūtras, Tantras and Śāstras; his heart must drip with compassion for innumerable beings whom he considers to be his only child; he must be well-versed in the Tripiṭaka and in the methods of the four types of Tantras; he must have realized the particular qualities of renunciation and attainment by direct experience of reality; he must be a man who is able to attract diligent students by the four qualities of liberality, well-mannered speech, conscientiousness and adequate interest.'

26. *lha'i sku phyag.rgya.chen.po.* See 'Phyag.rgya chen.po'i man.ṅag. gi bśad.sbyar rgyal.ba'i gan.mdzod', fol. 29b.

27. *bdag.med,* Skt. *anātman.*

28. i.e. the 'Dharmakāya'. See Chapter 20.

29. *yid,* Skt. *manas.*

30. 'Bodhicaryāvatāra' II, 41.

31. ibid., II, 42.

32. ibid., II, 44–5.

33. 'Suhṛllekha', 84.

34. 'Bodhicaryāvatāra' II, 34.

35. See above, Chapter 4, p. 47.

36. 'Bodhicaryāvatāra' II, 33.

37. 'Suhṛllekha', 14.

38. *zag.pa,* Skt. *āsrava.* There are four such elements: sensuality (*kāma*), belief in existence (*bhava*), opinionatedness (*dṛṣṭi*) and spiritual ignorance (*avidyā*).

39. *srota-āpanna.*

40. 'Suhṛllekha', 14.

41. ibid.

42. The following explanation is given: the poor man who goes to a rich one is symbolical of taking refuge; and the expulsion of poison by charms is symbolical of forming a healthy attitude directed toward enlightenment.

43. 'Suhṛllekha', 14.

44. *mi nag.po*: laymen who usually wear dark clothes.

45. i.e. merits and knowledge. See Chapter 10.

46. i.e. conflicting emotions and primitive beliefs about reality.

47. 'Bodhicaryāvatāra' III, 4.

48. ibid., III, 5.

49. ibid., III, 6.

50. i.e. attitude of aspiration and perseverance.

51. See Chapter 8, p. 103.

52. *ñon.moṅs.pa*, Skt. *kleśa*. The three principal *kleśas* are cupidity, malevolence and bewilderment.

53. *byaṅ.chub sñiṅ.po*, Skt. *bodhimaṇḍa*. A similar explanation is given in 'Bodhicaryāvatārapañjikā', p. 58.

54. i.e. non-localized Nirvāṇa (*apratiṣṭhitanirvāṇa*). The Hīnayāna conception of Nirvāṇa is either existence (Sarvāstivādins) or non-existence (Sautrāntikas). Existence and non-existence are extremes which the Middle Path taught by the Buddha, avoids. Since Hīnayāna does not avoid the extremes, only the Mahāyāna conception of Nirvāṇa can claim to represent the spirit of Buddhism.

55. See above, p. 116.

56. See Chapter 13 for the various types of ethics and manners.

57. See note 15.

58. The Sanskrit version is found in 'Bodhicaryāvatārapañjikā', p. 32.

59. See 'Bodhicaryāvatārapañjikā', p. 33, for the Sanskrit version.

60. See Chapter 10.

61. See Chapter 10 at the end.

62. The four evil actions are: destroying life, stealing, sexual incontinence and telling lies.

10

THE TRAINING IN AN ENLIGHTENED ATTITUDE

After an enlightened attitude has been formed, training starts in (A) aspiration and (B) perseverance.[1] The following is a guide to the first type:

> Five tasks complete the training in aspiration:
> Not to exclude beings from our thoughts;
> To be mindful of the usefulness of this attitude;
> To accumulate the prerequisites;
> Ever and again to purify this attitude and
> To accept and reject the four positive and negative qualities respectively.

The first is the method of not violating an enlightened attitude; the second is the means by which that attitude does not deteriorate; the third is the method for strengthening it the fourth for spreading and deepening it, while the fifth is the means by which it is not forgotten.

I. The method of not violating an enlightened attitude, which is called the training in thinking of sentient beings, is mentioned in the 'Ma.dros.pas žus.pa'i mdo' ('Anavataptanāgarājaparipṛcchāsūtra'):

> When a Bodhisattva possesses one virtue, he has all the most excellent Buddha qualities. Which one? The attitude which does not exclude sentient beings from his thoughts.

So to exclude sentient beings implies adopting an attitude of determining not to think of a person who has wronged one, and even after cooling down not to help or harm him when opportunity occurs.

Should you ask whether we can speak of excluding from our thoughts all sentient beings or only one, the answer is that except for Śrāvakas and Pratyekabuddhas not even eagles or jackals can do it. Therefore, by excluding only one sentient being from our thoughts, if it is not remedied within one hour, the enlightened attitude is violated. To call ourselves Bodhisattvas while so excluding sentient beings and following another discipline is altogether unreasonable. It is like killing your only child and preserving his things. Therefore, since sentient beings are useful to us, how can we ever allow an enlightened attitude to be violated by excluding them from our thoughts?[2] Since such an attitude may be violated by harming others, we must all the more develop compassion and establish the happiness and welfare of beings. This, indeed, is the nature of saintly people. As has been recorded:

> When harm has been done in return for a good deed,
> Even then it has to be answered by Great Compassion.
> The best men in the human world
> Return a good deed for an evil one.

II. How to safeguard an enlightened attitude from deteriorating, which is called the training in being mindful of the usefulness of forming an enlightened attitude, is mentioned in the 'Byaṅ.chub.lam. sgron' ('Bodhipathapradīpa', 12):

> In the Gaṇḍavyūha
> Maitreya has explained
> The virtues of forming
> An attitude of aspiration.

In this Sūtra the usefulness of forming an enlightened attitude has been illustrated by two hundred and thirty similes which, however, can be summarized under four main headings.

(i) The words, 'Oh son of a good family, an enlightened attitude is like the seed of all Buddha qualities'[3] and 'Because it extirpates all poverty it is like Vaiśravaṇa (god of riches)',[4] and other similes refer to the usefulness for ourselves.

(ii) 'Because it protects all the world it is like an asylum'[5] and 'Because it is the support of all sentient beings it is like a foundation'[6] and so on, refer to the usefulness for others.

(iii) 'Because it overcomes the enemy of emotional instability it is like armour'[7] and 'Because it fells the tree of misery it is like an axe'[8] and others refer to the usefulness in destroying all elements opposed to enlightenment.

(iv) 'By fulfilling all aspirations (64b) it is like a lucky jar'[9] and 'Because it makes all wishes come true it is like the Wish-Fulfilling Gem'[10] and so on, refer to its usefulness in making available all elements conducive to enlightenment.

By being mindful of all such virtues of usefulness this enlightened attitude is highly appreciated, held to be the most excellent possession and protected against deterioration when these virtues have been taken to heart. Therefore we must be mindful of this usefulness hourly at all times.

III. The method for obtaining a strong enlightened attitude, which is called the training in the accumulation of the two prerequisites, is discussed in the 'Byaṅ.chub.lam.sgron' ('Bodhipathapradīpa', 38):

> The accumulation of merits and acquisition of spiritual awareness
> Is the perfect cause.

'Accumulation of merits' is the method[11] of behaving in accordance with the ten fundamental rules[12] and produces the four expedients by which sentient beings feel themselves attracted by us,[13] while 'acquisition of spiritual awareness' belongs to the category of discriminating awareness born from wisdom[14] which is the knowledge that our motives are pure.[15] In this way the strength of an enlightened attitude develops by acquiring these two prerequisites which can, and should, be accumulated and then strengthened by muttering the prescribed mantras hourly at all times. In the 'Tshogs.kyi gtam' ('Sambhāraparikathā') it is stated:

> A Bodhisattva must always think:
> Today I will accumulate
> Merits and spiritual awareness
> And bring merits to all beings.

IV. (65a) The method of spreading and deepening an enlightened attitude, which is called the training in its purification, is mentioned in the 'Byaṅ.chub.lam.sgron' ('Bodhipathapradīpa', 18):

> After having formed an attitude of aspiration
> One has to increase it by many endeavours.

The training in how to do this is threefold: purification of mind as (i) the motive, (ii) the substance and (iii) correct conduct in and of enlightenment. By this triple purification an enlightened attitude is made to grow.

(i) The first means always to think benevolently and compassionately of sentient beings, even every hour.

(ii) The mind is purified as the substance of enlightenment in the following manner. Thrice by day and by night, in the desire to attain Buddhahood for the sake of all sentient beings, and once an hour to form an enlightened attitude, we should repeat the following words:

> Until I have attained enlightenment I take refuge
> In the Buddha, the Dharma, and the noble Sangha.
> By performing acts of liberality and other virtues
> May I realize Buddhahood for the benefit of the world.

(iii) The purification of mind acting correctly through enlightenment is twofold: that by which (a) others are benefited and (b) our own life is made pure.

(a) The first is to adopt an attitude which transmutes into the happiness and welfare of others all the good and wholesome we have done in the three divisions of time (past, present, future), our own body and the wealth of our enjoyments.

(b) The second is always to rely on ethics and manners and to shrink from evil and conflicting emotions.

V. The method of not forgetting an enlightened attitude, which is called the training in accepting four positive and rejecting four negative qualities (65b), is mentioned in the 'Byaṅ.chub.lam.sgron' ('Bodhipathapradīpa', 18):

> The training will have to be kept as it has been taught,
> So that it may be remembered in future existences.

The training has been explained in the ''Od.sruṅs.kyis žus.pa'i mdo' ('Kāśyapaparivartasūtra'):

> Which are the four negative qualities? Kāśyapa, when a Bodhisattva possesses them he will forget his enlightened attitude. They are, in brief, (i) to cheat spiritual teachers and persons worthy of worship; (ii) to make others feel ashamed without cause; (iii) out of spite to say improper things to a Bodhisattva who has adopted an enlightened attitude and (iv) to behave meanly to sentient beings.
>
> Which are the four positive qualities? Kāśyapa, when a Bodhisattva possesses them, an enlightened attitude will become manifest as soon as he has been born in any existence whatsoever, and he will never forget it until he has reached the quintessence of enlightenment. They are, in brief, (i) not to tell a lie willingly even to save one's life; (ii) to set all sentient beings on the path of the good and wholesome in general and of the Mahāyāna in particular; (iii) to consider a Bodhisattva who has formed an enlightened attitude as The Teacher, The Buddha, and to proclaim his virtues in the ten regions of the world; and (iv) to love all sentient beings without ever behaving meanly to them.

(i) The first negative quality means that if out of a deceiving attitude we tell lies to and cheat spiritual teachers, learned elders, instructors, donors (66a) and others who are worthy of worship, regardless of whether they hear these lies or not, feel flattered or not, are enhanced or humiliated and are deceived or not, the enlightened attitude is violated if this evil is not remedied within one hour. Its remedy is the first positive quality, namely to keep to the truth and never willingly tell a lie not even for the sake of our life.

(ii) The second negative quality is that the enlightened attitude is violated if, when you have caused, or even only tried to make, someone feel ashamed at the good done by another, you do not remedy it within an hour. Its remedy is the second positive quality, the attempt to set all sentient beings on the path of the good and wholesome in general and of the Mahāyāna in particular.

(iii) The third negative quality is out of spite to speak about the faults of anyone who has formed an enlightened attitude. Whether you discuss some defect in his manners or appearance, or talk about one of his faults secretly, openly or in your imagination, civilly or rudely, audibly or inaudibly and with or without enjoyment, the enlightened attitude is violated if this evil is not remedied within one hour. Its remedy is the third positive quality, namely, to consider a Bodhisattva who has adopted an enlightened attitude as The Buddha himself (66b) and to try to make his virtues known in the ten regions of the world.

(iv) The fourth negative quality is committing frauds with intent to deceive any sentient being. Whether the individual concerned observes it or not, or is harmed by it or not, the enlightened attitude is violated if it is not remedied within one hour. Its remedy is the fourth positive quality, namely, to love sentient beings. In other words, to have the intention and desire to confer benefits on others without thinking of our own advantage.

The tenth chapter, dealing with the Training in an Enlightened Attitude of Aspiration, from
The Jewel Ornament of Liberation or
The Wish-Fulfilling Gem of the
Noble Doctrine.

NOTES TO CHAPTER 10

1. See Chapter 11 for the training in this attitude.
2. Beings are useful to us in the sense that they give us an opportunity to learn patience. See Chapter 14.
3. 'Gaṇḍavyūhasūtra', p. 494, l. 1.
4. ibid., p. 494, l. 24.
5. ibid., p. 494, l. 10.
6. ibid., p. 494, l. 10.

7. ibid., p. 495, l. 7.
8. ibid., p. 495, l. 10.
9. ibid., p. 495, l. 3.
10. ibid., p. 495, l. 2.
11. *thabs*, Skt. *upāya*. The author refers to the well-known interpenetration of method and knowledge as the outcome of the realization of enlightenment. Method unsupported by knowledge is a fetter which causes man to make all sorts of mistakes, just as knowledge which does not find its expression in methodical work, remains barren and fetters man in a world of his fancies. See Chapter 17.
12. They are the perfection in right views, proper conduct, spiritual interest, the joys of an enlightened attitude, of giving concentrated attention to the unfoldment of an enlightened attitude and in the Dharma; the pursuance of the Dharma in its spirit; to live in accordance with it; to abandon pride and other selfish motives and to comprehend the inner meaning of the Buddha's teaching.
13. They are liberality, affability, conscientiousness and adequate interest.
14. *śes.rab*, Skt. *prajñā*. See note 11 for its relation to method.
15. Literally 'which is the knowledge of the purity of three aspects': in other words there must be no vested interest in the person who acts, the person toward whom the action is directed and in the action itself.

11

THE SIX PERFECTIONS

B. THE TRAINING in forming an enlightened attitude of perseverance is threefold: (i) in higher ethics, (ii) higher thoughts and (iii) deeper understanding. The 'Byaṅ.chub.lam.sgron' ('Bodhipathapradīpa', 36) says:

> When with an attitude of perseverance one adheres to the discipline
> And trains oneself in the three ways in ethics and manners
> A delight in this then grows.

(i) Training in higher ethics consists of the triad of liberality, ethics and manners, and patience.

(ii) That in higher thoughts involves meditative concentration; and

(iii) That in deeper understanding is discriminating awareness born from wisdom.

Strenuousness partakes of all three types. As is stated in the 'mDo.sde.rgyan' ('Mahāyāna-sūtrālaṅkāra' XVI, 7):

> With respect to the three types of training
> The Victorious Ones have spoken
> Of six perfections; the first type comprises the first three perfections;
> The last two partake of the remaining two trainings;
> One perfection applies to all three types of training (67a).

Therefore:

> Six heads determine
> The training in forming an enlightened attitude of perseverance:
> Liberality, ethics, patience,
> Strenuousness, meditative concentration and discriminating awareness born from wisdom.

In the 'Lag.bzaṅs.kyi žus.pa'i mdo' ('Subāhuparipṛcchāsūtra') is written:

> Subāhu, in order to become quickly and perfectly enlightened, a Bodhisattva Mahāsattva must always and continuously complete these six perfections. Which six? Those of liberality,

ethics and manners, patience, strenuousness, meditative concentration and discriminating awareness born from wisdom.

These six perfections are to be known in two ways: (A) by their concise meaning and (B) by explaining their nature in detail.[1]

A. In stating their concise meaning the following will serve as a guide:

Under six heads the six perfections are subsumed:
Fixed number and order,
Primary characteristics and etymology,
Division and grouping.

Their fixed number is given with respect to (i) higher forms of life and (ii) ultimate good; three referring to each.

(i) The three perfections which refer to higher forms of life are: liberality leading to great enjoyment, ethics and manners which adorn physical existence and patience which pleases those around us.

(ii) Those leading to ultimate good are: strenuousness which increases virtues, meditative concentration which produces tranquillity and (67b) discriminating awareness born from wisdom which gives mystic insight.

As is stated in the 'mDo.sde.rgyan' ('Mahāyāna-sūtrālaṅkāra' XVI, 2):

Most excellent wealth, body,
And surroundings.

Fixed order means the succession in which the perfections arise in our life. By liberality, not counting how much enjoyment we give, we bow to ethics and manners. Following these rules we grow patient and so become strenuous. This in turn develops the power of meditative concentration. When we enter the latter state we acquire discriminating awareness born from wisdom and see things as they are.

Fixed order also means orderly progression from the lower to the highest form. It also implies development from gross to subtle. The gross which is very easy to practise comes first, while that which is most subtle and so most difficult is last. As is said in the 'mDo.sde.rgyan' ('Mahāyāna-sūtrālaṅkāra' XVI, 14):

Basing itself on the former the following is born;
Because they proceed from the coarse to the subtle
And from the lower to the highest,
They follow this order.

The primary characteristics of the perfections beginning with liberality of a Bodhisattva are fourfold: (i) destroying the elements that are opposed to enlightenment, (ii) producing true knowledge which is not falsified by interpretation,[2] (iii) fulfilling all desires and (iv) maturing sentient beings in three ways.[3] As is stated in the 'mDo.sde.rgyan' ('Mahāyāna-sūtrālaṅkāra' XVI, 8):

Liberality destroys the opposing elements,
Produces true knowledge which is not falsified by interpretation,
Fulfils all desires
And brings beings to spiritual maturity in three ways (68a).

The etymology is as follows:[4]

It is called (i) liberality because it abolishes poverty (*dāridryam apanayatīti dānaṃ*), (ii) ethics because it leads to coolness (*śaityaṃ lambhayatīti śīlaṃ*), (iii) patience because it endures harshness (*kṣayaḥ kruddher iti kṣāntiḥ*), (iv) strenuousness because it applies itself to what is most sublime (*vareṇa yojayatīti vīryaṃ*), (v) meditative concentration because it holds mind in its own inner sphere (*dhārayaty adhyātmaṃ mana iti dhyānaṃ*) and (vi) discriminating awareness born from wisdom because by it the ultimately real is known (*paramārthaṃ jānāty anayeti prajñā*).

These six are known as perfections (*pāram-itā*) because they enable us to cross over to the other side of Saṃsāra. They are so-called in the 'mDo.sde.rgyan' ('Mahāyāna-sūtrālaṅkāra' XVI, 15):

Because of removing poverty,
Attaining coolness and enduring wrath,
Applying to the sublime and keeping mind in its own sphere,
And knowing the ultimate.

Division means that each perfection is subdivided into six, such as liberality of liberality, ethics of liberality and so on, so that there are thirty-six varieties. This is stated in the 'mÑon.rtogs.rgyan' ('Abhisamayālaṅkāra' I, 43):

The six perfections of liberality and so on
By taking them in their own way
Are divided into six other varieties
As forming a complete instrument (for winning enlightenment).

Grouping means that they belong to the two types of accumulation and acquisition, liberality and ethics to that of merits and discriminating awareness born from wisdom to that of spiritual awareness. Patience, strenuousness and meditative concentration belong equally to both. As is said in the 'mDo.sde.rgyan' ('Mahāyāna-sūtrālaṅkāra' XVIII, 39):

> Liberality and ethics
> Form the accumulation of merits; discriminating awareness born from wisdom brings transcending awareness.
> The other three (perfections) belong to both (groups).

The eleventh chapter, dealing with the Six Perfections, from
The Jewel Ornament of Liberation or
The Wish-Fulfilling Gem of the
Noble Doctrine.

NOTES TO CHAPTER 11

1. See Chapters 12 to 17.
2. *rnam.par mi.rtog.pa'i ye.śes*, Skt. *nirvikalpakajñāna*. See Chapter 20.
3. The three ways are the Śrāvakayāna, Pratyekabuddhayāna and Bodhisattvayāna.
4. This etymology, which of course is no etymology in the strict sense of the word, is taken from the commentary of 'Mahāyāna-sūtrālaṅkāra' XVI, 15.

12

THE PERFECTION OF LIBERALITY

B. HERE FOLLOWS the detailed explanation of each of the six perfections (62b):

The perfection of liberality
Is summarized under seven heads:
The consideration of its defects and qualities,
Its essence, its classification,
The primary characteristics of each class,
Its increase, purification, and
Result.

I. You must know that he who is not liberal will always suffer from poverty in this life and be poor and dejected if reborn as a human, but he is more likely to find himself amongst spirits. As is stated in the ''Phags.pa sdud.pa' ('Prajñāpāramitāsaṃcayagāthā', fol. 39a):

The miser is born in the world of spirits,
But should he become a human being he will be poor in that life.

And in the ''Dul.ba.luṅ' ('Vinayāgamottaraviśeṣāgamapraśnavṛtti'):

The answer of the spirit to Gro.bžin skyes.ri was:
  Miserly and avariciously
  We did not give a small gift.
  So we were born in the world of spirits.

Further, when we are not liberal we are unable to work for the benefit of others so that we do not attain enlightenment. As is said:

He who has never given a gift remains without wealth,
Is unable to attract beings,
To say nothing of his inability to attain enlightenment.

On the other hand, a liberal person will be rich in all existences and attain happiness. As is written in the ''Phags.pa sdud.pa' ('Prajñāpāramitāsaṃcayagāthā', fol. 40a):

The liberality of a Bodhisattva destroys rebirth among spirits
As well as poverty and all conflicting passions.
During his lifetime he wins infinite wealth.

In the 'bŚes.sbriṅ' ('Suhṛllekha', 6):

> Beyond a properly given gift
> There is (69a) no better friend than liberality.

And in the 'dbU.ma 'jug.pa' ('Madhyamakāvatāra' I, 10):

> Having seen that even wealth springs from liberality,
> And desiring the happiness of all beings
> So that nobody might be without happiness and wealth
> The Buddha Śākyamuni first spoke of liberality.

Further, when we are liberal we are able to work for the benefit of others and when they have become attracted by liberality they can be led to the Noble Doctrine. As is said:[1]

> Liberality brings suffering beings to maturity.

And when we are liberal it is easy to realize even unsurpassable enlightenment. As is stated in the 'Byaṅ.chub.sems.dpa'i sde.snod' ('Bodhisattvapiṭaka'):

> It is not difficult for a liberal man to attain enlightenment.

And in the ''Phags.pa dKon.mchog.sprin' ('Ratnameghasūtra'):

> Liberality is a Bodhisattva's enlightenment.

Finally, in the 'Khyim.bdag Drag.śul.can.gyis žus.pa'i mdo' ('Gṛhapati-Ugra-paripṛcchāsūtra') the virtues that lie in what has been given and the defects that are attached to what has been withheld, are contrasted. There we read:

> A gift really belongs to us and has intrinsic value (just because it has been given), while something left in the house does not and has no intrinsic worth. The one must not, but the other should, be guarded, and while the former must not be feared for, the latter is a cause of anxiety. Things given show the way to enlightenment, while those left in the house lead to damnation (Māra). The one turns into inexhaustible wealth while the other is soon exhausted.

II. The essence of liberality is to bestow wealth with an unattached mind. As is expressed in the 'Byaṅ.sa' ('Bodhisattvabhūmi'):

> What is the essence of liberality? It is an unattached and spontaneous mind and the dispensing of gifts and requests in that state of mind.

III. The classification of liberality is threefold in respect of (i) material goods, (ii) fearlessness and (iii) the Dharma.

It makes respectively (i) the physical existence, (ii) the lives and

(iii) the minds of others secure. Moreover, the former two types guarantee the happiness of others in this life, while the latter that in the next.

IV. The primary characteristics of liberality (i) in material goods is twofold: (A) improper and (B) proper. Of these the first has to be rejected and the second practised.

(iA) There are four varieties of improper liberality implying improper (i) intention, (ii) gift, (iii) recipient and (iv) manner of giving.

(i) Improper intention is (a) perverted and (b) base.

(a) To show liberality out of a perverted intention is to give in order to harm others, to gain fame in this life and to rival others. A Bodhisattva has rejected all three intentions. As is said in the 'Byaṅ.sa' ('Bodhisattvabhūmi'):

> A Bodhisattva does not give to kill, fetter (70a), punish, imprison and ostracize others; nor does he make gifts in order to gain fame and praise; nor to rival others.

(b) Liberality with a base intention is to give from fear of poverty in the next life and from a desire to be reborn as a human being or god and to enjoy that status. A Bodhisattva does not act in these two ways. As has been said:

> A Bodhisattva does not make gifts because he is afraid and terrified of poverty.

And,

> A Bodhisattva does not give to become Indra, a universal monarch, or Īśvara.

(ii) Other improper forms of liberality to be avoided are listed in the 'Byaṅ.sa' ('Bodhisattvabhūmi'), while the 'Rin.chen 'phreṅ.ba' ('Ratnāvalī') states concisely:

> To whom poison becomes useful,
> To him even this must be given;
> To whom dainty food is of no use,
> To him this must be withheld;
> Just as it is expedient to cut off a finger
> When it has been bitten by a viper,
> So also Śākyamuni said that to whom it is of use
> Even something unpleasant has to be done.
> But one does not do so on a mere request.

A Bodhisattva does not make gifts of poison, fire or weapons and so forth when asked, because these things harm both the receiver and others. When asked he does not give slings and arrows and other weapons, in short anything that serves to harm or to bring misery to others (70b). Nor does he give away or pawn his father, mother, children, wife or other members of his family without their willing consent. As long as he is wealthy he does not give trifles or things that have been saved up.

(iii) To avoid an improper recipient means that a living Bodhisattva does not give away his body or his limbs even if someone should ask him for them with an intention to vex the Mārakuladevatās (i.e. to practise necromancy); nor to those obsessed by Māra, nor to the insane. Since they are unable to make good use of the body and their minds are not free, any gift serves only to make them rave. A Bodhisattva also does not give food or drink to gluttons and drunkards.

(iv) To avoid an improper manner of giving means that we should not make a gift if we do not rejoice at doing so or while we are angry or upset; nor with scorn and unfriendliness to a bad person; nor even to a beggar while chiding, threatening and disheartening him.

(iB) In practising proper liberality three things have to be considered: (i) the gift, (ii) the recipient and (iii) the manner of giving.

(i) The gift is of two kinds: (a) inner and (b) outer.

(a) The inner is said to be our body. As is written in the 'Sred. med.kyi bus žus.pa'i mdo' ('Nārāyaṇaparipṛcchāsūtra'):[2]

> If necessary I will give my hand, foot, flesh, blood and other parts of my body to him who asks for them.

Further, when a Bodhisattva is still a novice and so has not yet realized his ultimate sameness with others, he is apt to give up his whole body (71a), but is advised not to do so when alive. This is stated in the 'sPyod.'jug' ('Bodhicaryāvatāra' V, 87):

> The body is not to be given up
> Out of misguided compassion.
> On the contrary, for the benefit of others
> It has to be made the basis for the realization of the ultimate goal.

(b) The outer gift is all that which has been rightfully acquired such as food, drink, dress, conveyances, children, wife and so on. In the 'Sred.med.kyi bus žus.pa'i mdo' ('Nārāyaṇaparipṛcchāsūtra')[3] we read:

> The outer gift are money, grain, silver, gold, jewels, ornaments, horses, elephants, sons and daughters.

Further, a Bodhisattva who is a householder gives both types according to their value. As is stated in the 'mDo.sde.rgyan' ('Mahāyāna-sūtrālaṅkāra' V, 85):

> A Bodhisattva who does not give his body and wealth
> To others, does not exist.

A Bodhisattva who has left the life of a householder gives up everything except his three robes. As is stated in the 'sPyod.'jug' ('Bodhicaryāvatāra' VIII, 16):

> Except his three robes he gives up everything else.

The reason is that, if he gave them, his interest for others would suffer.

(ii) Recipients are of four kinds: those distinguished (a) by virtues, as for instance a spiritual teacher and the Three Jewels; (b) by having been helpful like a father and mother; (c) by misery such as sick persons and orphans and (d) by harmfulness, namely, enemies and others of their type. This is called in the 'sPyod.'jug' ('Bodhicaryāvatāra' V, 81):

> The field distinguished by virtues and helpfulness.

(iii) The manner of giving is that you should give with either (a) good intention or (b) excellent behaviour.

(a) The first is (71b) to give in compassion for the sake of enlightenment and the benefit of sentient beings.

(b) The second is according to the 'Byaṅ.sa' ('Bodhisattvabhūmi'):

> A Bodhisattva, when the proper time has come, gives with confidence and respect, with his own hands and without harming others.

In this quotation the first virtue means that a Bodhisattva has confidence through the three divisions of time (past, present and future), that he has a lucid mind when he makes, and feels no regret after making, the gift.

'Respect' means with devotion.

'With his own hands' implies that he gives without ordering others to do so.

'When the proper time has come' means when he himself deems it proper.

'Without harming others' implies that the gift will not harm his household and their belongings. Further, though it be his own property, yet if his household (who enjoy it) should weep at it being given away, he will not do so. He also does not steal nor dishonestly appropriate their belongings. As is stated in the 'Chos.mṅon.pa kun.las btus.pa' ('Abhidharmasamuccaya', p. 59):

> Because of giving repeatedly, impartially and in order to fulfil the desire.

Here 'giving repeatedly' refers to the particular quality of the donor who makes gifts over and again; 'giving impartially' to the nature of the recipient—the donor makes a gift to people without showing partiality to the one or the other; and 'in order to fulfil the desire' to the particular object—the donor makes a gift according to the expectations and desires of the recipient.

This concludes my explanation of liberality in respect to material goods.

(ii) Liberality in fearlessness means to be a refuge to those who are frightened by robbers, wild animals, diseases and floods. As is written in the 'Byaṅ.sa' ('Bodhisattvabhūmi'):

> The gift of fearlessness is to be known as being a refuge to those who are frightened by lions, tigers, crocodiles, kings, robbers, floods and other disasters.

This concludes my explanation of the gift of fearlessness.

(iii) Liberality in the Dharma comes under four heads: (a) the object, (b) the intention, (c) the nature and (d) the manner of making the gift of the Dharma.

(a) The object means that the gift should be made to those who want, have respect for and explain the Dharma.

(b) The intention is to abjure evil and to rely on good. To abjure evil intentions means that we explain the Dharma with a mind free from such material considerations as wealth, fame and other worldly gains. As is stated in the ''Phags.pa sdud.pa' ('Prajñāpāramitāsaṃcayagāthā', fol. 20b):

> Without consideration for material gain he shows the Dharma to the world.

And in the ''Od.sruṅs.kyis žus.pa'i mdo' ('Kāśyapaparivartasūtra'):

> With a pure mind and free from materialistic considerations
> To make a gift of the Dharma, (is what) the Victorious One has proclaimed.

Having good intentions means to expound the Dharma out of compassion. As is said in the ''Phags.pa sdud.pa' ('Prajñāpāramitāsaṃcayagāthā', fol. 31a):

He makes a gift of the Dharma to the world in order to end misery.

(c) The nature of the Dharma means to explain the Dharma in such a way that the sense of the Sūtras and other texts is not lost and that their meaning is not perverted;[4] as is stated in the 'Byaṅ.sa' ('Bodhisattvabhūmi'):

To make a gift of the Dharma, means to explain it logically and not in a perverted way and to make the disciple hold firmly to the principles of training therein.

(d) The manner of explaining the Dharma means not to discuss it immediately you are asked for an explanation. In the 'Zla.ba sgron.ma'i mdo' ('Candrapradīpasūtra') we read:

When someone requests you
To make a gift of the Dharma,
At first you must say:
'I have not studied it deeply.'

And,

You must not talk immediately.
After having examined the recipient
Or knowing him
You may (72b) explain the Dharma even without being requested to do so.

When we explain the Dharma we must speak in a clean and pleasing place. The 'Dam.pa'i chos padma dkar.po' ('Saddharma-puṇḍarīkasūtra' XIII, 26) says we should only do so

In a clean and pleasing place
On a wide and comfortable seat.

Further, we must do so from the Dharma-seat; that is:[5]

Seated on a seat that has legs
And is covered with various rugs.

We also have to wash ourselves and put on good clothes. Then having become pure (in mind) we expound it carefully. This is confirmed in the 'bLo.gros rgya.mtshos žus.pa'i mdo' ('Sāgara-matipariprḍcchāsūtra'):

He who explains the Dharma must be pure, very careful, well-washed and well-dressed.

So also must be the surroundings. On sitting down we should recite the mantra that overcomes the power of Māra in order to make sure that no obstacles can arise. All this is stated in the 'bLo.gros rgya. mtshos žus.pa'i mdo' ('Sāgaramatiparipṛcchāsūtra'):

> 'Peace, peace, appeaser of enemies, conqueror of Māra, you who wear a garland of skulls, you resplendent one, you who look around, are pure and immaculate and remove all stains; you who look everywhere, who bind all evil and are yourself free from the fetters of Māra. You who are wholly pure, let all the devilish impediments vanish.'[6] Sāgaramati, when one repeats this mantra before the explanation starts and then expounds the Dharma, the Mārakuladevatās in a radius of one hundred miles cannot come to annoy and obstruct you. After the recitation you should explain the Dharma in a moderately loud voice.

This concludes my explanation of the gift of the Dharma.

V. To increase liberality means that if any of the three types of it are little they should be made copious. As is said in the 'Byaṅ.chub. sems.dpa'i sde.snod' ('Bodhisattvapiṭaka'):

> Śāriputra, an intelligent Bodhisattva makes even a little liberality copious. He (i) increases it by means of comprehensive understanding; (ii) expands it by discriminating awareness born from wisdom; and (iii) makes it infinite by transmutation.

Here, (i) 'To increase liberality by transcending awareness' means to know the three elements involved to be perfectly pure. That is to say, the donor, the object of the gift and the recipient are like phantoms.[7]

(ii) 'To expand it by discriminating awareness born from wisdom' in order to accrue much merit, means that the object of the gift is to establish all sentient beings on the spiritual level of Buddhahood, that there should be neither attachment to nor expectation of reward for the gift. This increases the merits that accrue. As is stated in the ''Phags.pa sdud.pa' ('Prajñāpāramitāsaṃcayagāthā', fol. 39a):

> He who does not harp on the gift he has made,
> Will never expect any rewards for it.
> Thus a man wise in the manner of giving gives everything;
> Though it be a trifle, the effects will be vast and immeasurable.

(iii) 'To make it infinite by transmutation' means that the gift cannot be measured when it is transmuted into unsurpassable enlightenment for the benefit of all sentient beings. Therefore it is said in the 'Byaṅ.sa' ('Bodhisattvabhūmi'):

> He does not make a gift while looking for a reward; he turns it over to unsurpassable perfect enlightenment.

The increase of liberality by transmutation is an inexhaustible process. In the ''Phags.pa bLo.gros mi.zad.pa'i mdo' ('Akṣayamatiparipṛcchāsūtra') we read:

> Śāriputra, just as (73b) a single drop of water which has fallen into the great ocean does not get lost or absorbed until the end of time, so also the precepts of the good and wholesome which have been transmuted into enlightenment will never become exhausted until one has become the quintessence of enlightenment.

VI. The 'sLab.pa kun.las btus.pa' ('Śikṣāsamuccaya', 21cd) says of the purification of liberality:

> One's merits become pure by a mode of behaviour
> Which expresses the essence of Śūnyatā and Compassion.

Such liberality supported by Śūnyatā and Compassion does not give rise respectively to Saṃsāra or Hīnayāna, but is pure in itself[8] and leads to the Nirvāṇa that is neither existent nor subsistent (Apratiṣṭhitanirvāṇa).

According to the 'gTsug.na rin.chen.gyis žus.pa'i mdo' ('Ratnacūḍaparipṛcchāsūtra') the expression 'supported by Śūnyatā' means that liberality is to be stamped by four seals:

> One makes a gift after having applied four seals. What are they? (i) The within or one's body; (ii) the without or the wealth of one's enjoyments; (iii) mind or the owner of the objective situation; and (iv) awareness of reality or enlightenment are to be stamped with the seal of Śūnyatā. When these four seals have been applied one makes a gift.

The term 'supported by Compassion' means that we give because we cannot bear the misery of sentient beings in general or in particular.

VII. The result of liberality is to be known as (i) fulfilment and (ii) effectiveness in our temporal life.

(i) Fulfilment is unsurpassable enlightenment. As is stated in the 'Byaṅ.sa' ('Bodhisattvabhūmi'):

> Thus when a Bodhisattva has completed the perfection of liberality he realizes unsurpassable perfect enlightenment.

(ii) Effectiveness in our temporal life means that by having made a gift of material goods our wealth of enjoyment becomes complete, even if we do not want it. Moreover, having attracted others by liberality (74a) we are able to make them strive for ultimate good.

This is expressed in the ''Phags.pa sdud.pa' ('Prajñāpāramitāsaṃcayagāthā', fol. 40a):

The liberality of a Bodhisattva destroys rebirth among spirits
As well as poverty and all conflicting passions.
During his lifetime he wins infinite wealth.
Liberality brings suffering beings to maturity.

And in the 'Byaṅ.sa' ('Bodhisattvabhūmi'):

By a material gift one becomes strong;
By one of clothes one acquires a good complexion;
By one of conveyances one becomes happy; and
By one of a lamp one can see.

By the gift of fearlessness we become unassailable by Māra and by obstacles. As is written in the 'Rin.chen 'phreṅ.ba' ('Ratnāvalī'):

By the gift of fearlessness to those who are frightened
One becomes unassailable by all Māras
And grows most strong.

By the gift of the Dharma we quickly meet the Buddhas, associate with them and speedily attain all that we desire. As is stated in the 'Rin.chen 'phreṅ.ba' ('Ratnāvalī'):

When the gift of the Dharma has been made to
Those who want it and shines unveiled,
We quickly join the company of the Buddhas
And find the fulfilment of our desires.

The twelfth chapter, dealing with the Perfection of Liberality, from
The Jewel Ornament of Liberation or
The Wish-Fulfilling Gem of the
Noble Doctrine.

NOTES TO CHAPTER 12

1. 'Ārya-Prajñāpāramitāsaṃcayagāthā', fol. 40a.
2. Cp. 'Bodhicaryāvatārapañjikā', p. 38.
3. Cp. ibid.
4. According to 'Laṅkāvatārasūtra', p. 96, the instruction in the Dharma is such that all ontological speculations are avoided and that attention is focused on the Four Noble Truths.

5. 'Saddharmapuṇḍarīkasūtra' XIII, 28.

6. This is a paraphrase of the Tibetanised Sanskrit of the mantra.

7. *sgyu.ma lta.bu*, Skt. *māyopama*. Buddhism avoids the fallacy of judging the world in which we live and act as being Māyā. Life in this world is like a spell cast over us, while our experiences are fleeting and change like a mirage. This will be realized the moment we attempt to throw off the enchantment. The statement that the donor, the gift and the recipient are like a mirage results from meditative practices by means of which the bluntness and crudeness of so-called 'objectivity' loses its hold over mind so that the relativity of everything is realized.

8. The Hīnayāna form of Buddhism, in particular the Theravāda, is notorious by its claim that compassion has no place in higher forms of spirituality. See my 'Philosphy and Psychology in the Abidharma' pp. 307 seq. The Nirvāṇa they claim is a negative quality, not the dynamic reality of the Mahāyānic *apratiṣṭhitanirvāṇa*, a Nirvāṇa which cannot be localized as something existent or subsistent.

13

THE PERFECTION OF ETHICS AND MANNERS

The perfection of ethics and manners
Is summarized under seven heads:
The consideration of its defects and qualities,
Its essence, its classification,
The primary characteristics of each class,
Its increase, purification, and
Result.

I. A LIBERAL PERSON who lacks ethics and manners will be reborn neither as a god nor as a man. This (74b) is stated in the 'dbU.ma 'jug.pa' ('Madhyamakāvatāra' II, 4):

> When a human being breaks his foot, namely ethics and manners,
> Even if he practises liberality, he will fall into evil states of life.

Further, when we have no ethics and manners we do not meet with the Noble Doctrine. As is asserted in the 'Tshul.khrims daṅ ldan.pa'i mdo' ('Śīlasaṃyuktasūtra'):

> Just as a blind man does not see forms
> So one does not see the Dharma, when one is unethical.

We also do not become liberated from Saṃsāra in the three world-spheres. This is stated in the same Sūtra:

> Just as a man without feet cannot walk,
> So also one does not become liberated when one lacks ethics.

Finally we do not attain unsurpassable enlightenment, because the road to Buddhahood is incomplete.

On the other hand, when we are ethical and well-mannered we are reborn in the most favourable circumstances. As is stated in the ''Phags.pa sdud.pa' ('Prajñāpāramitāsaṃcayagāthā', fol. 40a):

> Through ethics and manners one avoids rebirth as an animal or under
> The eight unfavourable conditions, and is always given the unique occasion of human life.[1]

When we are ethical and well-mannered we lay the foundation of real happiness and of ultimate good. This is written in the 'bŚes. sbriṅ' ('Suhṛllekha', 7):

> Ethics and manners, like the earth upon which the movable and unmovable rests,
> Have been declared to be the foundation of all virtues.

We are like a fertile field in which all virtues grow abundantly. This is expressed in the 'dbU.ma 'jug.pa' ('Madhyamakāvatāra' II, 6):

> When virtues ripen in the field of ethics and manners
> The enjoyment of their fruits will last uninterruptedly.

Many doors of meditative absorptions are opened to us. As is stated in the 'Zla.ba sgron.ma'i mdo' ('Candrapradīpasūtra'):

> Quickly one attains absorption undisturbed by conflicting emotions;
> This is the benefit of ethics and manners.

We attain whatever we are (75a) interested in and devoted to. As is said in the 'Yab.sras mjal.ba'i mdo' ('Pitāputrasamāgamanasūtra'):

> By the preservation of pure ethics and manners
> All interests are fulfilled.

Finally the realization of enlightenment becomes easy. In the same Sūtra we read:

> Since pure ethics and manners are very useful,
> The realization of enlightenment is not difficult.

Such and other virtues are also pointed out in the 'Tshul.khrims daṅ ldan.pa'i mdo' ('Śīlasaṃyuktasūtra'):

> An ethical man meets the Buddhas when they appear,
> He is the most beautiful ornament,
> The centre of all joys.
> He is honoured by all the world.

II. The essence of ethics and manners consists of four qualities listed in the 'Byaṅ.sa' ('Bodhisattvabhūmi'):

> One must know that the essence of ethics and manners comprises the following four qualities: (i) to accept properly from others; (ii) to be inspired by pure motivation; (iii) to mend one's own ways once one has fallen from one's code and (iv) to avoid so falling by being mindful and devoted.

These four qualities come under two heads: (A) acceptance and (B) preservation. The one (A) refers to the first quality (i), the other (B) to the last three qualities (ii–iv) mentioned in the above quotation.

III. The classification of ethics and manners is threefold: (A) restraint, (B) acquiring the good and wholesome and (C) working for the benefit of all sentient beings. The first type (A) makes our attitude firm and constant, the second (B) clears the ever-changing stream of our life and the third (C) brings all sentient beings to full spiritual maturity.

IV. The primary characteristics of each type of ethics and manners:

A. The ethics of restraint are (i) common and (b) uncommon.

(i) The common type (75b) refers to the seven sections of the Prātimokṣa. As is stated in the 'Byaṅ.sa' ('Bodhisattvabhūmi'):

> The ethics of the Bodhisattva discipline are to accept that of the Prātimokṣa. Its seven sections are the Bhikṣu, the Bhikṣuṇī, the Śikṣamāna, the Śramaṇera, the Śramaṇerikā, the Upāsaka and the Upāsikā. The last two groups are known as referring to the householder and Prāvrajika.[2]

They have all ceased to harm and hurt others. An ordinary individual does so for his own sake, but a Bodhisattva for others. As is said in the 'Sred.med.kyi bus žus.pa'i mdo' ('Nārāyaṇaparipṛcchā-sūtra'):

> Ethics are not to be observed for the sake of kingship, the bliss of heaven, the position of Indra, Brahmā or Īśvara; nor for enjoyment of wealth, for the world of forms and other experiences. They are not to be observed out of fear of hell, of rebirth among animals, or of the world of Yama. On the contrary, ethics are to be observed in order to become like the Buddhas and to bring profit and happiness to all sentient beings.

(ii) As to the uncommon type of ethics, the Teacher Ži.ba.lha (Śāntideva), following the doctrine of the Nam.mkha'i sñiṅ.po'i mdo (Ākāśagarbhasūtra), declares that there are eighteen basic evils of which five are as prominent as a king, five as a minister, and eight are like a novice. We have to learn to abjure all eighteen of them.[3] As is said:[4]

> To steal that which belongs to the Three Jewels
> And to reject the Noble Doctrine

The Sage has declared (76a) to be offences expiatable only by expulsion.

> To steal a robe from, to strike
> And to cast into prison
> A Bhikṣu even if he has fallen from his code of ethics;
> To make someone forsake the Order;

To commit the five heinous crimes;
To cling to wrong views;
To terrorize villages and hamlets—

The Victorious One has declared to be offences to be expiatable by expulsion.

To impart the teaching of Śūnyatā
To beings who have not made their mind fit for its reception;
To turn away from perfect enlightenment
Those who entered the path towards Buddhahood;
Having forsaken the Prātimokṣa
To direct someone to the Mahāyāna and
To say that conflicting passions will not be resolved
By the discipline the disciple has followed so far;
To induce someone to embrace an outsider's code;
To proclaim one's own virtues;
To smear others
For the sake of gain, honours and praise;
To speak such falsehood as
'Deep is my patience and realization';
To induce someone to punish a Śramaṇera;
To make (illegally) a present of the Three Jewels and to accept such a gift;
To cause someone to forsake his state of tranquillity;
To set the enjoyment of seclusion
Before those who are devoted to their studies:
These are the basic evils and
The cause of the great hell for beings.

Lord gSer.gliṅ.pa (Dharmakīrti), following the teaching of the 'Byaṅ.sa' ('Bodhisattvabhūmi'), declares that we have to learn to abjure four evils which are as bad as the offences expiatable by expulsion and forty-six others. The four are according to the 'sDom.pa ñi.śu.pa' ('Saṃvaraviṃśaka') which summarizes the 'Byaṅ.sa' ('Bodhisattvabhūmi'):

To glorify oneself and smear others
For the sake of gain and honours;
Not to give the right means of subsistence out of avarice
To those who are destitute and unprotected;
Angrily to censure others
Without listening to apologies; and
Forsaking the Mahāyāna (76b)

To give the appearance of being a follower of the Noble Doctrine.

The list of the forty-six evils begins:

Not to worship the Three Jewels thrice;
To follow one's desires. . . .[5]

B. Ethics aimed at acquiring that which is good and wholesome, comprise, in addition to what is laid down in the Bodhisattva discipline, everything serving to accumulate the good and wholesome in body and speech. They are described in the 'Byaṅ.sa' ('Bodhisattvabhūmi'):

Relying on and abiding by the ethics of a Bodhisattva, one strives to find satisfaction solely in listening to, pondering over and making a living experience of the Dharma; to receive spiritual teachers respectfully and to serve them; to help and nurse the sick; to give liberally and to proclaim the virtues of others; to rejoice at their merits and forbear their faults; to transmute the good and wholesome into enlightenment and to make the resolve to attain it; to worship the Three Jewels and to strive strenuously; to be scrupulous; to be eager with one's training; to be watchful with circumspection; to guard the gates of the senses and to know moderation in eating; not to sleep during the first and last parts of the night and strenuously to apply oneself to spiritual exercises; to meet saintly people and spiritual friends; to scrutinize one's own state of bewilderment and spiritual ignorance and to give up attachment to it—to realize, to guard, and to strengthen such traits as these are ethics which lead to acquiring the good and wholesome.

C. Ethics in order to work for the benefit of others are, in short, known as the eleven duties as laid down in the 'Byaṅ.sa' ('Bodhisattvabhūmi'):

(i) To participate in (77a) meaningful activity; (ii) to remove the misery of all sentient beings and (iii) to instruct those who do not know how to do so; (iv) to be grateful and to return favours; (v) to protect those who are frightened; (vi) to remove the misery of suffering and to provide for those who are in need; (vii) to grasp the Dharmacakra[6] and to fit it into one's attitude; (viii) to delight in proper virtues; (ix) to carry out the spiritual training correctly; (x) to refrain from making a display of magic powers and (xi) to aspire for the good.

Further, a Bodhisattva rejects the impure motivations of the three levels of activity (i.e. body, speech and mind) and relies on the three pure ones so that he may continue to have the confidence of others and may not fall away from his code of ethics and manners.

(i) Impure motivation resulting in bodily activity is silly behaviour such as unnecessary running about and other forms of restlessness. This a Bodhisattva rejects. Pure motivation means to be restfully composed and to have a smiling countenance. As is said:[7]

Thus one should be one's own master
And always show a smiling face;
Without frowning
One should be friendly and sincere to the world.

And the following rules should be observed, when looking at others:[8]

Look straight at sentient beings
And in a loving way
Thinking 'May it come about that by relying on them
I shall attain Buddhahood'.

When sitting:[9]

Without stretching one's legs
And crossing one's arms.

When eating:[10]

One must not eat with one's mouth wide open
Nor talk with it full (77b).

When moving about:[11]

In putting down a chair or some other piece of furniture
One must not make a noise.
Also a door must not be opened violently;
One should always be willing and without haughtiness.

When sleeping:[12]

One should lie in the position one likes best
Like the Lord when he passed into Nirvāṇa.

(ii) Impure motivation manifesting itself in speech is (a) talkativeness and (b) sharp words, both of which should be avoided.

(a) The evil of talkativeness has been pointed out in the ''Phags.pa dKon.mchog.sprin' ('Ratnameghasūtra'):[13]

The fool falls away from the Noble Doctrine,
His mind becomes rigid and coarse,

He is far away from tranquillity and insight:
Such are the evils of delight in talk.
He never respects spiritual teachers,
But develops delight in indecent speech,
Abides in what is worthless and lacks discrimination:
Such are the evils of delight in talk.

Many other verses follow in further explanation.

(b) The evil of harsh words is according to the 'Zla.ba sgron.ma'i mdo' ('Candrapradīpasūtra'):

He who sees bewilderment of any kind
Without considering it evil
Will reap the just fruit
Of his work.

And the 'Chos thams.cad 'byuṅ.ba.med.par bstan.pa'i mdo' ('Sarvadharmāpravṛttinirdeśasūtra'):[14]

When a Bodhisattva preaches offensively or enviously he is far from enlightenment.

Therefore talkativeness and the use of sharp words have to be abjured. But how then should we speak when our motive is pure? The answer is:

In a pleasing and coherent way
Making the meaning clear and acceptable,
Without passion and anger,
In a mild and moderate manner (78a).

(iii) Improper motivation manifesting itself in our thoughts is (a) hankering after gain and honour and (b) addiction to dreaminess, sloth and similar forms of muddled thinking.

(a) The first has been discussed in the 'lHag.pa'i bsam.pa bskul. ba'i mdo' ('Adhyāśayasaṃcodanasūtra'):[15]

Maitreya, a Bodhisattva must know that gain and honour produce desire, bewilderment and unenlightenment; they cause deception, have the disapproval of all Buddhas and destroy the basis of the good and wholesome; they are like a deceitful harlot.

Many other illustrations to the same effect might easily be quoted. Even if we acquire gain, we are not satisfied with it, as is stated in the 'Yab.sras mjal.ba'i mdo' ('Pitāputrasamāgamanasūtra'):

Just as water in a dream
Does not quench the thirst, even could one drink it,

So also one does not become satisfied
In clinging to the objects of sensual desires.

In examining and understanding the problem in this way, cupidity must be reduced and we must know moderation.

(b) The evil of dreaminess has been described as follows:[16]

He who is dreamy and slothful
Loses discernment, judgment
And finally comprehensive understanding.

And,[17]

He who delights in dreaminess and sloth
Becomes stupid, lazy, idle and discards discernment.
Demons find occasion to assail
And wound him in his solitude.

Therefore all this has to be abjured.

Pure motivation finding its expression in our thoughts (78b) is to have the courage of one's convictions and other qualities.[18]

V. Ethics and manners are increased by (1) transcending and (2) discriminating awareness born from wisdom and (3) transmutation.[19]

VI. They are purified when supported by Śūnyatā and Compassion.[20]

VII. Their result is (i) fulfilment and (ii) effectiveness in our situation in life.

(i) The first is unsurpassable enlightenment. As is stated in the 'Byaṅ.sa' ('Bodhisattvabhūmi'):

> When a Bodhisattva has completed the perfection of ethics and manners he realizes and awakens to unsurpassable perfect enlightenment.

(ii) Effectiveness in our temporal life means that we experience the most perfect happiness in Saṃsāra, even if we do not want it. As is declared in the 'Byaṅ.chub.sems.dpa'i sde.snod' ('Bodhisattvapiṭaka'):

> Śāriputra, a Bodhisattva who has become perfectly pure by ethics and manners will always experience the utmost perfect bliss of a godly or human life.

Not overpowered by even such worldly happiness, he sets out on the path towards enlightenment, as is stated in the 'Sred.med.kyi bus žus.pa'i mdo' ('Nārāyaṇaparipṛcchāsūtra'):

A Bodhisattva who observes this code of ethics and manners,

does not fall from a position of a universal monarch or of Indra; even in such situations he aspires scrupulously for enlightenment.

Further, a man who is ethical and well-mannered is worshipped and honoured by human and non-human beings. As is explained in the same Sūtra:

> A Bodhisattva who abides by this code of ethics and manners is always revered by gods, praised by serpent demons (79a) and Yakṣas, worshipped by Gandharvas and sought by Brahmins, noblemen, merchants and householders. He is always thought of by the Buddhas and esteemed in this world of gods and men.

The thirteenth chapter, dealing with the Perfection of Ethics and Manners, from
The Jewel Ornament of Liberation or
The Wish-Fulfilling Gem of the
Noble Doctrine.

NOTES TO CHAPTER 13

1. See Chapter 2 for the unfavourable conditions and the unique occasion of human existence.
2. See above, Chapter 8, p. 106.
3. Cp. 'Śikṣāsamuccaya', pp. 59 seq., where, however, nothing has been said as to the evil ways of a minister of state.
4. Cp. 'Śikṣāsamuccaya', p. 66.
5. The forty-six evils are also mentioned in the 'gSaṅ.sṅags.rig.pa. 'dzin.pa'i.sde.snod.las.byuṅ.ba'i.miṅ.gi.graṅs', fol. 13b. Those in the text attack the perfection of liberality. Of all the forty-six evils, seven are a violation of the perfection of liberality, nine of ethics and manners, four of patience, three of strenuousness, three of meditative concentration, eight of discriminating awareness and twelve of all the six perfections in a general manner.
6. The Dharmacakra is the Path of Seeing. See 'Abhidharmakośa' VI, 54c. On the meaning of this Path see also below, Chapter 18.
7. 'Bodhicaryāvatāra' V, 71.
8. ibid., V, 80.
9. ibid., V, 92cd.
10. ibid., V, 92ab.

11. ibid., V, 72.
12. ibid., V, 96.
13. In 'Śikṣāsamuccaya', p. 106, this passage is attributed to the 'Adhyāśayasamcodanasūtra'.
14. Cp. 'Śikṣāsamuccaya', pp. 90 seq.
15. Cp. 'Śikṣāsamuccaya', pp. 104 seq.
16. Cp. 'Śikṣāsamuccaya', p. 111.
17. ibid.
18. See Chapter 2.
19. See Chapter 12.
20. See Chapter 12.

14
THE PERFECTION OF PATIENCE

> The perfection of patience
> Is summarized under seven heads:
> The consideration of its defects and qualities,
> Its essence, its classification,
> The primary characteristics of each class,
> Its increase, purification and
> Result.

I. IF AN ETHICAL MAN is impatient, he is roused to anger and loses in a moment whatever merit he has acquired from previous liberal behaviour. Therefore it is said in the 'Byaṅ.chub.sems.dpa'i sde. snod' ('Bodhisattvapiṭaka'):

> Anger, indeed, destroys the basis of the good and wholesome that has been accumulated through hundred thousands of aeons.

And in the 'sPyod.'jug' ('Bodhicaryāvatāra' VI, 1):

> All the liberality and Buddha worship
> That has been practised and accumulated
> As merit through thousands of ages
> Is destroyed in a single burst of rage.

When we are impatient we are like a man pierced by a poisoned arrow, because malevolence has entered and then in our mental distress we do not experience joy, happiness or peace and cannot even sleep. Thus it is said:[1]

> When one adopts an attitude that has felt the sting of malevolence
> Mind does not experience peace (79b).
> Since one does not find joy and happiness
> One becomes sleepless and restless.

And,[2]

> In brief, there is no such thing
> As anger in happiness.

Through impatience hot anger arises because malevolence has penetrated to the core. Friends, companions and servants then get tired of us and we are not liked by them even though we spend money on them. So also it is said:[3]

> His friends get tired of him,
> And though he entices them by liberality, they do not stay.

Then as is said in the 'Byaṅ.chub.sems.dpa'i sde.snod' ('Bodhisattvapiṭaka'):

> Hc whose mind is angry is open to the assaults of Māra and obstacles come his way.

When we are impatient we never attain unsurpassable enlightenment because we do not rise to the six perfections which are the path to Buddhahood. This is stated in the ''Phags.pa sdud.pa' ('Prajñāpāramitāsaṃcayagāthā', fol. 29b):

> How can there be enlightenment for him who is malevolent and impatient!

On the other hand, when we have patience we possess the very best of the good and wholesome. As is said:[4]

> There is no evil like malevolence,
> And no austerity like patience;
> Therefore one should in various ways
> Earnestly pay attention to patience.

When we do so we attain happiness and ultimate good in our position in life. As is stated:[5]

> He who earnestly overcomes anger
> Is happy here and elsewhere.

Finally, when we have patience we attain unsurpassable enlightenment. This is declared in the 'Yab.sras mjal.ba'i mdo' ('Pitāputrasamāgamanasūtra'):

> Anger is not the path to Buddhahood!
> To think so always develops benevolence.
> Enlightenment is born from patience.

II. The essence of patience (80a) is to be prepared for every event. In the 'Byaṅ.sa' ('Bodhisattvabhūmi') is said:

> To be ready for everything without bothering about material considerations and filled with pure compassion is the essence of a Bodhisattva's patience.

III. The classification is threefold: patience which (i) is ready to cope with a harmful person, (ii) puts up with misery and (iii) is ready to investigate the nature of the whole of reality.

The first two mean to show patience by having investigated the real nature of (i) a harmful person and (ii) misery, and they are relative.

(iii) The third, which must be taken in an ultimate sense, is showing patience by having understood the harmony that runs through the whole of reality.

IV. The primary characteristics.

A. The first (i) type is to show patience by not wanting ourselves or our relatives to be beaten, reviled, angered or upbraided and by counteracting any wish for hurting. In other words, it is not quarrelling, not doing harm in retaliation and not being insistent.

Further, in the opinion of the Teacher Ži.ba.lha (Śāntideva) it is said to mean (a) to understand that those who harm us are not masters of themselves; to analyse the evil of (b) our actions, (c) our body and (d) our mental attitude; (e) to realize that there is no difference between one person having certain, and someone else other, faults; (f) to examine the usefulness (of harmful persons); (g) to understand them as benefactors; to realize (h) the chance they give us for aspiring Buddhahood and (i) their beneficial influence.

(a) The first point can be illustrated thus: (80b) A man who harms me, as Devadatta harmed Buddha, is not master of himself because of his malevolence, which, being related to an undesired object, is not something independent.[6] Therefore, since such a man is not master of himself, it is not right that I should retaliate. Thus it is said:[7]

> Everything is in the power of something else,
> And man is powerless.
> When one knows this, one does not become angry
> At everything which is a mere magic spell.

(b) To analyse the evil of our actions is to remember the harm I am now suffering was caused by similar action on my own part. Therefore, since it is my fault, it is wrong for me to retaliate. As is said:[8]

> Similar harm I did
> Formerly to sentient beings.
> Therefore it happens that now harm comes to me
> From tormenting beings.

(c) To analyse the evil resulting from having a body means realizing that if there were no body no one could strike it with a sharp or blunt weapon. Since however it does exist such harm may befall it and it is wrong to retaliate. As is stated:[9]

> His weapon and my body
> Are both the cause of misery.

Therefore when the one hits the other
With whom shall I become angry?

(d) To analyse the evil of our mental attitude means that our own disposition is not bound to an ideal body which must not be harmed by others but is affected unpleasantly by an ugly one. Therefore, since everything is the fault of our own disposition, it is wrong for me to retaliate. As is written:[10]

This abscess resembling a human body
Does not allow itself to be touched and is painful.
When blinded by desire I touch it
Pain is felt, so at whom shall I get angry?

(e) To understand that there is no difference between one person having certain, and someone else other, faults, is expressed in the following verse:[11]

Some do evil
And some become angry out of deludedness.
Who can be said to be without faults?
Who can be said to have them?

Therefore we should show patience and shun faults.

(f) To examine the usefulness (of harmful persons) means that we must be patient with them, so that evil becomes purified, after which the prerequisites for enlightenment are accumulated and finally we awaken to Buddhahood. In other words we have to show patience, because those who do harm are for the above-mentioned reasons persons of great usefulness. As is said:[12]

In showing them
Patience my evil is atoned for in many ways.

(g) To understand them as benefactors means that since enlightenment is not realized without the perfection of patience, which cannot be developed without a harmful person, the latter helps in the realization of the Dharma and is a benefactor. Therefore we have to be patient with the harm he does. As is said:[13]

Since he is a companion in my striving for enlightenment
I must delight in my enemy.
Because I have got one
The fruit of patience
Should first be bestowed on him.
Thus he is the cause for patience.

(h) To understand the chance they give for aspiring Buddhahood is expressed in the verse:[14]

> Moreover, what better repayment can there be
> Than the appeasement of beings,
> For they are sincere friends
> And incomparable helpers.

(i) To understand their beneficial influence is referred to in the verse:[15]

> Being pleased in many ways
> They have completed perfection.

And in the 'Byaṅ.sa' ('Bodhisattvabhūmi') we read:

> Patience is said to be developed by fostering the five ideas of (i) favouring a harmful person, (ii) following only the Dharma, (iii) impermanence, (iv) misery and (v) gathering beings around oneself.

(i) The first means to show patience by being favourably inclined to a harmful person because in former lives such a man may have been our father or mother, brother or sister, or teacher. Since the benefit I have derived from them cannot be assessed it is not fit that I now retaliate for the harm they do.

(ii) The second means that this harmful person does evil because of certain conditions and is bent on doing harm due to these circumstances, and therefore it is only proper to be patient because there does not exist some absolute entity such as a Pure Ego (Ātman), a mental substance, a life principle or a personality that is abusing, beating, reviling or finding faults.

(iii) The third is that sentient beings are transitory and subject to death and that the worst harm is to deprive them of their lives. Therefore, since sentient beings by their very nature must die it is not proper to kill them. Hence we have to show patience.

(iv) Misery means that all sentient beings are affected by its three types.[16] Not wanting them to experience the brand that ought to be removed, I must, because of this reflection on misery, have patience with the harm they do.

(v) The fifth idea means to accept all sentient beings as my wife, thinking that I shall work for their benefit in developing an attitude directed towards enlightenment. When we accept them in this way we show patience, because we reflect that it is not proper to retaliate for the smallest harm done.

B. The second (ii) type of patience, which puts up with misery, means not to be fatigued by hardships involved in realizing unsurpassable enlightenment (82a) and to accept them joyfully. This is stated in the 'Byaṅ.sa' ('Bodhisattvabhūmi'):

> To accept the eight hardships inseparable from life.

They are essentially the hardship of (i) finding clothes and food after renouncing the life of a householder, (ii) worshipping and revering the Three Jewels and the spiritual teachers, (iii) listening to the Dharma, (iv) explaining, (v) discussing and (vi) making a living experience of it, (vii) devoting ourselves to spiritual exercises instead of sleeping in the first and last parts of the night, and (viii) the hardships that result from striving to do all this for the sake of sentient beings. One must accept them without getting tired of the consequences such as fatigue, weariness, heat, cold, thirst, hunger and disturbance of mind. It is, for example, like accepting the misery of being bled in order to relieve the agony of a virulent disease. As is said in the 'sPyod.'jug' ('Bodhicaryāvatāra' VII, 22):

> The misery I have to endure in realizing
> Enlightenment is measurable:
> It is like probing a wound
> To stop the pain caused by what is lodged therein.

Thus a man who has accepted the misery connected with the Dharma has driven back the army of Saṃsāra and defeated the enemy of conflicting passions and is a great hero. Although in this world he is reckoned one, if he has killed an enemy who after all being human must die, he is not one in fact but merely a man brandishing a sword over a corpse. As is stated in the 'sPyod.'jug' ('Bodhicaryāvatāra' VI, 20):

> Those who destroy all misery
> And conquer the enemy of malevolence and other evils,
> Are victorious heroes,
> Others kill only a corpse.

C. The third (iii) type of patience, which is ready to investigate the nature of the whole of reality, is according to the 'Byaṅ.sa' ('Bodhisattvabhūmi') (82b):

> To be interested in the eight topics beginning with the qualities of the Three Jewels.[17]

It is further the acceptance of ultimate reality as by nature devoid of the two types of individuality.[18]

V. Patience is increased by (i) transcending and (ii) discriminating awareness born from wisdom and (iii) transmutation.[19]

VI. The purification is to be supported by Śūnyatā and Compassion.[20]

VII. The result of patience is (i) fulfilment and (ii) effectiveness in our situation in life.

(i) Fulfilment means the attainment of unsurpassable enlightenment. As is said in the 'Byaṅ.sa' ('Bodhisattvabhūmi'):

> By relying on great immeasurable patience maturing into great enlightenment, a Bodhisattva awakens to unsurpassable perfect enlightenment.

(ii) Effectiveness in our situation in life means that, though we do not look for it, we are beautiful, healthy, famous and long-lived, and attain the position of a universal monarch in all our lives. As is stated in the 'sPyod.'jug' ('Bodhicaryāvatāra' VI, 134):

> During his stay in Saṃsāra, by patience he finds amiability,
> Health and fame,
> Long life and
> The happiness of a universal monarch.

The fourteenth chapter, dealing with the Perfection of Patience, from The Jewel Ornament of Liberation or The Wish-Fulfilling Gem of the Noble Doctrine.

NOTES TO CHAPTER 14

1. 'Bodhicaryāvatāra' VI, 3.
2. ibid., VI, 5.
3. ibid., VI, 5.
4. ibid., VI, 2.
5. ibid., VI, 6.
6. While all that can be said is that a thing or a person is there and that it is my personal attitude whether I consider either as my friend or enemy or feel indifferent to them, my attitude is a complex phenomenon which is both subjective and objective in the sense of having some reference. Since the referential situation may be said to

belong to a mind (which is different from the object which I believe to be outside me and to which I as an individual cannot belong) and since such mind is both cognitive and emotive, it is possible to say that the object is undesirable. The correct statement would be that the perceptual, intuitive and referential situation is unpleasantly toned. Since many forces operate in such a situation, the latter is said to be 'under the power of something other than itself'.

7. 'Bodhicaryāvatāra' VI, 31.

8. ibid., VI, 42.

9. ibid., VI, 43.

10. ibid., VI, 44.

11. ibid., VI, 67.

12. ibid., VI, 48.

13. ibid., VI, 107cd–108.

14. ibid., VI, 119.

15. ibid., VI, 112cd.

16. See above, Chapter 5.

17. The eight topics are: The Three Jewels, the power of the Buddhas and Bodhisattvas, the meaning of Reality, the teaching of causal laws, the teaching of the results of causal laws, the goal striven after, the necessary prerequisites for goal-seeking and that which has been well said, i.e. the texts which are authoritative for the Bodhisattva ideal.

18. i.e. the non-individuality of an individual (*pudgala-nairātmya*) and of the constituents of reality (*dharma-nairātmya*). See Chapter 17.

19. See Chapter 12.

20. See Chapter 12.

15

THE PERFECTION OF STRENUOUSNESS

The perfection of strenuousness
Is summarized under seven heads:
The consideration of its defects and qualities,
Its essence, its classification,
The primary characteristics of each class,
Its increase, purification, and
Result.

I. WHOEVER IS NOT strenuous is lazy even though he be liberal and possesses all other qualities (83a). He can neither realize the good and wholesome, work for others, nor attain enlightenment. This is confirmed in the 'bLo.gros rgya.mtshos žus.pa'i mdo' ('Sāgaramatiparipṛcchāsūtra'):

> A lazy person is neither liberal nor knowledgeable. He does not work for others and is far from enlightenment.

On the other hand, when we are strenuous all positive qualities increase in splendour. As is said in the ''Phags.pa sdud.pa' ('Prajñāpāramitāsaṃcayagāthā', fol. 40a):

> By strenuousness the positive qualities do not get obscured;
> The royal treasure of infinite transcending awareness born from wisdom is obtained.

Another virtue is according to the 'mDo.sde.rgyan' ('Mahāyānasūtrālaṅkāra' XVI, 66) that

> By strenuousness one crosses the perishable and becomes free.

But above all we attain unsurpassable enlightenment. This is also stated in the 'mDo.sde.rgyan' ('Mahāyāna-sūtrālaṅkāra' XVI, 66):

> With strenuousness one awakens to enlightenment.

In the 'bLo.gros rgya.mtshos žus.pa'i mdo' ('Sāgaramatiparipṛcchāsūtra'):

> Unsurpassable perfect enlightenment is not difficult for those who make efforts, because, Sāgaramati, where there is strenuousness there is enlightenment.

And in the 'Gaṅ.pos žus.pa'i mdo' ('Pūrṇaparipṛcchāsūtra'):

Enlightenment is easy
For the hard-working.

II. The essence of strenuousness is to strive for the good and wholesome. As is laid down in the 'Chos.mṅon.pa kun.las btus.pa' ('Abhidharmasamuccaya'):[1]

> It is the remedy against laziness. It is directing one's mind to the good and wholesome.

And in the commentary to the 'mDo.sde.rgyan' ('Mahāyānasūtrālaṅkāra' XVI, 23) (83b):

> Its essence is striving for the good and wholesome.

It is the one remedy against laziness which is on the side of what is detrimental to enlightenment.

There are three varieties of laziness: (i) lassitude, (ii) idleness and (iii) gross laziness.

(i) The first is addiction to the pleasures of mental inertia such as sleepiness, restfulness and dreaminess. These have to be given up because in this life there is no time for them. In a Sūtra we read:

> Bhikṣus, consciousness diminishes, life runs down, the life forces give way, and even The Teacher's Doctrine disappears. Why is this so? Because one cannot realize ultimate reality without strenuousness and hard exercises.

And in the 'sPyod.'jug' ('Bodhicaryāvatāra' VII, 7):

> Since death comes quickly,
> Accumulate the prerequisites while there is time.

If you think that it will be sufficient to accumulate them just before you die, you should remember that when death comes there is no time to do so. As has been said:[2]

> Even if you were then to abjure laziness,
> What can you do since there is no time.

It is no sign of intelligence to think that you will not die until you have taken possession of the good and wholesome. As has been stated:[3]

> The Lord of Death who is not to be trusted
> Does not wait for whether or not something has been done;
> Whether one be ill or healthy
> Life is accidental and not to be trusted.

How then is laziness as lassitude to be rejected? It must be thrown off like a snake or a firebrand. This is stated in the 'sPyod.'jug' ('Bodhicaryāvatāra' VII, 71):

> Just like a serpent which has crept on one's lap
> Has to be quickly thrown away,
> So also, when dreaminess and lassitude have come,
> They must at once be discarded.

And in the 'bŚes.sbriṅ' ('Suhṛllekha', 104):

> When one's hair or clothes have suddenly caught fire
> One extinguishes it and throws everything away (84a),
> So one must strive to avoid the world,
> Though there is no harder task than this.

(ii) Idleness is faintheartedness from thinking how can dejected people like myself ever attain enlightenment even if we try to do so. We must take heart and give up idleness. This applies to:

> Even he who has become a fly, a wasp, a bee
> Or even a worm,
> Attains enlightenment so difficult to reach and so unsurpassable,
> When he develops the power of strenuousness.
> When one has become a man such as I
> Knowing what is useful and what is harmful, and
> Does not forsake a life devoted to enlightenment,
> Why should I not attain it?

(iii) Gross laziness is addiction to such evil and unwholesome practices as subduing enemies and hoarding money. They have to be abjured because they are the cause of real misery.

III. The classification is threefold: (A) armour, (B) applied work and (C) insatiableness.

(A) The first is most excellent motivation.

(B) The second is similar application; and

(C) The third means that the two preceding types are brought to highest perfection.

IV. The primary characteristics.

(A) The first means to put on this armour of strenuousness for the good and wholesome with the intention of wearing it until all sentient beings turn towards enlightenment. As is stated in the 'Byaṅ.chub.sems.dpa'i sde.snod' ('Bodhisattvapiṭaka'):

> Śāriputra, put on the armour of unfathomable benevolence, do not relax in strenuousness so that the most insignificant in Saṃsāra may come to enlightenment.

In the 'Go.cha bkod.pa bstan.pa'i mdo' ('Varmavyūhanirdeśa-sūtra'):

> A Bodhisattva (84b) puts on armour
> In order to gather all beings around him.
> Since beings are infinite
> So is his armour.

In the ''Phags.pa bLo.gros mi.zad. pas žus.pa'i mdo' ('Akṣaya-matiparipṛcchāsūtra'):

> One must not calculate in seeking enlightenment by thinking that for so many aeons I shall, and so many more shall not, put on the armour of the Bodhisattva, but one should buckle it on without thought, for thought cannot encompass it.

And in the 'Byaṅ.sa' ('Bodhisattvabhumi'):

> I shall rejoice at staying in hell for thousands of aeons if only to save one single being from misery, to say nothing of still longer periods and of still greater miseries. Such is a Bodhisattva's armour of strenuousness.

(B) Strenuousness as applied work is of three types: to make efforts (i) to reject conflicting emotions, (ii) to realize the good and wholesome and (iii) to work for the benefit of all sentient beings.

(i) The first means that since conflicting emotions such as passions and the activity aroused by them is the root of misery, we do not allow them to rise for ever. This is expressed in the 'sPyod.'jug' ('Bodhicaryāvatāra' VII, 60):

> When one is in the midst of conflicting emotions
> One must be firm in a thousandfold way,
> And not allow oneself to be assailed by them
> Just as a lion will not allow jackals to attack him.

Or again:[4]

> When one carries a pot full of oil
> And there is a sword over one's head,
> Just as one is afraid of being killed,
> So must one grasp the pot tightly.

(ii) To make efforts to realize the good and wholesome, means (85a) to strive for the six perfections regardless of health or life. And how have we to strive? In five ways: by strenuousness which is (a) ever active, (b) devoted, (c) unshakable, (d) does not turn back and (e) is indefatigable.

(a) The first is uninterrupted. As is said in the 'dKon.mchog.sprin' ('Ratnameghasūtra'):

> When a Bodhisattva is strenuous in all walks of life, he must make efforts without getting weary in body or mind. This is called a Bodhisattva's ever active strenuousness.

(b) The second means to act joyfully, eagerly and quickly. As is said:

> In order to complete his work
> He has to attend to it
> Like an elephant entering a lake
> When struck by the midday heat.

(c) It is unshakable when unmoved by interpretations,[5] conflicting emotions and misery.

(d) Strenuousness which does not turn back means that, whatever others think, we must not turn away by knowing how much we can be hurt, mocked or upset by others. This is clearly shown in the ''Phags.pa rDo.rje rgyal.mtsan.gyi mdo'.

(e) When it is indefatigable, a man who makes efforts does not have too high an opinion of himself.

(iii) The third type, working for the benefit of others, is to strive for eleven virtues such as aiding those who are helpless.

We now turn to (C) insatiable strenuousness. It means that we so strive for the good and wholesome (85b) until enlightenment is attained. Thus we read:

> If one is unsatisfied with sensual desires
> Which are like the teeth of a saw (cutting you to pieces),
> What can be said about the merits
> Of happiness and peace, which result from strenuousness (giving you boundless bliss)?

V. Strenuousness is increased by (i) transcending and (ii) discriminating awareness born from wisdom, and (iii) transmutation.[6]

VI. The purification is to be supported by Śūnyatā and Compassion.[7]

VII. The result of strenuousness is (i) fulfilment and (ii) effectiveness in our situation in life.

(i) Fulfilment is unsurpassable enlightenment. As is stated in the 'Byaṅ.sa' ('Bodhisattvabhūmi'):

> A Bodhisattva must complete the perfection of strenuousness and he will awaken to unsurpassable perfect enlightenment.

(ii) Effectiveness in our situation in life means obtaining supreme worldly happiness while still in Saṃsāra. As is stated in the 'mDo. sde.rgyan' ('Mahāyāna-sūtrālaṅkāra' XVI, 66):

Through strenuousness one wins the pleasures of worldly life.

The fifteenth chapter, dealing with the Perfection of Strenuousness,
from
The Jewel Ornament of Liberation or
The Wish-Fulfilling Gem of the
Noble Doctrine.

NOTES TO CHAPTER 15

1. I have not been able to find this quotation in the restored Sanskrit text of the 'Abhidharmasamuccaya', but it is found in Sthiramati's 'Vṛtti' on Vasubandhu's 'Triṃśikā', p. 27.
2. 'Bodhicaryāvatāra' VII, 7.
3. ibid., VII, 8.
4. ibid., VII, 70.
5. *rnam.par rtog.pa*, Skt. *vikalpa*.
6. See above, Chapter 12.
7. See above, Chapter 12.

16

THE PERFECTION OF MEDITATIVE CONCENTRATION

The perfection of meditative concentration
Is summarized under seven heads:
The consideration of its defects and qualities,
Its essence, its classification,
The primary characteristics of each class,
Its increase, purification and
Result.

I. HE WHO DOES NOT practise meditation, though he be liberal and possess all other qualities, falls into the power of restlessness and his mind is wounded by the fangs of conflicting emotions. As is said (86a) in the 'sPyod.'jug' ('Bodhicaryāvatāra' VIII, 1):

A man whose mind is upset
Lives between the jaws of conflicting emotions.

When we do not practise meditation, supersensible cognition[1] does not rise and then we are unable to work for sentient beings. This is stated in the 'Byaṇ.chub.lam.sgron' ('Bodhipathapradīpa', 44, 40):

When tranquillity is not realized
Supersensible cognition does not rise;
One who is without this power
Cannot work for sentient beings.

Further, when we do not practise meditation discriminating awareness born from wisdom[2] does not rise so that enlightenment is not attained. As is written in the 'bŚes.sbriṅ' ('Suhṛllekha', 107):

In the absence of concentration there is no discriminating awareness born from wisdom.

On the other hand, when we practise meditation the desire for vulgar things is abolished, supersensible cognition is born and many doors to meditative absorptions[3] are opened to our consciousness. As is stated in the ''Phags.pa sdud.pa' ('Prajñāpāramitāsaṃcayagāthā', fol. 40a):

By concentration vulgar objects of sense gratification are discarded,
Reasonableness, supersensible cognitions and meditative absorptions are realized.

Further, all conflicting emotions are conquered when we practise meditation and when with the help of it we have acquired discriminating awareness born from wisdom. As is said in the 'sPyod. 'jug' ('Bodhicaryāvatāra' VIII, 4):

> By insight coupled with tranquillity
> One knows that all conflicting emotions have been overcome.

By meditating we see reality in its true nature and compassion for sentient beings is born. This is stated in the 'Chos yaṅ.dag.par sdud.pa'i mdo' ('Dharmasaṅgītisūtra'):[4]

> When the workings of mind[5] have become harmonized, one sees things according to their true nature. A Bodhisattva then becomes steeped in Great Compassion for sentient beings.

Finally, we are able to establish in enlightenment beings who are to be brought to spiritual maturity (86b). As is expressed in the 'mDo.sde.rgyan' ('Mahāyāna-sūtrālaṅkāra' XVI, 40):

> By this very concentration all beings are established in the three types of enlightenment.[6]

II. The essence of meditative concentration is tranquillity by which mind abides within itself by the oneness[7] of the good and wholesome. So also in the chapter on the Essence of Concentration in the 'Byaṅ.sa' ('Bodhisattvabhūmi') we read:

> Oneness of mind, the indwelling of mind with the good.

Since such concentration is attained by rejecting agitating elements which are its enemies, all such disturbances have to be avoided. This is done by detachment. It means to detach (A) our senses from agitation and (B) our mind from its tendency artificially to divide reality.[8] This is stated in the 'sPyod.'jug' ('Bodhicaryāvatāra' VIII, 2):

> When body and mind have become detached
> The division of reality does not come about.

Of these two types of detachment, (A) that of the senses will be discussed under six heads: (a) the primary characteristic, (b) the cause, motive and (c) evil of agitation, (d) the primary characteristic, (e) cause, motive and (f) value of detachment.

(a) The first is to be agitated in the presence of our wife, children, servants and objects of enjoyment.

(b) The cause and motive is attachment to our family, retinue and so on; to material goods such as food and money; and to fame and praise. As is said:[9]

Because of attachment and the thirst for material goods
The world is not renounced.

(c) The evil is (i) general and (ii) particular.

(i) The first has been pointed out in the 'lHag.pa'i bsam.pa bskul.pa'i mdo' ('Adhyāśayasaṃcodanasūtra'):

> Maitreya, there are twenty evils of agitation (87a). One's movements, words and thoughts are not restrained. Conflicting emotions are rampant. One is addicted to worldly talk, open to the attacks of Māra and steeped in carelessness. One attains neither tranquillity nor insight. And so forth.

(ii) In a particular sense agitation is evil because attachment to sentient beings prevents us from attaining enlightenment. As is said in the 'Zla.ba sgron.ma'i mdo' ('Candrapradīpasūtra'):

Indulging in sensuous and sensual desires
And hankering for wife and children,
He who clings to home that should be despised,
Will never attain unsurpassable sublime enlightenment.

And in the 'sPyod.'jug' ('Bodhicaryāvatāra'):

When one is attached to beings
Reality remains obscured.

Therefore, attachment to all this has to be given up. As is said:

Since attachment does not aid me
Nor am I any help to it,
This foolish behaviour is to be thrown far away.

The benefits of its rejection are expressed in the 'Zla.ba sgron.ma'i mdo' ('Candrapradīpasūtra'):

Having quenched the thirst for wife and children,
The attainment of sublime enlightenment is not difficult
For those who, terrified by a home, have left it.

There are two types of the evil of attachment to material good and fame: (i) the inability to hold them and (ii) the misery that they cause.

They are both indicated in the 'sPyod.'jug' ('Bodhicaryāvatāra' VIII, 20 and 18):

(i) It is uncertain where those go
Who have many material goods and fame.

(ii) Wherever there is attachment
Association with it
Brings endless misery.

(d) The primary characteristic of detachment is to be free from these types of agitation.

(e) Its cause and motive are to live in solitude (87b). That means in a cremation ground, jungle, verandah or any other lonely place. Five hundred furlongs is called an ear-shot and 'solitude' is found one or two ear-shots away from a settlement. This definition is taken from the 'Chos.mṅon.pa.mdzod' ('Abhidharmakośa' III, 87).

(f) The value of detachment means that many advantages accrue from (i) living in solitude free from agitation and worshipping the Buddhas to enlighten ourselves and sentient beings, (ii) that discontent with Saṃsāra is born, the eight worldly goods[10] do not concern us any more and emotional conflicts do not grow stronger and (iii) that meditative absorption is achieved in our lifetime.

(i) The first advantage means to stay in solitude for the sake of sentient beings because our whole attitude tends towards enlightenment, and not to move more than seven steps from our place of retreat is better than worshipping the Samyaksambuddhas and offering them food, drink and flowers. In the 'Zla.ba sgron.ma'i mdo' ('Candrapradīpasūtra') also is said:

> The most distinguished among men, the Victorious One, is not worshipped
> With food, drink and garments,
> Flowers, incense and garlands.
> But he who adopts an enlightened attitude
> And who, for the sake of sentient beings, disgusted with the evil of conditioned existence
> Stays in solitude never moving more than seven steps away,
> Acquires more merits than by any other form of worship.

(ii) That discontent with Saṃsāra is born, the eight worldly goods do not concern us any more and emotional conflicts do not grow stronger, is expressed in the same Sūtra:

> Thus there is always discontent with the conditioned;
> There is no desire for anything in the world;
> Conflicting emotions do not increase (88a).

(iii) That meditative absorption, the first essential (in winning enlightenment), is quickly achieved, is also stated in the same Sūtra:

> Having given up the delights of village and city life,
> You should stay always detached in a forest grove;
> Like the unicorn, you should roam forever alone;
> And in a very short time you will attain sublime absorption.

This concludes my explanation of detachment as far as our physical side is concerned.

(B) The mind is detached from its habit of dividing reality as follows. When in solitude one should analyse why one is there. The reason for my having gone into retreat was fear of the disturbing influences of village and city life and other distractions as described in the 'Khyim.bdag Drag.śul.can.gyis žus.pa'i mdo' ('Gṛhapati-Ugra-paripṛcchāsūtra'):

> I have taken refuge in solitude because I was afraid of agitation, material goods and fame, evil companions and unwholesome associates; terrified by the three emotional conditions of sensuality, malice and delusion; by the four limitations called Skandhamāra, Kleśamāra, Mṛtyumāra and Devaputramāra;[11] and by the three unfavourable forms of existence—the denizens of hell, spirits and animals.

After being afraid and terrified in this way, we should, in our retreat, investigate the nature of our movements, speech and thought. We should ponder on whether we can realize our aim while like wild beasts, hunters and robbers we continue to kill, steal and so on, and whether we should therefore abstain from such activities (88b).

When considering the nature of our speech, we should ponder, while in solitude, on whether we can ever win through if like peacocks, parrots, blackbirds, larks and other birds we continue to speak foolish things, and whether we should therefore stop doing so.

In studying how our mind works, we should deliberate when alone on whether we shall achieve our goal if like deer, apes, monkeys, bears, hyaenas and other animals we continually harbour thoughts tainted by desire, malice, envy and other emotionally unbalancing powers and whether therefore we should cease so to behave.

This concludes my discussion on detaching mind from its habit of dichotomy.

When the above has been achieved, no agitation can come about. Then we enter into a state of concentration, after which our mind has to be purified. This means that when we have found out which is our strongest emotion, we must seek its remedy. (This is done in each case by meditating on its opposite quality). Thus (i) for sensuous and sensual attachments you concentrate on ugliness, (ii) for aversion on benevolence, (iii) for bewilderment on the so-called Law of Interdependent Origination (Pratītyasamutpāda),[12] (iv) for envy on the basic similarity between ourselves and others, (v) for haughtiness on how I fare and (vi) if the various emotions are of equal strength or if there is an excess of dichotomy we must concentrate attentively on breathing.[13]

(i) When our attachment to sensuous and sensual desires is great, we should meditate thus on ugliness. First we have to remember that our body consists of thirty-six impure substances such as flesh, blood, skin, bones, marrow, lymph, bile, phlegm, mucus, tears, excrements and so on. Then we must go to a cremation ground and after having seen a corpse that is putrid, corrupted (89a) and swollen, we should think that our body is of the same type and quality and does not go beyond this nature. Further, when the corpse has become a skeleton, the ligaments have parted and the bones been scattered piecemeal after becoming the colour of a shell or a pigeon, we should remember that our body is of the same type and quality and does not go beyond this nature.

(ii) When aversion and malice are strong in us we must pay concentrated attention to benevolence as the remedy. Of the three types of benevolence discussed above[14] in a general way, here benevolence extending to sentient beings is to be practised. First we have to think that those who are dear to our heart may realize benefits and happiness and we must experience that type of benevolence which corresponds to this desire. We have then to show it in turn to those who evoke mixed feelings and are vulgar, to our relatives and neighbours and finally to all who live in the ten regions of the compass, the East and so forth.

(iii) When bewilderment is rampant we must concentrate on the Law of Interdependent Origination (Pratītyasamutpāda). As is stated in the 'Sa'.lu.ljaṅ.pa'i mdo' ('Śālistambhasūtra', p. 91):

> Bhikṣus, he who knows this rice stalk knows the Law of Interdependent Origination. He who knows this Law knows the Dharma. He who knows the Dharma knows the Buddha.

There are two types of this Law proceeding respectively in (A) progressive and (B) inverted order, and leading to (A) Saṃsāra and (B) Nirvāṇa.

Of the first type (A) there are two varieties: (i) exterior and (ii) interior (89b). Of the latter there are also two types, an interior one connected with (a) necessary (*rgyu*, Skt. *hetu*) and (b) sufficient (*rkyen*, Skt. *pratyaya*) conditions.[15]

(a) The first is as follows:[16]

> Bhikṣus, because of this, that arises, because of the birth of that, this is born. In other words, ignorance causes motivation, and from this the process goes on until under condition of birth there

> follows old age, death, sorrow, lamentation, misery, mental unhappiness and distress. From these comes the vastness of our misery.

This has special reference to the world of sensuality and to those born from a womb.

There is at the very beginning (before birth) ignorance of or bewilderment at the knowable.[17] This in turn gives rise to sullied actions that are either wholesome or unwholesome, and is called 'motivation through ignorance'. The individual's conscious and unconscious mind when affected by these potentialities is termed 'consciousness with a motive'. It then develops in a way contrary to its original state and having entered a female's womb becomes an embryo and is called 'name and form conditioned by consciousness'. This 'name and form' grows into the senses of eye, ear and so on and is called 'the six working bases conditioned by name and form'. The meeting and interaction of the senses of sight and of the other senses, their respective objects and the knowing-perceiving principle is termed 'the aggregate conditioned by the six working bases'. This unit produces a feeling of either pleasure, displeasure or indifference, which is called 'feeling-sensation conditioned by the aggregate'. In feeling-sensation there is delight, longing and craving (for further such experiences), and this is (90a) called 'thirst conditioned by feeling'. Not becoming free from longing and not getting it off one's mind and ever and again seeking for the object (believed to satisfy this craving) is called 'acquisition and ascription conditioned by thirst'. When the object is thus procured, action which leads to activity by body, speech and mind follows and is termed 'living conditioned by acquisition and ascription'. The five psychosomatic components which have been grouped and organized by this activity are termed 'birth under living conditions'. The growth, maturing, ageing and dying of the psychosomatic components that have become manifest after birth, are death and are known as 'old age and death conditioned by birth'. To be afflicted inwardly by longing and attachment due to perception becoming dim at the time of dying is 'sorrow', which gives rise to 'lamentation'. The experience of unpleasantness associated with the five types of sense perception is 'misery', which when felt causes 'unhappiness'. All other emotional troubles lead to 'distress'.

There are three groups in this Law of Interdependent Origination: Ignorance, thirst and ascription cause emotional disturbances, motivation and life are activity, and consciousness with the six remaining elements in this Law are misery. Thus in the 'dbU.ma rten.'byuṅ' ('Pratītyasamutpādahṛdayakārikā') is said:

The Sage has said about this Law
That the twelve elements
Are to be known by three groups:
They are
Emotion, activity and misery.
The first, eighth, and ninth elements are emotional;
The second and tenth are active;
The remaining seven are miserable.

Their similes are as follows: ignorance is the sower, Karma or activity the field, and consciousness the seed. Thirst is like moisture (90b); name and form are the shoot and the other members are the leaves and petals.

There is no motivation without ignorance, and, in the same way, if there is no birth, all that lies between old age and death does not manifest. But if motivation becomes active through ignorance, then also birth, old age and death follow. But neither ignorance, motivation, birth, old age nor death are anthropomorphic agents who conceivably might think: 'I have created, or been created by, the one or the other.' Motivation is due to the presence of ignorance, and old age and death to that of birth. In this way the interior Law of Interdependent Origination is to be viewed as having necessary conditions.

(b) The interior Law of Interdependent Origination with sufficient conditions contains the six principles of solidity, cohesion, heat, movement, extension and organization.[18]

The principle or element of solidity forms the hard core of the body, cohesion makes it whole; combustion (heat) is responsible for our being able to digest what we eat and drink; movement leads to breathing in and out; extension is responsible for the cavities in the body; and the principle of organization for the five types of sense perception (91a) and our tainted capacity for becoming aware of them (*yid.kyi rnam.par śes.pa*, Skt. *manovijñāna*).[19] A body cannot be born without these constituents, but is the result of the combination of all six elements. But again none of these is an anthropomorphic agent who might think that he is responsible for any element. These conditions or elements just happen to work.

Should you ask whether the twelve elements of this Law combine in one lifetime, the answer is given in the ''Phags.pa sa.bcu'i mdo' ('Daśabhumikasūtra', p. 21J):

> Motivation under the condition of ignorance refers to the past; consciousness and feeling and all that is mentioned in between to the present; thirst and life and all that comes in between to the future. It continues beyond.

(B) The inverted form of the Law of Interdependent Origination leading to Nirvāṇa, means that a complete understanding of the nature of the whole of reality as Śūnyatā abolishes ignorance, thus gradually doing away with everything up to old age and death. As is said:[20]

> When ignorance disappears there is no motivation and so it goes on until with the removal of birth there is no old age and death, sorrow, lamentation, misery, unhappiness and distress. Thus this vast body of misery is abolished.

(iv) When envy is rampant in us, our remedy lies in paying concentrated attention to the goodness and sameness of ourselves and others. For we and they equally want happiness and dislike misery (91b). As is stated in the 'sPyod.'jug' ('Bodhicaryāvatāra' VIII, 90):

> First strive for and attend to
> The similarity between yourself and others.
> Since you and they feel the same way about happiness
> Treat others like yourself.

(v) When haughty our remedy is to concentrate on our relationships with others. Foolish people consider themselves important and suffer in this world by respecting only themselves. The Buddhas, however, deem others important and attain enlightenment by working for their benefit alone. As is said:[21]

> Fools think only of their own interest,
> While the Sage is concerned with the benefit of others.
> What a world of difference between them!

Therefore, while recognizing that it is wrong to consider ourselves superior, we should stop clinging to a self; while appreciating that it is right to think others important, we should regard them as ourselves. So also is stated in the 'sPyod.'jug' ('Bodhicaryāvatāra'):

> Having learned that we have faults, while others
> Are an ocean of virtues,
> We should cease clinging to ourselves
> And emulate others instead.

(vi) When our conflicting emotions are of equal strength or when we think too much in terms of dichotomy, we should practise breath control. The six stages of this exercise are listed in the 'Chos.mṅon. pa.mdzod' ('Abhidharmakośa' VI, 12):

> Counting, following the breath and holding it,
> Analysis, motivation and
> Purification.[22]

How to experience conflicting emotions without repressing, evoking or transferring them can be learned either orally from a teacher, which is the Mantra method or the Father-Son-Instruction of Mar.pa (and Mi.la.ras.pa), or from the 'lHan.cig.skyes.sbyor' and the Six Practices (Chos.drug)[23] of Venerable Nāropa.

These are the steps in the purification of mind and the attainment of meditative concentration.

III. Meditative concentration is of three types by which (A) we live happily in the present[24] (92a), (B) acquire qualities and (C) work for the benefit of sentient beings.

(A) The first is to make the stream of our consciousness a suitable vessel (for spiritual awareness).

(B) We then acquire the Buddhadharmas.[24a]

(C) The third involves working for the benefit of sentient beings.

IV. The primary characteristics of each type:

(A) Of the first type by which we now live in happiness we read in the 'Byaṅ.sa' ('Bodhisattvabhūmi'):

> The meditative concentration of the Bodhisattvas is (i) devoid of all dichotomy; (ii) produces relaxation of tension in the mind and its functions; (iii) is completely tranquil; (iv) without arrogance or (v) emotional evaluation; and (vi) is devoid of all determinate characteristics. By this one lives happily in this present life.

(i) Here, 'devoid of all dichotomy' means that we abide in the oneness of thought without mind swerving between the opposites of being and non-being.

(ii) 'Producing relaxation of tension in mind and its functions' means that the operational unfitness of mind and its function (due to tension) has wholly subsided.

(iii) 'Completely tranquil' means that mind has entered its own ultimate sphere.

(iv and v) 'Without arrogance and emotional evaluation' means without emotional conflicts due to dogmatism and worldliness.

(vi) 'Devoid of all determinate characteristics' means that one cannot attribute to it such joyous experiences as those belonging to the world of form (Rūpadhātu) and other realms.

The gate to all this is the fourfold concentration in meditation or the first, second, third and fourth *dhyānas*. The first is analytical and discursive, the second possesses delight, the third happiness and the fourth equanimity.[25]

(B) The concentration by which the Buddhadharmas are acquired (92b) is of two types: (i) extraordinary and (ii) ordinary.

(i) The first is the multifarious, inconceivable, boundless meditative absorption which falls under the ten powers.[26] Since the Śrāvakas and Pratyekabuddhas have not even heard their names, how can they attain them?

(ii) The ordinary type comprises the liberations, masteries, totalities, penetrations and so on[27] experienced by Śrāvakas. But though they are similar in name they are dissimilar in nature.[28]

(C) The concentration by which we work for the benefit of sentient beings is the creation of innumerable thought-forms by which eleven functions such as being an aid to others and so on are performed.

What then is tranquillity and insight resulting therefrom? Tranquillity is the fusing of mind with mind by pure absorption; the resulting insight is the discriminating awareness of reality as such, knowing thereby what should or should not be done. As is stated in the 'mDo.sde.rgyan' ('Mahāyāna-sūtrālaṅkāra' XVIII, 66):

> There is tranquillity and insight
> In relying on the real foundation (of life)
> Because of fusing mind with mind
> And discriminating the whole of reality.

Tranquillity is the essence of meditative concentration, while insight is essential to discriminating awareness arising from wisdom.

V. Concentration is increased by (i) transcending and (ii) discriminating awareness born from wisdom and (iii) transmutation.[29]

VI. It is purified when supported by Śūnyatā and Compassion.[30]

VII. The result is (i) fulfilment and (ii) effectiveness in our situation in life.

(i) Fulfilment is the attainment of unsurpassable enlightenment. As is stated in the 'Byaṅ.sa' ('Bodhisattvabhūmi'):

> A Bodhisattva who has completed the perfection of meditative concentration has awakened, will and does awaken to unsurpassable perfect enlightenment.

(ii) Effectiveness in our situation in life means that we are reborn as a god free from sensuality. The Teacher kLu.sgrub (Nāgārjuna) has declared:

> Through the four concentrations by which are given up
> Delight in hedonism and the misery of sensuality,
> One attains the same state as the Mahāphala,
> Brahmā, Prabhāsvara and Śubhakṛtsna gods.

The sixteenth chapter, dealing with the Perfection of Meditative Concentration, from
The Jewel Ornament of Liberation or
The Wish-Fulfilling Gem of the
Noble Doctrine.

NOTES TO CHAPTER 16

1. *mṅon.śes.pa*, Skt. *abhijñā*. See note 19 on Chapter 4 for this term.

2. *śes.rab*, Skt. *prajñā*. See Chapter 17 for a detailed discussion of the meaning and importance of this function.

3. *tiṅ.ṅe.'dzin*, Skt. *samādhi*. This is almost synonymous with *bsam.gtan*, Skt. *dhyāna*. But while the latter term may be said to refer to the ongoing process, the former is used more in connection with the final phase and the stage of attainment through the process of meditative concentration.

4. Cp. 'Śikṣāsamuccaya', p. 119.

5. *yid*, Skt. *manas*. Although the Buddhist texts state that the three terms for what we might call the mental-spiritual, viz. *sems* (Skt. *citta*), *yid* (Skt. *manas*), and *rnam.par śes.pa* (Skt. *vijñāna*), are synonymous (see 'Abhidharmakośa' II, 34), there is yet a marked difference in their working. *sems* (*citta*), apart from the fact that it is used philosophically to denote the basic mentalism of Mahāyāna Buddhism, corresponds very often to what we are wont to call 'attitude' or the fact that we are 'set' for something and that in this 'state' the psychological function-events operate in a manner as outlined by it. *rnam.par śes.pa* (*vijñāna*) is as the term implies 'discrimination', selecting one or the other characteristic from the welter of sensible data and making it the sole content of its operation; hence it is sensation-perception. The *yid* (*manas*) is interpreting the

data transmitted to its centre by the various senses (sensations). When this *yid* (*manas*) is no longer engaged in interpreting and working in a manner which we denote by pure sensation, the external reference or the belief we have about objects in space and time subsides and the *yid* (*manas*) becomes harmonized with its 'origin' or that which does not stand for any conception at all.

6. The three types of enlightenment are those of the Śrāvakas, the Pratyekabuddhas and the Bodhisattvas.

7. *rtse.gcig*, Skt. *ekāgratā*. This is a state of complete concentration in which there is no more any reference to anything but the ultimate which is of highest positive value, although no conception can be formed about it.

8. *rnam.par rtog.pa*, Skt. *vikalpa*. It is essentially the division of Reality into a subject and an object and considering this division as ultimate, the gap between subject and object remaining unbridgeable. Direct experience, which is emphasized by Buddhism, proves that the division is not ultimate. See also note 19 to Chapter 1.

9. 'Bodhicaryāvatāra' VIII, 3.

10. They are on the positive side: gain, fame, praise and pleasure; on the negative: loss, infamy, reproach and unhappiness.

11. Skandhamāra, Kleśamāra, Mṛtyumāra and Devaputramāra are names of certain limiting experiences which, as the term Māra implies, have a deadening influence on life. The skandhas are the five psychosomatic constituents of individual life (Corporeality (*rūpa*)—this often denotes merely the epistemological object of a perceptual situation, feeling (*vedanā*), sensation-ideation (*saṃjñā*), motivation (*saṃskārāḥ*) and consciousness (*vijñāna*).) To conceive of these constituents as ultimates in the manner of naïve realism instead of dealing with them as instrumental concepts, is 'the deadly influence of the psychosomatic constituents'. Similarly to put up with emotions (cupidity (*lobha*), malevolence (*dveṣa*) and bewilderment (*moha*)) instead of understanding their origin and using them as vehicles for gaining knowledge, is 'the deadly influence of emotions'. The analysis of the transitory nature of the psychosomatic constituents without realizing that the analytical process itself is nothing ultimate but only a means to sever attachment to these constituents, is because of its mere negative character equal to the killing of life and hence 'the deadly influence of spiritual death'. The experiences in meditation which have a 'divine' character because they go beyond the merely human concern, are also nothing ultimate in themselves. But by clinging to them instead of understanding them they turn into dead concepts which are likely to undermine the mental health of the

individual. Hence they are termed 'the deadly influence of divine powers'. It is necessary to overcome these deadly foes if spiritual freedom is to be won. See for instance 'Do.ha.mdzod ces.bya.ba spyod.pa'i glu'i 'grel.pa don.gyi sgron.ma' ('Dohākoṣa-nāma-caryāgīti-arthapradīpa-nāma-ṭīkā'), bsTan.'gyur, (Derge edition) rgyud ži, fol. 34a seqq.

12. In older works on Buddhism one finds 'Causal Nexus' as the translation of Pratītyasamutpāda. This is hardly correct, because an antiquated conception of causality was superimposed on the Buddhist one. The latter has certain similarities to the Humean conception of association, but it is important to note that the Buddhist Law of Interdependent Origination is not a description of reality but a leading principle (see John Hospers, 'An Introduction to Philosophical Analysis', p. 261, on this principle). Therefore, since it is only an attempt to eke out of nature as many uniformities as possible, it is the remedy against a state of bewilderment. In the course of sGam.po.pa's treatment of this Law it will become quite clear that Buddhist 'causality' by placing the emphasis on the relation rather than on the terms, is the reverse of the activity view and anthropomorphism which stood at the beginnings of science and which is dying out slowly in modern physics. (See L. S. Stebbing, 'A Modern Introduction to Logic', p. 261.)

13. The idea of first finding out what disturbs us most and then applying that which counteracts this influence, runs right through all schools of Buddhism. A similar list as given by sGam.po.pa is found in Buddhaghosa's 'Visuddhimagga' III, seq.

14. See Chapter 7.

15. The translation of *rgyu* (*hetu*) and *rkyen* (*pratyaya*) respectively as 'necessary condition' and 'sufficient condition', is only approximately correct. While *pratyaya* corresponds to what we call relation, *hetu* is a determinative sort of immanent teleology or directed control. The idea of 'immanent causality', where causality has nothing to do with final causes, mythical causal agents and other *ad hoc* invented 'explanations', has been expressed by Roy Wood Sellars, 'Causality and Substance', *Phil. Rev.*, **52**, 1–27. As has been shown in Chapter 1 of the present work, where Tathāgatagarbha is said to be the *hetu* of human striving, *hetu* is clearly a term for an integrative process from which at a higher level human behaviour will emerge in the humane form of Buddhahood or enlightenment.

16. 'Śālistambhasūtra', pp. 91–2.

17. Buddhism does not recognize the assumption that there is something unknowable. Knowledge, though not knowledge of

something, is at the core of human nature. Only as long as we have not penetrated to this core we speak of knower and knowable and erroneously believe that the two will never meet.

18. Lit.: earth, water, fire, wind, space and consciousness.

19. *yid.kyi rnam.par śes.pa*, Skt. *manovijñāna* lingers on in later and advanced Buddhist thought as a remnant of earlier forms of analysis. This term has two meanings: (i) *manas* which is *vijñāna*, i.e. our subjective frame of mind is a 'dis-criminating' (*vi-jñāna*) process; and (ii) *vijñāna* of the *manas*, i.e. similarly as every sensation is converted into a conscious awareness (*cakṣurvijñāna* 'visual consciousness', etc.), certain schools assumed that 'mind' also must have a centre which like that of sight is some 'organ'. This 'organ' was the *manas*. The two meanings of *manovijñāna* are fully explained in 'Vijñaptimātratā-siddhi', pp. 226, 289.

20. 'Śālistambhasūtra', p. 92.

21. 'Mahāyāna-sūtrālaṅkāra' V, 8.

22. Modification is the directing of mind from breathing to other phenomena connected with breath control; purification is entering upon the Path of Seeing (*darśanamārga*) and the Path of Practising (*bhāvanāmārga*). These two paths are discussed in Chapter 18.

23. On the Six Practices by Nāropa see Introduction, p. xiii, note 1. Father-Son-Instruction is the name for special teachings which a Guru gives to his disciple. 'lHan.cig.skyes.sbyor' is the title of a book by sGam.po.pa.

24. See 'Abhidharmakośa' II, 4; VI, 42c, 58b, 65b; VIII, 27c–28.

24a. See Chapter 1, note 39.

25. See 'Abhidharmakośa' VIII, 7–8. See also above, Chapter 3.

26. See 'Abhidharmakośa' VII, 28c–29, and 'Bhāṣya' (pp. 68 seqq.).

27. *rnam.par thar.pa* (*vimokṣa*), *zil.gyis gnon.pa* (*abhibhvāyatana*), *zad.par.gyi skye.mched* (*kṛtsnāyatana*) and *so.so yaṅ.dag.par rig.pa* (*pratisaṃvid*). They have been mentioned in 'Abhidharmakośa' VIII, 32 seq., 35–6; VII, 37–40. A further analysis and examination of their interrelationships is found in my 'Philosophy and Psychology in the Abhidharma', pp. 206 seqq.

28. The difference lies in the realistic-materialistic conception of Hīnayāna and the idealistic-mentalistic conception of Mahāyāna Buddhism.

29. See Chapter 12.

30. See Chapter 12.

17
THE PERFECTION OF AWARENESS

The perfection of discriminating awareness arising from wisdom[1]
Is summarized under seven heads:
The consideration of its defects and qualities,
Its essence, its classification,
The primary characteristics of each class,
Its scope, practice and
Result.

I. NO BODHISATTVA, though he have all the virtues which begin with liberality, including meditative concentration, will reach the status of the Omniscient One, unless he possesses discriminating awareness, because like a blind man without a guide, he cannot reach his desired destination. As is stated in the ''Phags.pa sdud.pa' ('Prajñāpāramitāsaṃcayagāthā', fol. 11b):

How will a million million blind men, or even more,
Ever enter a city, not knowing the road to it?
Since in the absence of discriminating awareness the other five perfections are blind,
Without this awareness, the blind men's guide, enlightenment cannot be attained.

On the other hand, when we are thus aware—like a crowd of blind men led by their guide to a city—we let all the good and the wholesome which starts with liberality lead us on to the Buddha Path (93b) and so reach the citadel of the Omniscient One. As is said in the 'dbU.ma 'jug.pa' ('Madhyamakāvatāra' VI, 2):

Just as a man with eyes that see,
Leads the whole crowd of blind men easily
To the desired country, so discriminating awareness
Gathering the eyeless virtues (of liberality and so on) leads them to Buddhahood.

And in the ''Phags.pa sdud.pa' ('Prajñāpāramitāsaṃcayagāthā', fol. 40a):

If one knows the nature of reality by means of discriminating awareness
One becomes fully liberated from the three world-spheres.

Why then, if this awareness is enough, should beneficial expediency[2] as expressed by liberality and other perfections, be necessary? The answer is that awareness alone is not enough. As is stated in the 'Byaṅ.chub.lam.sgron' ('Bodhipathapradīpa', 52):

> Since discriminating awareness without beneficial expediency
> And beneficial expediency without discriminating awareness
> Have been termed 'bondage',
> They must not be parted from each other.

How then do we become fettered when we part them? Any Bodhisattva who resorts to the one without the other falls into a one-sided Nirvāṇa, into the desired peace and quietism of the Śrāvakas, and is, as it were, bound to this Nirvāṇa. He will never reach the Apratiṣṭhitanirvāṇa.[3] Those, however, who acknowledge the existence of three paths claim that an individual (who makes a separate use of either expediency or awareness) remains fettered for ever, while those who acknowledge only one path claim that he stays in bondage for eighty-four thousand great aeons.[4]

If we resort to beneficial expediency without discriminating awareness we do not go beyond the level and the path of unintelligent ordinary beings but remain bound by the chains of Saṃsāra. As is stated in the 'bLo.gros mi.zad.pas žus.pa'i mdo' ('Akṣayamatiparipṛcchāsūtra'):

> While fettered to Nirvāṇa by discriminating awareness without beneficial expediency, or vice versa to Saṃsāra, one must make use of both (in order to be liberated).

And in the ''Phags.pa Dri.ma.med.par grags.pas bstan.pa'i mdo' ('Vimalakīrtinirdeśasūtra'):

> What is a Bodhisattva's bondage and what his liberation? Discriminating awareness unsupported by beneficial expediency is bondage, but when supported is liberation (94a), and the same applies when their order is reversed.

If therefore we resort to either without the other we are working for damnation (Māra). As is asserted in the 'kLu'i rgyal.po rgya. mtshos žus.pa'i mdo' ('Sāgaranāgarājaparipṛcchāsūtra'):

> Māra works in two ways, through beneficial expediency without discriminating awareness and vice versa. He who knows this renounces either without the other.

Or to give a simile: When we walk, our eyes and feet must cooperate if we are to reach the city of our choice. In the same way the eyes of discriminating awareness and the feet of beneficial expediency must work together when we want to go to the citadel of Apratiṣṭhitanirvāṇa. As is said in the 'Ga.ya.go.ri'i mdo' ('Gayaśīrṣasūtra'):

> The Mahāyāna Path, in brief, is twofold: Beneficial expediency and discriminating awareness arising from wisdom.

Now the latter does not arise by chance. Just as a fire will never blaze when only fed by a little fuel, but will be inextinguishable when stoked with masses of dry wood, so this great discriminating awareness does not arise from a few merits, but derives from many accumulated virtues, such as liberality, ethics and manners and so on, and will then burn away all impurities. We therefore have to foster liberality and the other virtues for the sake of discriminating awareness. As is stated in the 'sPyod.'jug' ('Bodhicaryāvatāra' IX, 1):

> All this
> The Buddha has declared for the sake of discriminating awareness arising from wisdom.

II. The essence of this awareness is referred to in the 'mÑon.pa kun.las btus.pa' ('Abhidharmasamuccaya', p. 6):

> What is this discriminating awareness arising from wisdom? It is the exact analysis of the whole of reality.

III. In the commentary of the 'mDo.sde.rgyan' ('Mahāyānasūtrālaṅkāra' XVI, 28) (94b) discriminating awareness is classified as (A) worldly and spiritual, the latter being (B) lower and (C) higher.

IV. The primary characteristics of each class:

(A) Worldly awareness or understanding is derived from the study of medicine, logic, linguistics and art.

(BC) The two spiritual types of awareness, better known as 'Buddhist Spirituality', are an awareness which is born from attending to the Noble Doctrine.

(B) The first stems from hearing, pondering over and paying attention to the Noble Doctrine like the Śrāvakas and Pratyekabuddhas. It is the penetrating awareness that the five psychosomatic constituents of our organism[5] are impure, unsatisfactory, transitory and essenceless.

(C) The second type arises from hearing, pondering over and paying attention to the Noble Doctrine in the Mahāyāna way. It is an awareness in which the whole of reality is experienced as being nothing (*stoṅ.pa*, Skt. *śūnya*) by nature, without origination, basis or foundation. As is expressed in the 'Śes.rab.kyi pha.rol.tu phyin.pa bdun.brgya.pa' ('Saptaśatikā-prajñāpāramitā'):

> The knowledge that the whole of reality is without origination
> is the perfection of discriminating awareness.

In the ''Phags.pa sdud.pa' ('Prajñāpāramitāsaṃcayagāthā', fol. 5b–6a).

> To understand that the whole of reality has no nature of its own
> Is to practise the perfection of discriminating awareness.

And in the 'Byaṅ.chub.lam.sgron' ('Bodhipathapradīpa', 56):

> When it is thoroughly understood that
> The Skandhas, Dhātus, and Āyatanas[6]
> Are without origin,
> This knowledge that there is by nature only Śūnyatā
> Is called discriminating awareness arising from wisdom.

V. The scope of discriminating awareness.

As we have seen there are three types, but the one that really counts is spiritual awareness. This will be discussed under six heads: refutation (A) of existence and (B) non-existence; the fallacy of believing (95a) (C) in non-existence and (D) existence as well as non-existence; (E) the path of liberation and (F) the nature of liberation or Nirvāṇa.

(A) The refutation of existence.[7] This is laid down by Lord Atīśa after deep logical analysis in his 'Byaṅ.chub.lam.sgron' ('Bodhipathapradīpa', 57):

> There is no reason why that which already exists, should come into existence;
> The same holds good for what is non-existent like a sky-flower.

To understand this you must realize that existence and all beliefs therein involve two types of ens,[8] both of which are by nature nothing (Śūnyatā). Being mind they are of two types, (i) subjective and (ii) objective.

(i) There are many theories about this mind or subjective ens. It is the continuity of the psychosomatic constituents as organized by consciousness;[9] it means 'doing-nothing-and-doing-everything',[10] perception-sensation and fickleness. As is stated in the 'mDo sil.bu':

> Subjective ens is continuity,
> The continuation of fickleness.

To take this subjective ens as something lasting, unique and belonging to you, is the meaning of 'a mind'. It brings about conflicting emotions leading to activity (karma) and therefore to misery.

Thus the root of all unsatisfactoriness and evil is the subjective ens or the mind. As is stated in the 'rNam.'grel' ('Pramāṇavarttikā'):

> When there is a self, one knows someone other from it,
> From the I and Thou arises belief (in independent existence)
> and antagonism (to everything that threatens this belief);
> From the union (of these two)
> All evil comes about.

(ii) An objective ens means (what is popularly known as) a physical object outside (the perceiving subject) and a mind inside (that subject). These two are 'objective' because they bear their own characteristics. As is stated in the 'mDo sil.bu' (95b):

> Bearing one's own characteristics is 'objective ens'.

Thus, to believe in the existence of subject and object (both of which become the 'object' of investigation) and to be attached to them, is 'objective ens'.

To explain how both types of ens are by nature Śūnyatā, (a) first it is necessary to refute the idea that there is such a thing as a subjective ens. In his 'Rin.chen 'phreṅ.ba' ('Ratnāvalī') the Teacher kLu.sgrub (Nāgārjuna) has said:

> The I and the Mine exist—
> This is contrary to reality.

In other words, this alleged I is not found. If a subjective ens, self or mind really existed it ought to be discoverable when ultimate truth is seen. But when the mind sees ultimate truth and appreciates what reality means, it does not find a subjective ens or mind because there is no such thing. As is said in the 'Rin.chen 'phreṅ.ba' ('Ratnāvalī'):

> When true knowledge sees reality as it is
> Duality does not arise.

In other words, when truth or Mind are seen the belief in I and Mine does not arise.

Moreover, if a self or a mind existed as an ens, it should be possible to prove that it arose (i) by itself, (ii) by some other agency, (iii) by the combination of these two or (iv) by the three divisions of time (past, present and future).

(i) That it has not come about by itself is evident because it is either existent or not. If not, it cannot become the cause (for its existence), and if it exists it cannot be the result (of the non-existent cause), because the one contradicts the other.[11]

(ii) That it has not come about by some other agency is clear because it is without a cause. What does this mean? A cause exists in relation to an effect and as long as there is no effect there is no cause. And when there is no cause, no effect can be brought about, as has been shown in the preceding argument.[12]

(iii) That it has not come about by the combination of the two reasons mentioned (i.e. by itself and simultaneously by some other agency), is clear from the fallacy involved in either view.

(iv) That it is not produced by the three divisions of time is evident because the past is like a rotten seed having no creative power; (96a) and the future is like a barren woman's son; nor can the present do so, because nothing would be gained by it. As is stated in the 'Rin.chen 'phreṅ.ba' ('Ratnāvalī'):

> Since it is not obtained by itself, from others, or both,
> Nor by the three aspects of time,
> The belief in a Self collapses.

Here the expression 'is not obtained' is equivalent to 'is not produced'.

Or, the problem can be understood thus. Does this alleged self exist (as an independent entity) in the body, in the mind or in a name?

(a) Our body is of the nature of the four elements. That which is solid in it is the element earth; that which is moist, water; that which is warm, fire; and breathing and movement are wind. There is no (anthropomorphic) self or mind in these four elements (of the body) nor in the outer unorganized ones of earth, water, fire and wind.

(b) Should you then argue that this self is in the mind, the answer is that a mind is nowhere found (as an entity), because it has never been seen as such by ourselves, others or both. Therefore since a mind is not found, nor is a self (for the latter is supposed to be in a mind).

(c) Finally, if you think that this self is in a name you should know that a name is merely an arbitrary sound made conventionally to stand for something. Since a name does not exist as an independent entity, it cannot be connected with a self (which also does not exist independently).[13]

These three arguments prove that a subjective ens or a mind does not exist.

(b) That an objective ens exists is disproved by explaining that (i) neither a physical object outside (the perceiving subject) (ii) nor a mind inside (that subject) exists.

(i) As to the first, some people claim that objects exist physically.

The Vaibhāṣika declares: Atoms by nature are spherical, undivided, singular and exist physically. A mass of them is an object (of perception) such as colour-form and so on. When massed together there are intervals between each one. They appear to be in one place, like a yak's tail in the pasture. They remain in a mass because they are held together by the Karma of sentient beings.[14]

The Sautrāntika claims that when atoms mass together there are no intervals between them, although they do not touch each other.[15]

Although these people make such statements, no proof is forthcoming. Atoms must be singular or plural. If singular they must have spatial divisions or not. If so they must have an eastern, western, southern, northern, upper and lower part. With these six parts their claim to singularity collapses. If they have no spatial divisions, all material things ought to be of the nature of a single atom. But this clearly is not so. As is stated in the 'Ñi.śu.pa'i rab.tu byed.pa' ('Viṃśatikākārikā', 12):

> When one atom is joined with six others
> It follows that it must have six parts;
> If it is in the same place with six,
> The mass must be the same as one atom.

If you assume that there are many, there must have been one which by accumulation formed the mass. But since you cannot find a single atom physically, neither many atoms nor a single physical object having the nature of one can be found.[16]

If you think, you will find that what you experience directly is Mind.[17] Due to bewilderment,[18] an object in space and time is seen as an appearance[19] because Mind rises in such a way. This is clear from (1) scriptural authority, (2) reason and (3) examples.

(1) Scriptural authority is the 'Phal.po.che'i mdo' ('Buddhāvataṃsaka'):

> Oh sons of the Victorious One, this triple world is only Mind.

And the 'Lań.kar gśegs.pa'i mdo' ('Lańkāvatārasūtra' X, 155a, 153b):

> Mind defiled by traces and dispositions
> Appears as an object.
> As the latter does not exist (independently), there is only Mind;
> It is an error to see something as an outer (independent) object.

(2) Reason is the reassurance that the appearance of an outer object (97a) is a manifestation of bewilderment, because that which does not exist appears and is there. Similarly all appearance is but

bewilderment, because that which is there disappears, while that which appears changes, vanishes or is differentiated.

(3) Example means that all is like a dream or a magic show.

Thus it has been shown that a physical object is not found in reality.

(ii) The second point is that certain people claim that mind as the inner perceiving agency, is self-cognizing, self-illuminating and existent.[20]

There are three reasons why this is not so: (a) there is no such thing as mind in a temporal sense, (b) it has not been observed by anyone and so is not something existent and (c) since there are no objects (as independent entities) there is also no mind (as an independent subject and somehow mysteriously related to an object).

(a) To elaborate the first point: Does this mind which you claim to be self-cognizing and self-illuminating, exist for one moment or many? If for one, it must share the three divisions of time (past, present and future) or not. If it does, we can dismiss the existence of a single moment, but must assume a multitude of them. As is stated in the 'Rin.chen 'phreṅ.ba' ('Ratnāvalī'):

> Just as a moment has an end
> So it must have a beginning and a middle;
> Since thus it becomes triple,
> The world is not contained in a single moment.

If, on the other hand, the latter is outside the three divisions of time, it becomes non-existent. Therefore, since it is not found, neither is mind. If you say that there are many moments, then since one is not found, a multitude due to an accumulation of many can also not be found. And since there is no multitude, there is also no mind.

(b) The second point is that this so-called mind may be sought anywhere, outside or inside the body, in between the two and above or below. To investigate its shape or colour properly (97b), you must search until final and true knowledge arises and learn to change the object of your search in the manner taught by the Guru. But however hard you try you cannot see or lay your hand on it: there is nothing in the least substantial or visible there like a colour. But you can see and lay your hand on anything existent; in other words the seeker is the sought and goes beyond the realm of the intellect. Since Mind is beyond the realms of knowledge and speech you cannot see it (as something) wherever you may seek. As is stated in the ''Od.sruṅs.kyis žus.pa'i mdo' ('Kāśyapaparivartasūtra'):

> Kāśyapa, Mind is neither internal, external nor in between the two. Kāśyapa, Mind cannot be investigated, pointed out or seized; it is non-appearing, non-perceptive and non-localized. Kāśyapa, Mind has not been, will not be and is not seen by any Buddha.[21]

In the 'Dam.pa'i chos yoṅs.su 'dzin.pa'i mdo':

> Therefore mind is null and void.
> Knowing it to be non-existent
> It is taken to be without any essence
> And devoid of any substantiality.
> Entities devoid of substantiality
> Are not found (as entities).
> If the whole of reality is investigated in this way
> It is found to have this nature (of not standing for any conception).
> Avoiding the extremes (of existence and non-existence)
> The wise man keeps to the middle course.
> To be devoid of substantiality (and insubstantiality)
> Is the path to enlightenment.
> This is what I say.

And in the 'Chos.ñid mi.g'yo.ba'i mdo' ('Dharmatāsvabhāvaśūnyatācalapratisarvālokasūtra'):

> The whole of reality is unoriginated by nature,
> Does not abide materially,
> Is devoid of all actions and duties,
> Is beyond concepts and non-concepts.

Therefore, since nobody has ever seen Mind, to say that it is self-cognizing and self-illuminating, is meaningless. As is expressed in the 'Byaṅ.chub.spyod.'jug' ('Bodhicaryāvatāra' IX, 23):

> When one does not see anything,
> To say that it is illumining or not
> Is like dallying with a barren woman's child (98a).
> To speak of it is meaningless.

And Telopa exlaims:

> Indeed, this transcending awareness which is awareness in itself
> Is beyond the path of speech, is no field of speculation.[22]

(c) The third point is as follows. Since no outer object such as colour-form is found (existing as an independent entity), neither is mind which might take hold of it. As is written in the 'Chos.kyi dbyiṅs.kyi raṅ.bžin dbyer.med.par bstan.pa'i le'u' ('Dharmadhātu-prakṛti-asambhedanirdeśa-nāma-mahāyānasūtra'):

> Investigate whether this mind is green, yellow, white, red, brown or like a crystal; whether it is pure, impure, eternal, transitory, formed or formless. (Then you will find that) Mind is formless and cannot be demonstrated, is non-appearing, untouchable, non-perceptive, neither external, internal nor in between the two; it is nowhere to be found, but is absolutely pure and without liberation.[23] So is the Dharmadhātu.

And in the 'Byaṅ.chub.spyod.'jug' ('Bodhicaryāvatāra' IX, 61):

> When there is nothing knowable, what can we know?
> How then can one speak with knowledge?

And (ibid., IX, 62):

> Since there is nothing knowable
> There can be no knowledge.

Thus there is no such thing as mind.

After this refutation of existence, follows

(B) the refutation of non-existence.

It may be argued that since the two types of an ens do not exist, they may still be non-existent.[24] But non-existence is not found. This is because the two types of an ens or mind can only be said to be non-existent if they first had and later had not existed. But since that which has been called the two types of an ens or a mind has never been found (98b) existing by itself, it is beyond the extremes of existence and non-existence. Saraha exclaims:[25]

> Those who believe in existence are stupid like cattle,
> But those who believe in non-existence are still more stupid.

In the 'Laṅ.kar gśegs.pa' ('Laṅkāvatārasūtra' X, 595) we read:

> Outer objects cannot be said either to exist or not,
> Mind also cannot be grasped in any way.
> The rejection of all opinions
> Is the characteristic of unoriginatedness.

And in the 'Rin.chen 'phreṅ.ba' ('Ratnāvalī'):

> When one does not find existence
> Where will one find non-existence?

(C) The fallacy of believing in non-existence.

If you think that the belief in existence is the root of Saṃsāra, while that in non-existence is liberation from Saṃsāra, you will have to be reminded that the latter view is worse than the former one. Not only did Saraha say so, there are many other arguments. In the 'dKon. mchog brtsegs.pa' ('Ratnakūṭa') is stated:

> Kāśyapa, it is better to assume the existence of an individual though this view is as big and obvious as the mountain Sumeru. Yet the pride which comes from believing in Śūnyatā (as a non-existing entity) is worse.[26]

Further,[27]

> By the evil of thinking that Śūnyatā exists
> Persons of low discrimination degenerate.

And in the 'rTsa.ba'i śes.rab' ('Mūlamadhyamakakārikā' XIII, 8):

> Those who believe in Śūnyatā
> Are said to be incurably ill.[28]

How is this? In medical practice a disease is cured when both it and the medicine have been eliminated from the body, but if the medicine is not digested, the disease is not cured and death follows. It is the same with Śūnyatā, which should remove belief in existence. If you cling to Śūnyatā (misunderstanding it as a mere negative concept) you will fall into evil ways. As is stated in the 'Rin.chen 'phreṅ.ba' ('Ratnāvalī'):

> The believer in existence is reborn in happy surroundings
> The believer in non-existence meets misfortune in his next life (99a).

Therefore the latter view is worse than the former.

(D) The fallacy of the belief in existence and non-existence.

These two beliefs have a common fault, because they fall into the extremes of eternalism and nihilism. As is stated in the 'rTsa.ba'i śes.rab' ('Mūlamadhyamakakārikā' XV, 10):

> Existence is the view of eternalism,
> Non-existence that of nihilism.

To fall into these extremes is a sign of foolishness, and a fool is not liberated from Saṃsāra. As is expressed in the 'Rin.chen 'phreṅ.ba' ('Ratnāvalī'):

> He is a fool who believes
> That this world which is like a phantom
> Either does or does not exist.
> When there is such foolishness, there is no liberation.

(E) The path of liberation.

We become liberated by keeping to the Middle Path, not straying into extremes. As is said in the 'Rin.chen 'phreṅ.ba' ('Ratnāvalī'):

> By knowing things as they really are,
> By not relying on the two extremes, liberation is achieved.

And,

> Therefore he who does not cling to extremes, becomes liberated.

And in the 'rTsa.ba'i śes.rab' ('Mūlamadhyamakakārikā' XV, 10):

> Therefore the wise man does not cling
> To existence or non-existence.

The Middle Path that avoids extremes is discussed in the ''Phags. pa dkon.mchog brtsegs.pa' ('Ratnakūṭa'):

> Kāśyapa, what is the proper approach to a Bodhisattva's Dharma? It is the Middle Path, the investigation of the whole of reality, topic by topic. Kāśyapa, what is the Middle Path (and how can we follow it when thus) investigating reality? Further questions are asked, then comes a passage which says: Eternalism is one extreme, nihilism another. That which lies in between cannot be logically tested or demonstrated, does not appear as something and is non-perceptive. Kāśyapa, this (99b) is the Middle Path (by following which one can) investigate the whole of reality. Kāśyapa, the self is one extreme, the non-self is another and so on with other extremes. Finally, Kāśyapa, Saṃsāra is one extreme, Nirvāṇa is another. That which lies in between cannot be logically tested or demonstrated, does not appear as something and is non-perceptive. Kāśyapa, this is the Middle Path (by following which one can) investigate the whole of reality, topic by topic.

And 'Ži.ba.lha' ('Śāntideva') declares:[29]

> Mind is neither within nor without,
> Nor is it found anywhere else.
> It is neither mixed with other things, nor apart from them.
> It is not anything whatsoever and therefore
> Beings are by nature in Nirvāṇa.

Although not to harbour any ideas about extremes is the Middle Path, yet this Path is no concept to be investigated. It cannot be grasped by a consciousness which conceives it as something and it stays beyond the realms of the intellect and discursiveness. As is stated by Atīśa:

Mind remains extinct if past, unoriginating if future and present it is difficult to investigate. It has no colour, no shape and like celestial space it is not found as something concrete.

And in the 'mÑon.rtogs.rgyan' ('Abhisamayālaṅkāra' III, 1):

Neither here nor there,
Nor in between the two.
Because of knowing it to be the same in all three states of time,
It is acknowledged the Perfection of Discriminating Awareness.

(F) The nature of liberation or Nirvāṇa.

Since nothing in this world of Saṃsāra is either existent or non-existent, is that which is called Nirvāṇa something that exists or not? Some people believe that Nirvāṇa is something existent (100a). But this is not so as may be seen from the 'Rin.chen 'phreṅ.ba' ('Ratnāvalī'):

If Nirvāṇa is neither existent nor
Non-existent, how can it be existent?

Moreover, if it is something existent, it would be conditioned and if conditioned, it is perishable. The 'rTsa.ba'i śes.rab' ('Mūlamadhyamakakārikā' XXV, 5) says:

If Nirvāṇa is existent
It is something composite.

But Nirvāṇa is also not non-existent. In the same work is stated:[30]

There is also not non-existence.

What then is Nirvāṇa? It is that which cannot be conceptualized as existence or non-existence, being beyond the world of the intellect and devoid of any possibility of verbalization. It is defined in the 'Rin.chen 'phreṅ.ba' ('Ratnāvalī') as

The disappearance of beliefs in existence and non-existence.

In the 'Byaṅ.chub.sems.dpa'i spyod.pa.la 'jug.pa' ('Bodhicaryāvatāra' IX, 35):

When existence and non-existence
Are no longer present before the mind,
Then, since there is nothing else,
All conceptualization has come to an end.

In the ''Phags.pa Tshaṅs.pas žus.pa'i mdo' ('Brahmaparipṛcchāsūtra'):

Parinirvāṇa means that all characteristics have completely subsided and all unrest has disappeared.

And in the 'Dam.pa'i chos padma dkar.po' ('Saddharmapuṇḍarīkasūtra', p. 95):

> Kāśyapa, Nirvāṇa is the awareness that the whole of reality has the flavour of sameness.

Thus, Nirvāṇa is not something which can be found (as an ens) by inventing, destroying, rejecting or accepting (some tenet), but it can be described as stopping all intellectualistic processes. As is stated in the 'rTsa.ba'i śes.rab' ('Mūlamadhyamakakārikā' XXV, 3):

> Without rejection and acceptance,
> Without nihilism and eternalism,
> Without cessation and origination—
> That is Nirvāṇa.

Since there is neither origination nor cessation, neither rejection nor acceptance (100b), Nirvāṇa is self-authenticating, spontaneous and unchanging. As is written in the 'Nam.mkha' rin.po.che'i mdo':

> There is nothing to be removed
> And nothing to be posited.
> It is seeing reality as reality
> And when one sees thus one is liberated.[31]

Although there are such terms as discriminating awareness (*śes.rab*) and Mind (*rań.sems*),[32] they belong to the realm of logic, while the real Discriminating Awareness or Mind is beyond all that can be known and expressed. This is made clear in the 'Rab.rtsal. gyis rnam.par gnon.pas žus.pa'i mdo' ('Suvikrāntivikramaparipṛcchāsūtra'):

> Perfection of Discriminating Awareness arising from wisdom cannot be expressed in words. It is beyond them.

And in the 'sGra.can.'dzin.gyis yum.la bstod.pa':

> Praise to the Mother of the Victorious One of all times,
> Who is the Perfection of Discriminating Awareness inexpressible by words even if one attempted to speak,
> Who is without origin and end, of the nature of celestial space,
> And who is the sphere of transcending awareness which is experienced by and in ourselves.

This ends my discussion of the scope of discriminating awareness arising from wisdom.

VI. As to the development of mind or discriminating awareness you might ask whether it is necessary to develop it, since after all the whole of reality is Śūnyatā. The answer is Yes. Silver ore has the nature but not the appearance of silver, so that if one wants to have some silver, one must melt the ore. In the same way reality has always been Śūnyatā by nature and beyond words, but beings must know and develop this awareness, for Śūnyatā appears under various disguises and so is variously experienced with difficulty. Therefore, when you have understood the meaning of discriminating awareness you have to develop this awareness. This development has four stages: (A) preparatory, (B) the actual application, (C) the conclusion and (D) the signs of progress.

(A) The preparatory stage is to bring the mind to rest. How, is described in the 'Śes.rab.kyi pha.rol.tu phyin.pa bdun.brgya.pa' ('Saptaśatikā-prajñāpāramitā') (101a):

> A son or daughter of a good family must stay in solitude, delight in seclusion, sit cross-legged without pondering over the differentiating attributes of things and so on,

or is laid down in works on the preparation for the Mahāmudrā experience.[33]

(B) The method of the actual application is also laid down in the instructions about the Mahāmudrā: it involves not thinking about existence or non-existence, acceptance or rejection, thus leaving the mind without strain. This is stated by Telopa:

> Do not think, scheme or cognize,
> Do not pay attention or investigate; leave mind in its own sphere.

To rest the mind (the same author explains):

> My son, since by that on which you ponder
> I am neither fettered nor need be freed,
> (I advise you,) cure your fatigue
> In the unmoved, uncreated, spontaneous (reality).

kLu.sgrub (Nāgārjuna) says:

> Just as an elephant becomes gentle again after his rut,
> Mind rests in itself when its coming and going has stopped.
> Having understood it thus, what else do I need?

Further he states:

> Do not make a division anywhere and do not think about anything,
> Do not become agitated, remain at ease within yourself.
> The real has no origin and is self-authentic.
> It is the place where the Victorious Ones of the three times have gone.

Ri.khrod dbaṅ.phyug (Śabari) declares:

Do not see any fault anywhere,
Do not take anything to heart,
Do not hanker after the signs of progress such as heat—[34]
Although this may be said to be what is meant by non-attention,
Yet do not fall a prey to laziness;
Be attentive by constantly using inspection.[35]

In the 'sGom.don.grub.pa' we read:

At the time of practice nothing is to be practised,
Conventionally it is said to be attentive practice.

Saraha also declares:

When there is attachment, discard it;
When awareness is there, all is reality;
Apart from reality nothing is known.

And Atiśa stated:

It is (101b) profound and beyond verbalization;
Radiant and uncreated,
Without origin and end, pure from the beginning;
The Dharmadhātu, by nature Nirvāṇa, is without (a beginning) a middle and an end.
Since it is beyond the vision of the intellect
Look at it with eyes undimmed by sluggishness and frivolity.[36]

And,

In the Dharmadhātu which is beyond words
Rest your mind as (also being) beyond verbalization.

Thus putting mind into the Dharmadhātu, is the correct method of practising the perfection of discriminating awareness. As is written in the 'Śes.rab.kyi pha.rol.tu phyin.pa bdun.brgya.pa' ('Saptaśatikā-prajñāpāramitā'):

Where there is no accepting, no grasping (i.e. conceiving) and no rejecting, there is the practice of the perfection of discriminating awareness. Not to stay with anything is the practice of this awareness. Not to think and not to conceptualize is the practice of this perfection.

In the ''Phags.pa brGyad.stoṅ.pa' ('Aṣṭasāhasrikā-prajñāpāramitā') it is called

'Not to practise anything' and 'attentive contemplation of the sky'.[37]

How can we fix our attention on the sky? The answer is given in the same work:

> The sky is beyond the reach of discursive thinking as is the perfection of this awareness.[38]

And in the ''Phags.pa sdud.pa' ('Prajñāpāramitāsaṃcayagāthā', fol. 5b):

> Not to think about origination or unorigination
> Is to live by the perfection of this awareness.

The Teacher Ṅag.gi dbaṅ.phyug (Vāgīśvara) also declared:

> Not to think about the thinkable
> Nor about the unthinkable—
> When one does not think about either
> Śūnyatā is seen thereby.

If you ask how, the answer is given in the 'Chos yaṅ.dag.par bsdud.pa'i mdo' ('Dharmasaṅgītisūtra'):

> Seeing Śūnyatā is not seeing anything (102a).

And,

> Exalted One, not seeing anything is real seeing.

And,

> Not to see is seeing reality.

In the 'dbU.ma bden.chuṅ':

> Not to see is said to be seeing
> In the Śin.tu zab.pa'i mdo.

And in the ''Phags.pa sdud.pa' ('Prajñāpāramitāsaṃcayagāthā', fol. 16b):

> Seeing the sky,—is what people say.
> How to see the sky,—find out what it means.
> To see all things in this way is the teaching of The Buddha.

(C) The conclusion means that by seeing all things as enchantment, merits such as liberality are accumulated to the best of our power. As is stated in the ''Phags.pa sdud.pa' ('Prajñāpāramitāsaṃcayagāthā', fol. 4a):

> He who knows the five psychosomatic constituents as being the result of a magic spell
> Does not consider them to be different from each other

And has no ideas about multiplicity (and singularity), is calm and restful
And lives by the perfection of awareness arising from wisdom.

In the 'Tiṅ.ṅe.'dzin rgyal.po'i mdo' ('Samādhirājasūtra'):

Just as a magician produces visible objects
(Such as) horses, elephants, carts and other things
Which though they appear are non-existent,
So should you experience the whole of reality.

And in the 'sPyod.pa'i de.kho.na.ñid':

Merits proceed uninterruptedly
In a mind without discursiveness and habit-memory.

When by such a practice (of discriminating awareness arising from wisdom) the transcending awareness of mystic illumination (*mñam*, Skt. *samāhitajñāna*) and the subsequent presentational knowledge (*rjes*, Skt. *pṛṣṭhalabdhajñāna*)[39] have become undifferentiated, we become free from pride. As is said:

Without a haughty thought that I have achieved mystic illumination.
And why? Because the nature of the whole of reality has been experienced and understood.

Thus, to live only a single moment in the sphere of the ultimately real, Śūnyatā or Perfection of Awareness (102b) is of more worth and has more immeasurable merits than to listen to the Dharma, read it or practise liberality and the other virtues which are the foundation of the good and wholesome. So also is stated in the 'De.kho.na.ñid bstan.pa'i mdo' ('Tattvaprakāśa'):

Śāriputra, he who practises Absorption in the Ultimate (*de.kho.na.ñid.kyi tiṅ.ṅe.'dzin*) for as little time as it takes to snap one's finger produces greater merits than he who listens to the Dharma for an aeon. Śāriputra, instruction therefore is to be given seriously as to this Absorption. Śāriputra, all the Bodhisattvas who have been said to become Buddhas, abide in this Absorption.

In the 'rTogs.pa chen.po rgyas.pa'i mdo':

To enter meditative concentration for a time
Is more worthwhile than to save the life
Of beings in the three world-spheres.

In the 'gTsug.tor chen.po'i mdo':

It is more meritorious to dwell on the meaning of the Dharma for one day than to listen to or think about it for many aeons, because thereby (another journey along) the road of birth and death is postponed for a long time.

And in the 'Dad.pa.la 'jug.pa'i mdo' ('Śraddhābalādhānāvatāramudrāsūtra'):

> The yogi who pays attention to Śūnyatā only for a moment accumulates greater merits than the beings in the three world-spheres who restrict themselves to the necessities of life.

It has been pointed out that no merits can liberate us while Śūnyatā is absent from our minds. This is confirmed in the 'Chos 'byuṅ.ba.med.par bstan.pa'i mdo' ('Sarvadharmāpravṛttinirdeśa'):

> Even if one has kept the rules of ethics for a long time
> And has practised meditation for millions of aeons,
> When one does not understand this topic (Śūnyatā) properly,
> In the (Buddhist) doctrine no liberation is possible.
> He who knows (103a) the whole of reality to be nothing concrete,
> Will never become attached to it (and fettered).

In the 'Sa'i sñiṅ.po 'khor.lo bcu.pa':

> Doubts are dispelled by the practice of meditative absorption,
> Nothing else can do this.
> Therefore, since meditative absorption is the most excellent practice,
> The wise attend to it diligently.

And,

> To practise Śūnyatā for one day is more meritorious than to write, read, listen to, explain and discuss it.

When you possess such Śūnyatā there is nothing that is not included in it.

It is taking refuge. As is stated in the 'Ma.dros.pas žus.pa'i mdo' ('Anavataptanāgarājaparipṛcchāsūtra'):

> A Bodhisattva knows reality to be without individual nature, existence, life principle and personality.[40] Like a Tathāgata, to see things as unformed, uncharacterized and without a nature of their own, is taking refuge in the Buddha with a mind at peace. The nature of the Tathāgata is Dharmadhātu with which reality is in accord. This in turn is to take refuge in the Dharma with a mind at peace. Relying on the Dharmadhātu and the Śrāvakayāna as unconditioned, and seeing the conditioned and un-

conditioned as not being an unbridgeable duality, is to take refuge in the Sangha with a mind at peace (103b).

It is also the formation of an enlightened attitude. As is declared in the 'Sems.bskyed chen.po'i mdo':

Kāśyapa, the fact that the whole of reality is like celestial space without any differentiating attributes, radiant and pure from its very beginning, is the formation of an attitude directed towards enlightenment.

Attention to divine visions in the Developing Stage (*bskyed.rim*, Skt. *utpannakrama*) and muttering of mystic formulas (*mantra*) also concerns Śūnyatā, as is shown in the 'Kye.rdo.rje' ('Hevajratantrarāja'):

No practice, no practiser,
No gods and also no mantras (as entities).
In that which is beyond verbalization
The gods and mantras stay:
Vairocana, Akṣobhya, Amoghasiddhi,
Ratnasambhava and Amitābha.[41]

In the 'Saṅs.rgyas mñam.sbyor' ('Śrī-Sarvabuddhasamāyogaḍākinījālasaṃvara-nāma-uttaratantra'):

Since Yoga (union with the ultimate) is not achieved
With idols,
By exerting himself for enlightenment
The yogi becomes a living god.

And in the 'rDo.rje rtse.mo' ('Vajraśekhara-mahāguhyayogatantra'):

The nature of all mystic formulas
Is the Mind of all Buddhas;
It is that which produces the realization of the essence of reality.
That which possesses Dharmadhātu
Is said to be the nature of the mystic formulas.

Making sacrifices also concerns Śūnyatā, as is expressed in the 'gSaṅ.ba bdud.rtsi rgyal.po'i rgyud' ('Amṛtaguhyatantrarāja'):

Sacrifice is so called
Because it bestows real perfection
And overpowers discursiveness.
To burn wood and other ingredients is not performing sacrifices.

The six perfections as the way (towards enlightenment) also come under Śūnyatā, as is stated in the 'rDo.rje tiṅ.ṅe.'dzin.gyi mdo':

When one does not move from Śūnyatā
The six perfections are united.

In the 'Tshaṅs.pa khyad.par sems.kyis žus.pa'i mdo' ('Brahmaviśeṣacintiparipṛcchāsūtra'):

> Not to intend is liberality (104a). Not to live with differences is ethics and manners and not to create them is patience. Neither to reject nor to accept is strenuousness. Not to be attached is meditative concentration. Non-discursiveness is awareness arising from wisdom.

In the 'Sa'i sñiṅ.po'i mdo':

> Attention to Śūnyatā by the wise consists in not relying on or becoming permanently attached to worldliness, thereby preserving ethics and manners.

And, in the same work:

> A mind which has found peace through realizing that reality has but one emotional value and no differentiating attributes by which one entity is alienated from another, does not abide anywhere and is not attached to anything. This patience (and acceptance of reality) brings great benefit. The strenuousness of the wise consists in giving up all attachment:
> A mind which does not stay anywhere and is attached
> Is called 'the field of merits'.
> For the benefit and happiness of all beings
> You should practise meditative absorption; take upon yourself this burden and develop a correct view.
> To burn away all conflicting emotions is the sign of the wise.

It is also the ceremony of greeting. As is stated in the 'Nam.mkha' rin.po.che'i mdo':

> Like water poured into water
> Or oil into oil
> This transcending awareness which is awareness in and through itself
> As a vision of the wholesome, is greeting.

It is also like making an offering. This is asserted in the 'Yab.sras mjal.ba'i mdo' ('Pitāputrasamāgamanasūtra'):

> To rely on Śūnyatā
> And to be interested in the sphere of the Buddhas,
> Is performing unsurpassable worship
> To the Teacher (of mankind, the Buddha).

And in the 'bDud.rtsi gsaṅ.ba'i rgyud' ('Amṛtaguhyatantrarāja'):

To give pleasure and not to burn
Incense is real worship.
The proper functioning of mind (104b)
Is the sublimest and best worship.

When you possess this Śūnyatā, all the evil you have done has been confessed. As is said in the 'Las rnam.par dag.pa'i mdo' ('Karmāvaraṇaviśuddhi'):

He who wants to make a confession
Should eagerly look to what is pure.
To look at purity
Is the best type of contrition.

It is also keeping one's vows about ethics and manners. As is stated in the 'lHa'i bus žus.pa'i mdo' ('Susthitamatidevaputraparipṛcchāsūtra'):

Where mind is not proud of being or not being disciplined
There is the pure ethics of Nirvāṇa.

And in the ''Khor.lo bcu.pa'i mdo':

Though he may live in a house without shaving his head, wearing religious clothes and thinking about ethics, yet if endowed with the Noble Dharma, he is a real Bhikṣu.

It is also hearing, pondering over and paying attention to the Dharma, as is said in the 'Rab.tu mi.gnas.pa'i rgyud':

When the food of genuine peace is eaten
All tenets are satisfied.
A fool clings to words which he does not understand.
(After all,) everything is Mind.

And also Saraha sings:[42]

It is reading, paying attention to and practising the Dharma.
It is also learning it by heart.
There is no concept which can express the Dharma.

It is also exorcism, as recorded in the 'gSaṅ.ba bdud.rtsi rgyal.po'i rgyud' ('Amṛtaguhyatantrarāja'):

When the nature of Mind has been realized
As making offerings and performing exorcism
And all other sorts of works and duties,
(Then you understand that) everything is encompassed by it (105a).

Now since everything is included in the attentive contemplation of reality or the nature of Mind, why have we mentioned so many stages of discriminating awareness? The reason is to guide those who unfortunately know nothing of the ultimate nature of things. As is said in the 'Ye.śes snaṅ.ba rgyan.gyi mdo':

The exposition of conditioned origination
And the teaching about the gradual steps (towards enlightenment)
Are given for the stupid.
How can there be gradual progress
In ultimate reality which is self-authenticated?

In the 'bDe.mchog sdom.pa 'byuṅ.ba' ('Mahāsaṃvarodayatantrarāja'):

Thus, in my real nature vast like celestial space
I have obtained the reality of eternal freedom.

In the 'Nam.mkha' rin.po.che'i mdo':

As long as one has not entered the ocean of Dharmadhātu, the spiritual levels and the paths are said to be stages differing from each other, but when one has entered the ocean of Dharmadhātu then there are no spiritual levels or paths.

And Atīśa declared:

When the mind is composed and centred on the one
There is no need to work for the good with body or speech.

(D) The signs of progress in the practice of discriminating awareness are that we care for the good and wholesome, are less exposed to emotional conflicts, feel compassion for sentient beings, draw nearer reality, give up all unrest, become unattached and cease to covet anything in this life. This is taught in the 'Rin.chen 'phreṅ.ba' ('Ratnāvalī'):

By paying attention to Śūnyatā
One becomes heedful of the good and wholesome.

VII. The result of discriminating awareness is (i) fulfilment and (ii) effectiveness in our situation in life.

(i) Fulfilment is the attainment of unsurpassable enlightenment. As is stated in the 'Śes.rab.kyi pha.rol.tu phyin.pa bdun.brgya.pa' ('Saptaśatikā-prajñāpāramitā'):

Mañjuśrī, when the perfection of discriminating awareness is practised (105b), a Bodhisattva Mahāsattva quickly awakens to unsurpassable perfect enlightenment.

(ii) Effectiveness in our situation in life means that all happiness and all good is manifest. As is written in the ''Phags.pa sdud.pa' ('Prajñāpāramitāsaṃcayagāthā', fol. 33b):

All the good that is found among the Sons of The Buddha,
Śrāvakas, Pratyekabuddhas, gods and men,
Stems from the perfection of discriminating awareness arising from wisdom.

The seventeenth chapter, dealing with the Perfection of Discriminating Awareness arising from Wisdom, from
The Jewel Ornament of Liberation or
The Wish-Fulfilling Gem of the
Noble Doctrine.

NOTES TO CHAPTER 17

1. *śes.rab*, Skt. *prajñā*. The reasons for translating this key term of Buddhist philosophy by 'discriminating awareness arising from wisdom' have been given in note 3 of the Introduction. As the following pages will make clear, *prajñā* is always a function, never a quality, although this does not mean that the former is not qualitatively determined. It has also to be borne in mind that in Buddhist thought quality is not due to the decrees of some extranatural power. The quality of *prajñā* depends upon whether it functions in harmony or conflict with the all-transcending and all-encompassing nature of reality. To be more exact, *prajñā* is a transcending function (*Überleitungsfunktion*). Here 'transcending' is not primarily a metaphysical quality, but signifies the possibility that by the help of *prajñā* we may 'pass beyond' the borders of our habitually unenlightened attitude and enter the realm of spirituality and enlightenment.

2. *thabs*, Skt. *upāya*. This refers to the active aspect of Buddhism. But in stating the meaning thus, we face a difficulty which lies in the ambiguity of our word 'active'. Usually we mean by it 'doing something' and a man who is not engaged in bringing about a change in an existing situation by means of an expenditure of energy is supposed not to be active. In Buddhism, activity is always viewed in the light of its motivation. This distinguishes Buddhist activity from the modern concept of it, which only sees the external 'achievements' and

overlooks the internal driving-force, whether this be a sense of insecurity or the greed for money and power. Such activity is, as the following words of sGam.po.pa explain, 'bondage'; man is really a slave of his passions. But he is free and active (not driven) when he lives by his real nature revealed through discriminating awareness (*prajñā*). And inasmuch as *prajñā* is not the application of or the arrival at a certain set of dogmas, but Śūnyatā, i.e. nothing that can be twisted into some content of the intellect, *thabs* or 'beneficial expediency', is not some publicly applauded act of altruism, but ever-present compassion. The co-extensiveness and ultimate coincidence of beneficial expediency (*thabs*, *upāya*) or compassion (*sñiṅ.rje*, *karuṇā*) and discriminating awareness (*śes.rab*, *prajñā*) or Śūnyatā (*stoṅ.pa.ñid*) is paramount in Tantrism.

3. On this term see Chapter 9, note 54.

4. Some Buddhists believed that certain individuals would never attain liberation. sGam.po.pa does not subscribe to this view. For him every sentient being has the chance to attain salvation by his own efforts. See also above, Chapters 1, note 21; 8, note 15; and 12, note 7.

5. *ñe.bar len.pa'i phuṅ.po*, Skt. *upādānaskandha*. The term *upādāna* in this compound, refers, on the one hand, to the organization of the five psychosomatic constituents into our organism, and on the other is synonymous with *kleśa* 'conflicting emotions'. Thus in a certain sense our organism is always emotionally unstable. See 'Abhidharmakośa' I, 8, and 'Bhāṣya' and my 'Philosophy and Psychology in the Abhidharma', pp. 182, 266 seqq.

6. The Skandhas are the five psychosomatic constituents: *rūpa* 'colour-shape', *vedanā* 'feeling', *saṃjñā* 'sensation-ideation', *saṃskārāḥ* 'motivation' and *vijñāna* 'consciousness'. The Dhātus are the 'elements' organized (or unorganized) into a living organism; and the Āyatanas are the interaction between the Skandhas and Dhātus.

7. *dṅos.po*, Skt. *bhāva*. This term has a wider range of meaning than our 'existence'. It also denotes 'materiality', 'substantiality'. An understanding of this refutation will be helped by bearing in mind that 'existence' is no predicate. The Buddhists are here in agreement with modern philosophy.

8. *bdag*, Skt. *ātman*. This has been variously conceived in different systems of philosophy. As far as the non-Buddhist systems were concerned the tendency has been to regard Ātman as a Pure Ego. This the Buddhists rejected. For them reality or the ultimate always remained ineffable and the attempt to determine it as this or that was declared by them to be a sign of low intelligence and defective logic.

9. See above, note 5.

10. *mi.byed.dgu.byed.*

11. In a different context we find this argument in Western philosophies. Here it is used against the Causal Argument of the existence of God. See John Hospers, 'An Introduction to Philosophical Analysis', p. 330, note 20.

12. This argument should not lead us astray in assuming that Buddhism does not recognize causality. The Buddhist conception differs from our common one in that it does not accept an external causal agent which acts as a *deus ex machina*. There is agency, but it is within the process itself; it *is* this process. In passing it may be remarked that Buddhist Tantrism, the peak of Buddhist philosophy, recognizes causality as a timeless concept. Here causality is not abolished but it cannot be expressed in conventional terms. It is circular rather than plotted on linear time.

13. A name or a word is a conventional assignment. There are no right or wrong words for things.

14. Cp. 'Abhidharmakośa' I, 43, and 'Bhāṣya' (p. 90).

15. ibid., p. 92.

16. This problem has been dealt with more exhaustively in Diṅnāga's 'Ālambanaparīkṣā', 2a, and the commentary by Vinītadeva.

17. *raṅ.gi sems*. Literally translated this would mean 'one's mind'. The commonest temptation is then to interpret it as 'one's own mind' and arrive at some mentalistic solipsism. However, it does not mean 'my' or 'your mind', but 'Mind'. The capital letter is used here to distinguish it from the 'individual mind' and to point out that it does not mean an entity. It is, to use philosophical jargon, noetic nothingness as a necessary condition for the attainment of knowledge. As the noetic *act* this nothingness (*raṅ.gi sems*, Śūnyatā) is termed *raṅ.rig* (*raṅ.gi rig.pa*). As happened so often with philosophers all over the world, a linguistic expression has led them to postulate metaphysical systems and heap invective on those who do not accept them. So also in Buddhism this term *raṅ.rig* has been explained by certain schools as 'mind cognizing itself', 'mind' being, as it were, one entity and the 'itself' another.

18. *'khrul.pa*, Skt. *bhrānti*. On this term see Chapter 1, note 6.

19. *snaṅ.ba*, Skt. *pratibhāsa*. See Chapter 1, note 7.

20. This is said by the Mādhyamikas to be the view of the Vijñānavādins. It may, however, be doubted whether the Mādhyamikas gave a fair rendering of the Vijñānavāda philosophy. It is true the Vijñānavādins postulated Mind to exist *substantialiter* (*dravyataḥ*), thus continuing the Vaibhāṣika realism, which goes against all logical

analysis, but that they thought of Mind as cognizing itself seems to have been imputed to them by the Mādhyamikas who fell into a linguistic trap in their eagerness to keep philosophy from becoming stagnant.

21. Mind is not an entity, at best it is a symbol pointing to something ineffable.

22. This is a famous verse which Tilopa spoke while giving spiritual instruction to Nāropa. See 'mKhas.grub kun.gyi gtsug.brgyan/paṇ.chen Na.ro.pa'i rnam.thar/ṅo.mtshar smad.byuṅ', fol. 38a. It has been commented upon by Padma dkar.po in his 'bSre.'pho'i lam.skor.gyi thog.mar lam dbye.bsdu', fol. 90a seqq. The name of the author is written variously in Tibetan works: Te.lo.pa, Ti.lo.pa and Ti.lli.pa.

23. Cp. Saraha's 'sKu'i mdzod 'chi.med rdo.rje'i glu' ('Kāyakoṣāmṛtavajragīti'), bsTan.'gyur (Derge edition), rgyud, vol. ži, fol. 110b:

> However one may seek and investigate, it has no reference to an object,
> It has no origin, it does not conceive
> And it is without a cause for not conceiving.
> Memory and association is like a phantom, but this awareness
> Is nothing phantom-like, is without (the necessity of) being liberated, without memory and association, is radiant light.

24. Although non-existence is the denial of existence, the fact that we can think of that which does not exist, has led certain philosophers to assume a 'mode' of existence, termed subsistence. The original term, *dṅos.med*, Skt. *abhāva*, oscillates between the two meanings 'non-existence' and 'subsistence'. In rejecting 'subsistence' Buddhism shares the view of modern logical analysis. See Alfred Jules Ayer, 'Language, Truth and Logic', pp. 43 seq.

25. 'Mi.zad.pa'i gter.mdzod man.ṅag.gi glu' ('Dohākoṣa-upadeśa-gīti'), bsTan.'gyur (Derge edition), rgyud, vol. ži, fol. 29a.

26. Śūnyatā is not an entity, be it existent or non-existent (subsistent). It is a term or symbol used in instructing others. To conceive the name as the thing is to close one's eyes to Śūnyatā. In other words, Śūnyatā is pure transcendence; the moment we conceive it as something we divest it of its transcending character and develop a theory which is open to all sorts of attacks.

27. 'Mūlamadhyamakakārikā' XXIV, 11.

28. That is to say, those who make Śūnyatā a content of their mind, thereby turning it into an ordinary object of cognition, increase

the disease from which they suffer. The disease is their rationalism which leads to spiritual suicide.

29. 'Bodhicaryāvatāra' IX, 103–4.

30. 'Mūlamadhyamakakārikā' XXV, 7.

31. This verse is often quoted. It is also found, as far as the beginning is concerned, in 'Mahāyānottaratantraśāstra' I, 154.

32. See above, note 17.

33. The Mahāmudrā experience is the central theme of Buddhist Tantrism.

34. *drod*, Skt. *uṣmagata*. 'Heat' in the meditative process is a sign of success. As to its importance see 'Abhidharmakośa' VI, 17; and my 'Philosophy and Psychology in the Abhidharma', p. 334: 'Thus as the first indication of success there arises heat (*uṣmagata*), which is not only felt bodily but is both a distinct mental event and a force that burns away emotional instability. This heat may last for quite a long time—as long as the concentrative state of absorption continues—and will gradually increase until it reaches its maximum value or "top" (*mūrdhan*). Both the initial and the top heat bear on the Four Truths, each Truth revealing four aspects, so that a total of sixteen aspects obtains', and pp. 362 seq.: 'The first quality ("heat", *uṣmagata*) is the realization that the objective constituents of our perceptual situations are not external, physical objects, but "mental addresses" (*manojalpa*) in the sense that what had been called the intrinsic character or the nature of a thing (*svalakṣaṇa*) and its general characteristic (*sāmānyalakṣaṇa*) are "discourses" within a purely perceptual "world". This stage is also termed "clarity" (*āloka*) and is synonymous with an acceptance of that which has been found by a thorough investigation into the nature of things (*dharmanidhyānakṣānti*).'

35. *dran.pa*, Skt. *smṛti*. This is a highly ambiguous term. In ordinary usage it means 'memory', 'remembrance', 'recollection'. Without going into an analysis of the equally ambiguous term 'memory', 'remembrance' and 'recollection' are distinguished from each other in that 'remembrance' primarily applies to the act or the process of remembering, while 'recollection' not only refers to the act of remembering but also emphasizes the act or process of bringing back into the mind something which has been forgotten. (See Webster's 'Dictionary of Synonyms'.) However, Padma dkar.po in his 'Phyag. rgya.chen.po'i man.ṅag.gi bśad.sbyar rgyal.ba'i gan.mdzod', fol. 88a, points out that this meaning of *dran.pa* does not hold for meditation. Here it means not to let go of the object of one's contemplation. The same definition is given in 'Abhidharmakośa' II, 24. In order to

distinguish the two meanings of *dran.pa*, Skt. *smṛti*, I have, following the analysis of C. D. Broad in his 'The Mind and its Place in Nature', p. 295, adopted the term 'inspection' whenever the word is used in connection with meditative processes. That one word should be used for two different things is unfortunate, but due to a certain relation between memory and inspection. In this connection C. D. Broad's words (loc. cit., p. 299) may be quoted: 'Inspection itself is not memory. The purely inspective situation does not refer to the past; it merely professes to describe the apparent characteristics of its own objective constituent. But the objective constituent of an inspective situation is very often the objective constituent of a co-existing memory-situation. And the epistemological object of this memory-situation is such that, if anything corresponds to it, this corresponding object is the objective constituent of an immediately previous perceptual situation or of some other immediately previous situation such as a memory-situation. In so far as we profess to be learning by inspection about the apparent characteristics of the objective constituent of a perceptual or memory situation, we are relying, not on inspection alone, but on inspection and memory.' When Prof. Broad on p. 300 about inspection says that 'I try to keep the perceptual situation as nearly constant as I can, and to inspect the objective constituent of *that* situation or of others as like as it is possible', he has given a most exact definition of the Buddhist technical term *dran.pa* (*smṛti*) as used in texts on meditation: *dran.pa ni ma.yeṅs.pa ste* 'Inspection is not to let go' ('Phyag.rgya.chen.po'i man.ṅag.gi bśad.sbyar rgyal.ba'i gan. mdzod', fol. 88a, cp. 33a).

36. Sluggishness and frivolity are the enemies of meditative absorption. They are mentioned as such in 'Phyag.rgya.chen.po'i man.ṅag.gi bśad.sbyar rgyal.ba'i gan.mdzod', fol. 87a.

37. 'Attentive contemplation of the sky' is a technical term which refers to an experience in which the object has lost its external reference and which we are wont to call 'pure sensation'. The sky as a vast expanse of blue is particularly suited to produce this experience as its uniformity does not distract us.

38. Although the exact term would be 'discriminating awareness' I have dropped the attribute here and in several other passages, because we cannot speak of discrimination where there is not anyone any more. The Buddhist technical term does not encounter this difficulty, because it is more than mere discrimination and so can be used for that which is beyond it.

39. These two types of knowledge are different for the Bodhisattvas, they only become one for the Buddhas. In other words Buddhahood

is not a state where, oblivious to the world, one is immersed in the vision of something ineffable and overwhelming, but it means living in the world out of transcendence. A further discussion of these two types of awareness is given in Chapter 20.

40. All these determinations have their root in ontological speculations which Buddhism abhors. That reality is without this or that does not mean that reality is one thing and this or that another. Reality has nothing to do with the concepts we create about it and then believe to encompass it.

41. The deities and their mantras appear out of and fade back into Śūnyatā. The deities mentioned here are also terms for certain phases in the Developing Stage (*bskyed.rim*, Skt. *utpannakrama*) of Hevajra. See the 'Kye.rdo.rje lha dgu'i mṅon.rtogs dkyil.'khor.gyi cho.ga daṅ bcas.pa dṅos.grub.kyi gter.mdzod', fol. 3a seqq.

42. Dohākoṣa, verse No. 19.

18
THE FIVE PATHS

AFTER A MAN has begun to look towards enlightenment and has wrestled with the various disciplines, he gradually attains the levels of spirituality and follows the paths which lead to a Bodhisattva's enlightenment. These five are

> The Paths of Preparation, Application,
> Seeing, Practice and
> Fulfilment.

They are taught in the 'Byaṅ.chub lam.sgron' ('Bodhipathapradīpa') as follows. The Path of Preparation means that an individual of the lower and middle orders (of spiritual qualities) lays the foundation for enlightenment by paying attention to the Dharma, then adopts an enlightened attitude of aspiration and perseverance and finally strives to accumulate the two types of merit.[1] The Path of Application is indicated (in the 'Bodhipathapradīpa') by the words:

> By gradually obtaining the experience of meditative heat,[2]

and the Paths of Seeing, Practice and Fulfilment are referred to by the following words:

> Attains the (spiritual level) 'The Joyful One' and the others.[3]

(A) The Path of Preparation.[4]

An individual who belongs to a spiritual family,[5] first adopts an enlightened attitude (106a), then listens to the instructions of his teacher and strives for the good and wholesome until he acquires the spiritual awareness which comes with the experience of meditative heat.[6] This stage is fourfold according to whether this experience has been attained through intuitive understanding, devoted interest, benevolent and compassionate intention or spiritual attainment. It is called the Path of Preparation because on it the good and wholesome accumulate so that the aspirant becomes a suitable vessel for receiving all that goes with an intuitive understanding of reality which begins with and is accompanied by the feeling of meditative heat. Another reason is the ground of the good and wholesome which leads to liberation. At this stage twelve of the essentials for enlightenment[7] are dealt with: (i–iv) the four objects of inspection (*dran.pa ñe.bar gžag.pa bži, smṛtyupasthāna*), (v–viii) the four attempts at rejection and acquisition (*yaṅ.dag.par spoṅ.ba bži, samyakprahāṇa*) and (ix–xii) the four types of absorption (*rdzu.'phrul.gyi rkaṅ.pa bži, ṛddhipāda*).

The four objects of inspection are that which constitutes our physical life, feelings and disposition, and that which we call the whole of reality. These are part of the lower Path of Preparation.

The four attempts at rejection and acquisition are to give up the evil and unwholesome that has already arisen and not to allow more to rise, to create and then increase the good and wholesome in opposition. These belong to the middle Path of Preparation.

The four types of absorption are by strong interest, strenuousness, disposition and investigation. They are on the superior Path of Preparation.

(B) The Path of Application.[8]

It follows the superior one of Preparation. In it originates an intuitive understanding of the Four Truths and the four corresponding qualities conducive to climax a spiritual awareness of reality,[9] which are meditative heat (106b), a patient acceptance and highest worldly realization.[10] This is called the Path of Application because at this stage one concentrates on understanding the Truths.

Further at this stage of meditative heat and its climax there are five controlling powers:[11] confidence, energy, inspection, meditative absorption and discriminating awareness, while at that of patient acceptance and highest worldy realization the same are effective as unshakable forces.[12]

(C) The Path of Seeing.[13]

It opens up after highest worldly realization has been attained. It entails tranquillity[14] which has as its object the Four Truths and the corresponding insight.[15] Each Truth has four aspects, viz. a patient acceptance which produces the awareness that everything is unsatisfactory (*duḥkhe dharmajñānakṣānti*), the (actual) awareness that everything is unsatisfactory (*duḥkhe dharmajñāna*), a subsequent patient acceptance leading to the awareness that even the higher worlds (Rūpadhātu and Ārūpyadhātu) are unsatisfactory (*duḥkhe anvayajñānakṣānti*) and the actual awareness of the unsatisfactoriness of the higher worlds (*duḥkhe anvayajñāna*), so that there is a total of sixteen types of awareness (*jñāna*) and patient acceptance (*kṣānti*).[16] This is called the Path of Seeing because the four Noble Truths which have not been sighted before, are seen now. At this stage there are seven elements of enlightenment,[17] namely, inspection, discriminating awareness, energy, enthusiasm, relaxation, meditative absorption and equanimity.

(D) The Path of Practice.[18]

It begins as soon as that of Seeing is followed (107a). It consists of (i) a worldly and (ii) a spiritual path.

(i) The worldly path of practice covers the first, second, third and fourth grades of meditative concentration (*dhyāna*), the infinities of space, consciousness, no-thing-whatsoever-ness and neither-sensation nor non-sensation. In its practice there are three necessary divisions: (a) crushing those conflicting emotions which remain after seeing the Truths and which can be overcome only by attentiveness (*sgom. spaṅs.kyi ñon.moṅs, bhāvanāheya kleśa*); (b) achieving the special virtues of the 'Immeasurables' (benevolence, compassion, joy, equanimity) and (c) laying the foundation for the spiritual path.

(ii) The spiritual path of practice means tranquillity, which has as its object the two types of spiritual awareness[19] and the corresponding insight. Moreover, on the Path of Seeing, each of the Four Truths has two 'acceptances' (*kṣānti*) and two 'awarenesses' (*jñāna*). Of these sixteen aspects the eight *kṣāntis* are merely seeing and therefore belong to the Path of Seeing proper, while the eight *jñānas* are related to the four types of meditative concentration (*dhyāna*) and the three formless attainments[20] and belong already to the Path of Practice. Further, the practice of intuitively understanding the nature of reality forms the awareness that everything is unsatisfactory, while the deepening of this awareness is the subsequent spiritual awareness that the higher worlds are also unsatisfactory.[21]

The stage of neither-sensation nor non-sensation is worldly, because sensation is unstable and unclear.

All this is called the Path of Practice because it entails practising the understanding acquired on the Path of Seeing (107b). At this stage the eight sections of the Noble Eightfold Path have to be followed: right view, conception, speech, action, life, exertion (circumspection-)inspection and meditative absorption.[22]

(E) The Path of Fulfilment.[23]

It follows the Absorption which is as indestructible as a Vajra (Vajropamasamādhi) and consists of the awareness that all the causes of misery have lost their power (*zad.pa śes.pa, kṣayajñāna*) and that they will never rise again (*mi.skye.ba śes.pa, anutpattijñāna*).

Vajropamasamādhi is the occasion for the Path of Abandonment[24] which follows that of Practice, and is subsumed under those of application and unobstructedness.[25] This state of absorption is considered to be like a Vajra, because it is indestructible, hard and stable, has the same emotional value throughout and is all-pervasive.

'Indestructible' means that it cannot be obstructed by worldliness; 'hard' that it cannot be destroyed by any impurities; and 'stable' that it cannot be shaken by discursiveness. 'Having the same emotional value throughout' means that it possesses one and the same emotional feeling tone (of bliss), and 'all-pervasive' that its reference is the ultimate nature of everything knowable.

The awareness that all the causes of misery have lost their power (*kṣayajñāna*) which results from this absorption, has as its object the Four Truths by virtue of the fact that all 'causes' have disappeared.

The awareness that these causes will never be effective again (*anutpattijñāna*) also has as its object the Four Truths because misery has been given up.

Another reason for these names is that the 'cause' has lost its power (*kṣaya*) and that no 'effect' is produced (*anutpatti*).

All this is termed the Path of Fulfilment because training has ceased and the path leading to the citadel of Nirvāṇa has been travelled to its end (108a). At this stage there are ten attainments for which we need no longer train ourselves (*mi.slob.pa'i chos, aśaikṣa-dharma*), starting with right view and ending with right meditative absorption, increased by right liberation (*mi.slob.pa'i rnam.par grol. ba, aśaikṣī samyagvimukti*) and right mystic illumination (*mi.slob.pa'i yaṅ.dag.pa'i ye.śes, aśaikṣa samyagjñāna*).[26]

These ten attainments form four immaculate groups:

(i) Right speech, action and life are the Group of Ethics and Manners;
(ii) Right (circumspection-)inspection and meditative absorption that of Meditative Absorption;
(iii) Right view, conception, and exertion that of Discriminating Awareness; and
(iv) Right liberation is the Group of Freedom and right mystic illumination the (sub)Group of Seeing in the Illuminated Knowledge of Liberation.[27]

The eighteenth chapter, dealing with the Aspects of the Paths, from
The Jewel Ornament of Liberation or
The Wish-Fulfilling Gem of the
Noble Doctrine.

NOTES TO CHAPTER 18

1. More precisely, the aspirant strives to accumulate merits by practising the perfections and to acquire spiritual awareness through meditative concentration.

2. 'Bodhipathapradīpa', 69b.

3. ibid., 69c.

4. *tshogs.lam, sambhāramārga.*

5. *rigs, gotra.* The meaning has been discussed in Chapter 1.

6. *drod, uṣmagata.* See Chapter 17, note 34.

7. *byaṅ.chub.kyi phyogs.kyi chos, bodhipākṣika dharma.* All in all there are thirty-seven essentials of enlightenment. Twelve have been mentioned here. Another ten belong to the Path of Application: the next seven to the Path of Seeing and the remaining eight to the Path of Practice. All of them have been mentioned by sGam.po.pa in their proper context.

8. *sbyor.lam, prayogamārga.*

9. *rjes.su mthun.pa ṅes.'byed, nirvedhabhāgīya.* According to the 'Bhāṣya' ad 'Abhidharmakośa' VI, 20, *nirvedha* means 'decidedly true penetration of the aim' because the Four Truths are clearly distinguished and hence doubts are resolved. See also my 'Philosophy and Psychology in the Abhidharma', pp. 328 seqq., 334, 343, 362.

10. *drod* (*uṣmagata*), *rtse.mo* (*mūrdhan*), *bzod.pa* (*kṣānti*), and *'jig. rten.chos.mchog* (*laukikāgradharma*). See also Chapter 17, note 34. I have explained the importance of these four states of experience in my 'Philosophy and Psychology in the Abhidharma', pp. 334 seq., as follows: 'Both "heat" and its "maximum value" are pathways on which we can proceed as well as fall back. Their main function is to lead us to a more vivid realization and a deeper understanding of the nature of the constituents of our reality. After the "maximum value" has passed through three degrees of intensity it is on the highest degree that there occurs an event of the greatest importance and of momentary duration. It is the acceptance (*kṣānti*) of the validity of the Truths which have been directly experienced, and which also has three degrees of intensity. Out of the last there results an experience which is termed "highest worldly realization" (*laukikāgradharma*) which like the preceding event is of momentary duration. Acceptance and highest worldly realization are the culminating points of modifiable processes. Heat and its maximum value may be directed to an understanding of the Truths in such a way that the ultimate and highest level of knowledge may be achieved. However, due to the fact that through those experiences of heat and its maximum

value we come to understand certain aspects of reality which we had not observed or taken the time to attend to, we may at any moment come to an acceptance of that which we perceive even if it would be possible to proceed to a deeper understanding. In other words, we may stop before we have exhausted all possibilities. Once this happens we are stuck. It is, therefore, necessary to postpone acceptance as long as possible. The point where acceptance sets in is not only the final limit to the preceding process, it also separates one class of individuals from the other ones. It is out of the levels of spiritual penetration, i.e. from the demarcation line of the setting in of acceptance, that the spiritual classes of individuals (*gotra*) such as the Śrāvaka, Pratyekabuddha and the Buddha lineages come about.'

11. *dbaṅ.po, indriya.*

12. *stobs, bala.* The distinction between 'controlling powers' and 'unshakable forces' emphasizes the nature of meditation as a modifiable process. The 'controlling powers' direct the course of meditative concentration, while the 'unshakable forces' set in with 'acceptance' (*kṣānti*) whereby we stop pursuing meditation further.

13. *mthoṅ. lam, darśanamārga.*

14. *ži.gnas, śamatha.*

15. *lhag.mthoṅ, vipaśyana.*

16. The term *duḥkhe* refers to the First Noble Truth of the Misery and Unsatisfactoriness of our world of desires (Kāmadhātu). When it is replaced by *samudaye* we have the Second Noble Truth of the Origination of Misery and Unsatisfactoriness; by replacing this with *nirodhe* we come to the Third Noble Truth of the Cessation of Misery and Unsatisfactoriness; and by replacing this in turn with *mārge* we have the Fourth Truth of the Path towards the Cessation of Misery and Unsatisfactoriness. Since each Truth has two *kṣāntis* and two *jñānas*, the first *kṣānti* and *jñāna* referring to Kāmadhātu and the second *kṣānti* and *jñāna* to the Rūpadhātu and Ārūpyadhātu (accessible through meditation in its double aspect of form and formlessness) we have eight *kṣāntis* and eight *jñānas*, which counted together form the sixteen aspects of the Truths. See also my 'Philosophy and Psychology in the Abhidharma', p. 338.

17. *byaṅ.chub.kyi yan.lag, bodhyaṅga.*

18. *sgom.lam, bhāvanāmārga.*

19. The two types of spiritual awareness are here *dharmajñāna* and *anvayajñāna*, the former referring to the world of sensuality (Kāmadhātu) and the latter to the meditative worlds (Rūpadhātu and Ārūpyadhātu).

20. The four types of meditation (*dhyāna*) are the first, second, third and fourth *dhyānas* and the three formless attainments are the infinities of space, consciousness and no-thing-whatsoever-ness. They have been discussed in Chapter 6, p. 80.

21. The same explanation is found in 'Abhidharmakośa' VI, 26.

22. The reason why *samyaksmṛti* (Tib. *yaṅ.dag.pa'i dran.pa*) has been translated 'inspection' has been given in note 35 of Chapter 17. Although strictly speaking the Noble Eightfold Path is born from meditation, it goes beyond the meditative process and affects the whole life of the individual. I have added here 'circumspection' in order to show that in a wider context circumspection will help to preserve 'inspection'.

23. *mthar phyin.pa'i lam, niṣṭhāmārga.*

24. *spoṅ.ba'i lam, prahāṇamārga.* It is here that one gets rid of all impediments to the attainment of Nirvāṇa. See my 'Philosophy and Psychology in the Abhidharma', p. 326.

25. *bar.chad med.pa'i lam, ānantaryamārga.* See my 'Philosophy and Psychology in the Abhidharma', pp. 327, 337, 346 seq. 372, 375.

26. 'Abhidharmakośa' VI, 75, and 'Bhāṣya' (p. 295).

27. ibid., VI, 76 (p. 297).

19

THE SPIRITUAL LEVELS

THESE FIVE PATHS lead through thirteen spiritual levels, which are summarized thus:

> The two levels of the beginner and of devoted interest and behaviour,
> The ten belonging to the Bodhisattvas and
> That of a Buddha.

They are indicated in the 'Byaṅ.chub.lam.sgron' ('Bodhipathapradīpa', 69c) by the words:

> Attains (the spiritual level) 'The Joyful One' and the others.

'The Joyful One' is the first spiritual level and 'the others' refer to the two lower and ten higher levels.

Of these the beginner's level is the stage of the Path of Preparation because here the stream of our life and consciousness is brought to maturity.

The level of devoted interest and behaviour is the Path of Application because on it attention is devoted unceasingly to the meaning of Śūnyatā (108b). During this period, avarice and the other vices which oppose the perfections, as well as the particular type of emotional instability which can be overcome by a mere glimpse of Truth,[1] and primitive beliefs about reality which are all merely imagined, are subdued so that these disturbing factors do not rise again.

The Bodhisattvas' ten levels range from the first, 'The Joyful One', to the tenth, the 'Cloud of Dharma'. This is stated in the ''Phags.pa sa.bcu.pa'i mdo' ('Daśabhūmikasūtra', p. 5):

> Oh sons of the Victorious One, these ten levels are those of the Bodhisattvas, The Joyful One and the others.

The first spiritual level is the beginning of the Path of Seeing, which entails a realistic understanding of the meaning of Śūnyatā.

The second to the tenth level is the Path of Practice of that which has already been understood.

These ten levels of the Bodhisattvas are to be known in (i) a general and (ii) a particular way.

(i) The general way consists of understanding (a) the essence, (b) the significance of the term 'level' and (c) the reason for there being ten of them.

(a) The essence is learnedness characterized by meditative absorption which results from the awareness of the non-individuality of all constituents of reality.

(b) They are called 'levels' because each is the foundation of the qualities that belong to it and each leads to the one above or beyond it. Another meaning is that those on them constantly enjoy a transcending awareness, chewing the cud like a cow in a pen. They run through what they know like a horse on a racecourse. Or, since this awareness is the birthplace (109a) of all virtues, it is called 'level' like an arable field.

(c) There are ten levels because of the special preparations required for each.

(ii) The particular way has nine divisions for each spiritual level: (a) the special name, (b) significance, (c) preparation, (d) attention, (e) purification, (f) understanding, (g) rejection, (h) place of birth and (i) power.

(Ia) The special name of the first is 'The Joyful One' (*rab.tu dga'.ba, pramuditā*).

(Ib) Its special significance is that there is joy, because with the attainment of this level we are near enlightenment and the welfare of others is safeguarded. As is stated in the 'mDo.sde.rgyan' ('Mahāyāna-sūtrālaṅkāra' XX–XXI, 32):

By being near enlightenment
And seeing the welfare of others assured,
Joy is born;
Therefore this level is called The Joyful One.

(Ic) The special preparation involves attending to the preparatory actions such as never having deceitful intentions. As is laid down in the 'mṄon.rtogs.rgyan' ('Abhisamayālaṅkāra' I, 48 seq.):[2]

By ten preparations
This first level is attained.

(Id) The special attention means that although Bodhisattvas on this level practise the ten perfections,[3] they devote most of their time to that of liberality. They desire to satisfy all sentient beings. As is said in the ''Phags.pa sa.bcu.pa'i mdo' ('Daśabhūmikasūtra', p. 20):

On the first level liberality is the most important perfection (109b). But this does not mean that the other nine are not practised.

(Ie) The special purification is described in the 'Sa.bcu.pa' ('Daśabhūmikasūtra', p. 19):

> On the level 'The Joyful One', by virtue of a broad outlook and a strong determination, many times ten million million Buddhas appear. Having seen them the Bodhisattva venerates and honours them with great devotion and respects their followers. The foundation on which the good and wholesome rest is dedicated to unsurpassable enlightenment. The Bodhisattva hears the Dharma from the Buddhas, takes it to heart, holds it and attends assiduously to it. Gathering sentient beings around him[4] with the four methods, he brings them to maturity.

Thus the foundations of the good and wholesome become very extensive by (i) venerating and conferring benefits on the Buddhas, the Dharma and the Sangha for many aeons, (ii) bringing sentient beings to spiritual maturity, and (iii) dedicating the foundations to unsurpassable enlightenment. As is stated:[5]

> Just as a craftsman heats fine gold in the fire, and the more he does so the purer, clearer and more useful it becomes, so a Bodhisattva's foundations of the good and wholesome on the first level become very pure, bright and useful for all kinds of activity.

(If) The special understanding means, generally speaking, to realize that the ten levels (110a) are identical as far as mystic illumination (*mñam.gžag*, *samāhitajñāna*) is concerned, but differ in subsequent presentational knowledge (*rjes*, *pṛṣṭhalabdhajñāna*). Thus on the first level the Dharmadhātu is considered as 'universal' (extending everywhere). By this the 'sameness' of self and others is realized. Hence the 'dbUs.mtha'' ('Madhyāntavibhāga') speaks of

> Universal(ity).

(Ig) The special rejection means that on this level eighty-two types of conflicting emotions, all of them capable of being overcome by a mere glimpse of Truth,[6] are abandoned completely, while the outer layer of primitive beliefs about reality is stripped like bark from a tree. Also there is freedom from the five types of fear. As is stated in the ''Phags.pa sa.bcu.pa'i mdo' ('Daśabhūmikasūtra', p. 12):

> Attainment of the level of 'The Joyful One' at once dispels the five fears of (i) not making a living, (ii) bad reputation, (iii) death, (iv) evil lives and (v) subjection to anxiety while in this world (Saṃsāra).

(Ih) The special place of birth means that a Bodhisattva who has attained this level, becomes a universal monarch in India and removes the reproach of miserliness from sentient beings. As is expressed in the 'Rin.chen 'phreṅ.ba' ('Ratnāvalī'):

> By this spiritual maturity
> They become universal monarchs in the human world (Jambudvīpa).

Although this particular place of birth may be thought of as inherent to this level, yet the Bodhisattvas incarnate again and again for the benefit of those who are to be educated and brought to maturity, as is related in the 'sKyes.rab' ('Jātakamālā').

(Ii) (110b) The special power means that:[7]

> A Bodhisattva on the level of 'The Joyful One' willingly strives hard. Since he has renounced life as a householder, he experiences in a fraction of a moment a hundred meditative absorptions and sees a hundred Buddhas and recognizes their sustaining power.[8] He shakes a hundred world systems, walks over a hundred Buddha realms and illumines a hundred world spheres. He brings a hundred beings to spiritual maturity, lives for a hundred aeons and knows them from beginning to end. He opens a hundred doors to the Dharma and manifests a hundred times, on each occasion gathering a hundred Bodhisattva followers.

(IIa) The special name of the second spiritual level is 'The Stainless One' (*dri.ma med.pa, vimalā*).

(IIb) Its special significance is stainlessness because it is free from the reproach of violated ethics and manners. Therefore

> Because it is free from the impurity of violated ethics
> It is called the Stainless Level.[9]

(IIc) The special preparation means following eight preparatory practices such as devotion to ethics and manners, gratitude and other virtues, as is stated:[10]

> Ethics, gratitude, patience,
> Joy and great compassion.

(IId) The special attention means particular concentration on the perfection of ethics and manners without neglecting the other nine.

(IIe) The special purification means greatly extending the foundations of the good and the wholesome (111a).

> Just as fine gold is purified still further by being dipped in vitriol and remelted, so on this second level a Bodhisattva's

foundations of the good and wholesome are further enlarged, purified and made more fit for work.[10a]

(IIf) The special understanding is to appreciate the Dharmadhātu as of the highest value. The Bodhisattva thinks: 'I must exert myself to attain it in every way.' Therefore,

> The highest value.[11]

(IIg) The special rejection means that on this second level and up to the tenth, the sixty types of conflicting emotions which can be overcome by practising Truth,[12] are rejected as far as their overt form is concerned, though their possibilities of manifestation remain as yet untouched. The inner layer of beliefs about reality is stripped like the under-bark of a tree.

(IIh) The special place of birth means that a Bodhisattva as a rule becomes a universal monarch in one of the four mythical continents, restrains beings from the path of evil actions and puts them on that of the ten wholesome actions.[13] As is stated:

> By this spiritual maturity
> Adorned with seven precious jewels
> They become universal monarchs for the welfare of beings.

(IIi) The special power leads to his attaining a thousand meditative absorptions in a fraction of a moment.

The rest is as above (Ii) where a thousand is to be read instead of a hundred.

(IIIa) The special name of the third spiritual level is 'The Illumining One' (*'od byed.pa, prabhākarī*).

(IIIb) Its special significance is that the Dharma and meditative absorption are very bright and shed a clear light on others. As is stated:[14]

> Because it produces the bright light of the Dharma
> It is called the Illumining Level (111b).

(IIIc) The special preparation involves striving in five ways such as never tiring of listening to the Dharma. As is said:[15]

> Insatiable to listen to the Dharma,
> Imparting it without considering material gain.

(IIId) The special attention means to single out patience in particular without neglecting the other nine perfections.

(IIIe) The special purification results once more in the foundations of the good and wholesome becoming very pure.

Just as fine gold loses no weight from being purified, so a Bodhisattva's foundations of the good and wholesome do not decrease but become even purer and more fit for work.[16]

(IIIf) The special understanding means that he is aware of how instruction in the Dharma emanates from the Dharmadhātu. He will plunge through three thousand fires to listen to its praise. Therefore[17]

Instruction in the Dharma derives from the highest value.

(IIIg) (There is no special rejection.)[18]

(IIIh) The special place of birth means that a Bodhisattva usually becomes Indra, king of gods. As is said:

As king of gods he is skilled
And diverts beings from sensual desires.

(IIIi) The special power enables him to experience a hundred thousand meditative absorptions.

The rest as above with the change in number.

(IVa) The special name of the fourth spiritual level is 'The Flaming One' (*'od 'phro.ba, arciṣmatī*).

(IVb) Its special significance is that (112a) the flames of the knowledge of what leads to enlightenment burn the two veils of conflicting emotions and primitive beliefs about reality. Hence

Thus the elements leading to enlightenment
Are like a consuming fire.
Endowed with which, this level
Is called The Flaming One, because it consumes duality.[19]

(IVc) The special preparation consists of ten practices such as:

Living in solitude, having few desires, knowing moderation and
Adhering to a discipline properly purified.[20]

(IVd) The special attention means being strenuous without neglecting the other nine perfections.

(IVe) The special purification once more concerns the foundations of the good and wholesome. As is said:[21]

Just as gold worked by a clever jeweller into an ornament gains in value from his skill, so a Bodhisattva's foundations of the good and wholesome are superior to those on lower levels.

(IVf) The special understanding means that he regards reality as beyond appropriation and so stops thinking of it as an entity. As has been stated:[22]

Not to be appropriated.

(IVg) (There is no special rejection.)

(IVh) The special place of birth means that a Bodhisattva generally becomes a king of gods among the Suyāma. As is said:

> He becomes a king of gods among the Suyāma
> And is skilled in crushing
> The belief that the body alone is real[23] (112b).

(IVi) The special power is the attainment of a million meditative absorptions.

(Va) The special name of the fifth spiritual level is 'The One Difficult to Conquer' (*śin.tu sbyaṅ dka'.ba, sudurjayā*).

(Vb) Its special significance is derived from this name, because on this level there are two difficulties, (i) striving to bring sentient beings to spiritual maturity while (ii) not becoming emotionally unstable when they make a mess of everything done for them. As is stated:

> To assure the benefit of sentient beings
> And to guard one's mind
> Are difficult for judicious people.
> Therefore this level is called The One Difficult to Conquer.[24]

(Vc) The special preparation means renouncing ten acts such as associating with householders for the sake of gain. As is laid down:

> To long for acquaintances and homes,
> To live in places of unrest.[25]

(Vd) The special attention is specializing in meditative concentration while not forgetting the other nine perfections.

(Ve) The special purification deals once again with the good and wholesome.

> Just as fine gold wiped clean by a skilful worker and studded with precious stones is incomparable and cannot be surpassed by other gold, a Bodhisattva's grounding in the good and wholesome becomes very pure, being tested by beneficial expediency and discriminating awareness, and is superior to that of the lower levels.[26]

(Vf) The special understanding is that reality is not diverse. He knows the ten types of 'sameness'. As is said:

> Non-diversification of kinds.[27]

(Vg) (There is no special rejection.)

(Vh) The special place of birth means that as a rule he becomes a king of the Tuṣita gods:

By this spiritual maturity
He becomes a king among the Tuṣita gods
And refutes the unbalanced views
Of all non-Buddhists.

(Vi) The special power is realizing one thousand ten-million meditative absorptions in the fraction of a moment.

(VIa) The special name of the sixth spiritual level is 'The One Which is Present' (*mṅon.du gyur.pa, abhimukhī*).

(VIb) Its special significance is that on this level a Bodhisattva is neither in Saṃsāra nor Nirvāṇa, since these are present there in a pure state. As is written:

Because by relying on the perfection of discriminating awareness arising from wisdom
Saṃsāra and Nirvāṇa are
Both present,
This level is called The One Which is Present.[28]

(VIc) The special preparation is practising six virtues such as liberality and giving up six vices such as desiring to reach the levels of Śrāvakas or Pratyekabuddhas.

By perfecting liberality, ethics and manners, patience, strenuousness,
Meditative concentration and discriminating awareness.[29]

(VId) The special attention means devotion to discriminating awareness without ignoring the other nine perfections.

(VIe) The special purification is as explained above:

Just as fine gold studded by a skilful craftsman with beryl is incomparable and cannot be equalled by plain gold (113b), so also a Bodhisattva's grounding in the good and wholesome on this level becomes very pure and radiant, having been tested by beneficial expediency and discriminating awareness, and cannot be surpassed by Bodhisattvas on lower levels.[30]

(VIf) The special understanding involves knowing that reality is neither sullied nor clean and that since there is dependent origination, there is nothing in itself which becomes either the one or the other. Therefore it has been said:

Neither sullied nor purifiable.[31]

(VIg) (There is no special rejection.)

(VIh) The special place of birth means that he usually becomes a king among the Sunirmita gods and is skilled in pricking the pride of beings:

> By this spiritual maturity
> He becomes a god among the Sunirmitas
> And quells pride.
> His attainment cannot be spoiled by Śrāvakas.

(VIi) The special power produces one hundred thousand ten-million meditative absorptions in the fraction of a moment.

(VIIa) The special name of the seventh spiritual level is 'The One Which Goes Far' (*riṅ.du soṅ.ba, dūraṅgamā*).

(VIIb) Its special significance is that we go far, because on this level is the one and only path along which we can come to the end of our exertions:

> Because it is the one on which to go,
> This level is called The One Going Far.[32]

(VIIc) The special preparation means giving up the twenty types of attachment such as belief in a self, and relying on the twenty positive factors such as the knowledge that the opposite to these beliefs are the three gates to liberation.[33] The former is indicated by the words

> Belief in a self, in an anthropomorphic entity,[34]

and the latter by

> Knowledge of the three gates to liberation.[35]

(VIId) The special attention means concentrating on the perfection of beneficial expediency without neglecting the other nine.

(VIIe) The special purification is as before (114a):

> Just as fine gold studded with the most precious jewels by a skilful worker is more beautiful than all other ornaments in the whole of India, so a Bodhisattva's grounding in this seventh level cannot be surpassed by that of Śrāvakas, Pratyekabuddhas and Bodhisattvas who have not yet reached this level.[36]

(VIIf) The special understanding is to realize the meaning of non-differentiatedness and to know that the differentiating characteristics of the entities constituting reality, detailed in the Sūtras, are basically the same. Hence

> Non-differentiated.[37]

(VIIg) (There is no special rejection.)

(VIIh) The special place of birth means that a Bodhisattva almost always becomes a king of the Vaśavartin gods and is skilled in understanding the type of knowledge possessed by Śrāvakas and Pratyekabuddhas:

By this spiritual maturity
He becomes a king of the Vaśavartin gods
And the principal teacher
Who understands the Noble Truths.

(VIIi) The special power is experiencing one hundred thousand million ten-million meditative absorptions in the fraction of a moment.

(VIIIa) The special name of the eighth spiritual level is 'The Unshakable One' (*mi.g'yo.ba, acalā*).

(VIIIb) Its special significance is that it cannot be shaken by conceptions concerned with differentiating attributes or their absence. As is stated:

Because it cannot be shaken by the two types of conceptualism
It is called 'The Unshakable One'.[38]

(VIIIc) The special preparation involves eight subjects such as how sentient beings behave:

To know the mind of all beings,
To enjoy supersensible cognitions[39] (114b).

(VIIId) The special attention is to develop devoted resolution without neglecting the other nine perfections.

(VIIIe) The special purification is as before:

Just as an ornament of fine gold on the head or neck of an Indian rajah is superior to those worn by lesser people, so a Bodhisattva's foundations of the good and wholesome cannot be surpassed by those of Śrāvakas, Pratyekabuddhas and Bodhisattvas on lower levels.[40]

(VIIIf) The special understanding means that because a Bodhisattva comprehends that the whole of reality is beyond habit-making forms of thought and as limitless as celestial space, he is neither angry at nor afraid of Śūnyatā not standing for any conception at all. This attitude is termed: the joyful acceptance of the unoriginatedness of the whole of reality. By this acceptance a Bodhisattva realizes that there is neither decrease nor increase in reality. He does not observe anything that might become sullied or purified, less or more. Therefore also it is said:

Neither decrease nor increase,[41]

And,

The place of four masteries.[42]

These are over (i) absence of habit-making forms of thought, (ii) pure Buddha realms, (iii) transcending awareness and (iv) appropriate activity.

A Bodhisattva on this eighth level realizes that it means eliminating habit-making forms of thoughts and mastery over pure Buddha realms.[43] And further it is said that he obtains ten powers (115a) over (1) length of life, (2) mind, (3) necessities, (4) karma, (5) birth, (6) creative imagination, (7) resolution, (8) miracles, (9) knowledge and (10) presentation.[44]

(VIIIg) (There is no special rejection.)

(VIIIh) The special place of birth means that generally he becomes Brahmā:

By this spiritual maturity
He becomes Brahmā, a ruler over a chiliocosm.
He is incomparable in administering
To the needs of Arhants and Pratyekabuddhas.

(VIIIi) The special power results in attaining in a fraction of a moment as many meditative absorptions as there are atoms in ten ten-million trichiliocosms.

(IXa) The special name of the ninth spiritual level is 'The One having Good Discrimination' (*legs.pa'i blo.gros, sādhumatī*).

(IXb) Its special significance is in its well-defined knowledge:

This level is called 'The One with Good Discrimination'
Because on it there is good well-defined knowledge.[45]

(IXc) The special preparation involves twelve things such as infinite devoted resolution, as is said:

Infinite devoted resolution,
Knowledge of the language of gods.[46]

(IXd) The special attention is devotion to the perfection of power without ignoring the other nine.

(IXe) The special purification is as before:

Just as an ornament of fine gold on the head or neck of a universal monarch is superior to those of all other rulers in the four continents, so a Bodhisattva's grounding in the good and wholesome, adorned by a brilliant halo of transcending awareness, cannot be surpassed by all the Śrāvakas, Pratyekabuddhas and Bodhisattvas on a lower level.[47]

(IXf) The special understanding involves mastery over transcending awareness,[48] since the four types of well-defined knowledge have already been acquired. These four are given in the ''Phags.pa sa.bcu.pa'i mdo' ('Daśabhūmikasūtra', p. 77):

> Well-defined knowledge of the Dharma and the subjects for discussion, how to speak distinctly and to present the case.[49]

(IXg) (There is no special rejection.)

(IXh) The special place of birth means that a Bodhisattva usually becomes Brahmā, king of gods and lord over a biliochosm:

> By this spiritual maturity
> He becomes Brahmā, lord over a biliochosm.
> He cannot be prevented by Arhants and others
> From answering all the questions which beings have in their minds.

(IXi) The special power produces in a fraction of a moment as many meditative absorptions as there are atoms in ten ten-million uncountable Buddha realms.

(Xa) The special name of the tenth spiritual level is 'Cloud of Dharma' (*chos.kyi sprin, dharmamegha*).

(Xb) It is so called because a Bodhisattva on this level lets the Dharma fall like rain and extinguishes the very subtle glow of conflicting emotions still held by sentient beings. Another reason is that it is covered by meditative absorption and mantras like the sky with clouds (116a):

> Because it is covered by two factors, like the sky by clouds,
> This level is called Cloud of Dharma.[50]

(Xc) The special preparation is discussed not in the 'mNon.rtogs. rgyan' ('Abhisamayālaṅkāra') but in the ''Phags.pa sa.bcu.pa'i mdo' ('Daśabhūmikasūtra', p. 82):

> Oh sons of the Victorious One, in this way a Bodhisattva for nine levels analyses and discerns limitless knowables with a discriminating mind.

It then defines the tenth level as that of attaining the all-inclusive knowledge of all causal characteristics, because here a Bodhisattva is initiated by the light rays of the Buddhas in the ten regions of the world. A more detailed account of this level which is also known as the Level of Initiation, is given in the 'Sa.bcu.pa'i mdo' ('Daśabhūmikasūtra', pp. 95 seq.). Also in the 'Rin.chen 'phreṅ.ba' ('Ratnāvalī') it is stated:

> Because the Bodhisattva
> Is initiated by the Buddha rays.

(Xd) The special attention is to concentrate on the perfection of transcending awareness without neglecting the other nine (116b).

(Xe) The special purification is as before:

> An ornament made by the artist of the gods, studded with precious jewels and worn by a king of the gods cannot be compared with the jewelry of other gods and men. Neither can the transcending awareness of a Bodhisattva on the tenth level be diverted by all sentient beings, Śrāvakas, Pratyekabuddhas and Bodhisattvas on lower levels.[51]

(Xf) The special understanding is that this level is the basis of the fourth mastery.[52] In whichever way the Bodhisattva likes he manifests himself in various shapes and in so doing fulfils the needs of sentient beings.

(Xg) (There is no special rejection.)

(Xh) The special place of birth means that a Bodhisattva as a rule becomes Maheśvara, king of gods, and is skilled in pointing out the perfections to sentient beings, be they Śrāvakas, Pratyekabuddhas or Bodhisattvas on lower levels:

> By this spiritual maturity
> He becomes one of the Śuddhavāsin gods;
> The Supreme Lord and
> The master of infinite transcending awareness.

(Xi) The special power means that in a fraction of a moment he attains as many meditative absorptions as there are atoms in ten times one hundred thousand one hundred thousand million ten-million uncountable Buddha realms.

Further, from every pore of his skin he is able to pour out a continual stream (117a) of innumerable Buddhas and Bodhisattvas. He can make visible many living beings, gods and men. As Indra, Brahmā, Maheśvara, a king, a Śrāvaka, a Pratyekabuddha or a Tathāgata he can teach the Dharma as necessary to those who are to be taught. So also is written in the 'dbU.ma 'jug.pa' ('Madhyamakāvatāra' XI, 9):

> From the pores of their skin they can produce Buddhas
> Surrounded by innumerable Bodhisattvas,
> Gods, men and demons,
> In every single moment.

This concludes my discussion of a Bodhisattva's ten spiritual levels.

The Buddha level is the stage of the Path of Fulfilment. On it the veils of conflicting emotions which can be torn by practising Truth,[53] and of primitive beliefs about reality which flow like the sap in a tree,[54] can be rent and discarded when the Vajropamasamādhi concentration begins.

The attainment of this level is described in the 'Byaṅ.sa' ('Bodhisattvabhūmi'):[55]

> It is reached through the three main divisions (asaṃkhyeya)[56] of a Mahākalpa. In the first, after the stage of devoted interest and corresponding behaviour has been passed, the first spiritual level, 'The Joyful One', is attained by constant effort, not by inaction. In the second, the levels from the first to the seventh, 'The One Which Goes Far', are passed by and the eighth level, 'The Unshakable One', is attained with absolute certainty, because a Bodhisattva with pure intentions makes definite efforts. In the third, the eighth and ninth levels are passed by and the tenth, 'The Cloud of Dharma', is attained (117b). Of those who make very great efforts, some will skip several intermediate aeons (*antarakalpa*), others even one great aeon (*kalpa*), but none an Asaṃkhyeya.

The nineteenth chapter, dealing with the Spiritual Levels, from
The Jewel Ornament of Liberation or
The Wish-Fulfilling Gem of the
Noble Doctrine.

NOTES TO CHAPTER 19

1. Certain forms of emotionally disturbing processes can be neutralized by seeing Truth (*mthoṅ.spaṅs.kyi ñon.moṅs.pa, darśanaheya kleśa*), but others only by practising Truth (*sgom.spaṅs.kyi ñon.moṅs.pa, bhāvanāheya kleśa*). While we are accustomed to make a sharp distinction between feelings and emotions on the one hand, and intellectual cognitive processes on the other, in Buddhism the differentiation is more flexible; apart from cupidity-attachment (*rāga*) and aversion-hatred (*dveṣa*), which we would at once consider as emotions proper, there is also bewilderment-delusion (*moha*) which, if we want to accept as an emotion, we must call an 'intellectual' one. It is the 'intellectual emotion' and all that it entails is overcome by 'seeing Truth', while the deep-rooted emotions of

cupidity-attachment, aversion-hatred and, above all, conceitedness can only be overcome (sublimated) by practising Truth, which means that we make that which we have sighted a living experience and mould our life accordingly.

2. According to this text the ten preparations are: (i) right intention, (ii) beneficence, (iii) impartiality, (iv) renunciation, (v) association with spiritual friends, (vi) striving for the Dharma, (vii) an attitude of non-attachment, (viii) a desire for the Buddhakāya (i.e. Buddhahood as spiritual integration manifest in all actions), (ix) teaching the Dharma and (x) truthfulness.

3. These are the first six of liberality, ethics and manners, patience, strenuousness, meditative concentration, discriminating awareness and the four of beneficial expediency, devoted resolution, power and transcending awareness.

4. *bsdu.ba'i dṅos.po, saṃgrahavastu.* They have been given in note 13 of Chapter 10.

5. 'Daśabhūmikasūtra', p. 20.

6. See above, note 1.

7. 'Daśabhūmikasūtra', p. 22.

8. *byin.brlabs, adhiṣṭhāna, adhiṣṭhita.* It is through this power which permeates and sustains everything, that the ultimate understanding of Reality is possible. See 'Lam.zab.kyi rnam.par bśad.pa zab.lam.gyi sñe.ma', fol. 15b.

9. 'Mahāyāna-sūtrālaṅkāra' XX–XXI, 33.

10. 'Abhisamayālaṅkāra' I, 51. The remaining three are (i) reverence, (ii) devoted attention to the Guru and (iii) liberality.

10a. 'Daśabhūmikasūtra', p. 30.

11. 'Madhyāntavibhāga.'

12. See above, note 1.

13. The ten wholesome actions have been mentioned in Chapter 6, p. 79.

14. 'Mahāyāna-sūtrālaṅkāra' XX–XXI, 33.

15. 'Abhisamayālaṅkāra' I, 52–3. The remaining three are (i) purification of all Buddha realms, (ii) not to feel disgusted with Saṃsāra (and hence to have resort to escapism) and (iii) self-respect and decorum.

16. 'Daśabhūmikasūtra', p. 37.

17. 'Madhyāntavibhāga.'

18. This level and the following ones consolidate that which has been achieved on the preceding levels. The most subtle remnant of that which gives rise to emotional conflicts, can only be overpowered on the Buddha level. There is no special rejection because on the

preceding levels the coarser and subtler emotionally disturbing elements have been neutralized ('abandoned'), otherwise this level would not have been reached.

19. 'Mahāyāna-sūtrālaṅkāra' XX–XXI, 34.

20. 'Abhisamayālaṅkāra' I, 53–4. The remaining six are (i) never to give up the training one has undertaken, (ii) to despise sensuality (as an aim in itself), (iii) to pass beyond worldliness, (iv) to discard all beliefs in existence (as a predicate), (v) not to become faint-hearted and (vi) not to hold certain views (i.e. not to be opinionated).

21. 'Daśabhūmikasūtra', p. 41.

22. 'Madhyāntavibhāga.'

23. *'jig.tshogs.lta.ba, satkāyadṛṣṭi.* See also 'Abhidharmakośa' V, 7, and 'Bhāṣya' (p. 17), and my 'Philosophy and Psychology in the Abhidharma', pp. 136 n. 2, 320, 341.

24. 'Mahāyāna-sūtrālaṅkāra' XX–XXI, 35.

25. 'Abhisamayālaṅkāra' I, 55–6. The remaining seven are (i) self-aggrandizement, (ii) disdaining others, (iii) to walk the path of evil actions, (iv) conceit, (v) erroneous views, (vi) evil-mindedness and (vii) succumbing to conflicting emotions.

26. 'Daśabhūmikasūtra', p. 46.

27. 'Madhyāntavibhāga.' The ten types of 'sameness' are listed in 'Daśabhūmikasūtra', p. 47. They mean that all the constituents of reality are the same so that no ideological image can be said to be valid (*animitta*), they have no characteristic marks as something ultimate (*alakṣaṇa*), are non-orginating (*anutpāda*) and non-originated (*ajāta*), are detached (from everything determinate) (*vivikta*), pure from their beginningless beginning (*ādiviśuddhi*), beyond verbalization (*niṣprapañca*) structuralization and destructuralization (*anāvyūhanirvyūha*), manifest themselves (not as something naïvely real but) as a magic spell, a dream, a reflection, an echo, a reflection of the moon in water and an image (*māyāsvapnapratibhāsapratiśrutkodakacandrapratibimbanirmāṇa*), and that they are the same in their non-duality of existence and non-existence (*bhāvābhāvādvaya*).

28. 'Mahāyāna-sūtrālaṅkāra' XX–XXI, 36.

29. 'Abhisamayālaṅkāra' I, 57–9. The six vices are (i) to desire or (ii) fear the state of a disciple or (iii) an Arhant, (iv) to become faint-hearted, (v) to be unhappy over having renounced everything and (vi) to turn away those who are in need, even if poor oneself.

30. 'Daśabhūmikasūtra', p. 54.

31. 'Madhyāntavibhāga.'

32. 'Mahāyāna-sūtrālaṅkāra' XX–XXI, 37.

33. The three gates to liberation are technically known as *śūnyatā*,

apraṇihita and *ānimitta*. Literally translated these terms mean that there is nothing predicable inasmuch as the ultimate cannot be defined and, though not bleak emptiness, is nothing in comparison to what we are accustomed to (*śūnyatā*), that in the ultimate there are no leanings towards anything (*apraṇihita*), and that it cannot be grasped by ideologies such as eternalism, persistence, Pure Ego theories, all of which are a passing whim rather than an indication of real philosophizing (*ānimitta*). Each gate opens to an understanding of the Buddhist fundamental tenets that reality has nothing to do with a Pure Ego (*anātman*), that everything conditioned is unsatisfactory (*duḥkha*) and impermanent (*anitya*). This relation I pointed out in my 'Philosophy and Psychology in the Abhidharma', p. 309: 'By *śūnya* the fact is realized that everything conditioned, be it natural objects or postulated selves, have no individuality of their own persisting over and beyond the conditions that brought those entities about. By *apraṇihita* the fact is realized that everything conditioned is unable to yield lasting happiness and hence is misery, and by *ānimitta* is understood that everything is transitory.'

34. 'Abhisamayālaṅkāra' I, 59–61. The remaining eighteen are: belief in (i) an agent, (ii) a life force, (iii) an individuality, (iv) nihilism, (v) eternalism, (vi) ideologies, (vii) (external) causality, (viii) reality staying in (i.e. being restricted to and making up) the psychosomatic constituents, (ix) elements and (x) their interaction or (xi) in the three world-spheres, (xii) attachment to them, (xiii) faint-heartedness, (xiv) inordinate desire for the Three Jewels, (xv) ethics and manners and (xvi) opinionatedness about them, (xvii) dissension with Śūnyatā and (xviii) the evil of contradiction.

35. 'Abhisamayālaṅkāra' I, 62–5. The twenty positive subjects are: (i) knowledge of the three gates to liberation, (ii) triple purity (for instance, the person who makes a gift must have a pure mind, so must the recipient, and the act of giving itself must be performed without any expectations of a reward in this world or the next), (iii) compassion, (iv) unpretentiousness, (v) awareness of the intrinsic sameness of all constituents of reality, (vi) of the uniqueness of reality, (vii) of its unoriginatedness and (viii) of the patient acceptance of reality as it is, (ix) demonstrating that all entities have only one causal characteristic (namely that of bewilderment), (x) uprooting of all habit-making forms of thought, (xi) renouncing all ideation, (xii) opinionatedness and (xiii) conflicting emotions, (xiv) pondering over tranquillity, (xv) skill in developing insight, (xvi) spiritual awareness arising from a trained mind and (xvii) from complete non-attachment, (xviii) desirelessness, (xix) going to other

spiritual realms however and whenever one likes, and (xx) everywhere to reveal one's real nature.

36. 'Daśabhūmikasūtra', p. 62.

37. 'Madhyāntavibhāga.'

38. 'Mahāyāna-sūtrālaṅkāra' XX–XXI, 37.

39. 'Abhisamayālaṅkāra' I, 66–7. The remaining six preparations are: (i) realizing the wholesome Buddha realms, (ii) serving the Buddhas because of thoroughly discerning (the spiritual implications), (iii) knowing the controlling powers, (iv) purifying the Buddha realms, (v) living by realizing that everything is like a magic spell, and (vi) willingly to accept this life.

40. 'Daśabhūmikasūtra', p. 72.

41. 'Madhyāntavibhāga.'

42. ibid.

43. The two other masteries, mentioned in the preceding paragraph, are won on the two following levels. See (IXf) and (Xf).

44. A more detailed explanation is given in Chapter 3, pp. 33 seq.

45. 'Mahāyāna-sūtrālaṅkāra' XX–XXI, 37.

46. 'Abhisamayālaṅkāra' I, 68–9. The remaining nine subjects are: (i) having realizations which come continually like the stream of a river, (ii) taking rebirth in a select womb, (iii) having the good fortune of coming into a good family, (iv) being surrounded by a spiritual atmosphere, (v) having good surroundings and attendants, (vi) taking a good birth, (vii) renunciation, (viii) sitting under the Bodhi-tree and (ix) perfection of all virtues.

47. 'Daśabhūmikasūtra', p. 81.

48. See above, note 43.

49. A more detailed analysis is given in 'Abhidharmakośa' VII, 37–40, and 'Bhāṣya' (pp. 89 seqq.).

50. 'Mahāyāna-sūtrālaṅkāra' XX–XXI, 38.

51. 'Daśabhūmikasūtra', p. 94.

52. See above, note 43.

53. See above, note 1, for an explanation.

54. Here the last vestige of primitive beliefs and conflicting emotions is abolished. The more obvious, but also the subtler, forms had already been overcome on the first and second levels. See above (Ig) and (IIg).

55. Quoted in 'Daśabhūmikasūtra', Appendices, p. 25.

56. Asaṃkhyeya is the name of a certain number, 10 in the 59th power.

20

PERFECT BUDDHAHOOD

(e) 'The result is Sambuddhakāya.'[1]

AFTER THE PATHS have been traversed and the levels successfully been reached, awakening in the essence of the Three Kāyas takes place. As is stated in the 'Byaṅ.chub.lam.sgron' ('Bodhipathapradīpa', 69d):

> Buddha-enlightenment is not far away.

Regarding 'Buddha' there is this index:

> Under seven heads
> The Samyaksambuddhakāyas are discussed:
> Ultimate nature, the meaning of the word Buddha, the classification,
> The definition, the exact number, the primary characteristics
> And the particularity.

I. The ultimate nature of a Samyaksambuddha is most excellent (i) renunciation and (ii) spirituality.

(i) The renunciation means complete escape from the fog caused by conflicting emotions and primitive beliefs about reality. This occurs after the paths and spiritual levels have been passed and Vajropamasamādhi[2] attained. Since the fog enveloping the attainments[3] has dispersed and all other hindrances have been removed, nothing remains to obscure the light.

(ii) There are various opinions about (118a) the spirituality or transcending awareness of a Buddha. Some say he has, others that he has not, habit-making thoughts[4] as well as transcending awareness of everything that can be known. Others state that the latter is an interruption in the normal stream of consciousness, while still others say that in a Buddha there has never been anything that could be said to be there.

On the authority of both Sūtras and Śāstras a Buddha's transcending awareness is explained as follows. In the ''Phags.pa sdud.pa' ('Prajñāpāramitāsaṃcayagāthā', fol. 12b):

> If you want to attain a Buddha's sublime transcending awareness
> Have confidence in the Perfection of Discriminating Awareness.

In the 'Śes.rab.kyi pha.rol.tu phyin.pa stoṅ.phrag brgya.pa' ('Śatasāhasrikā-prajñāpāramitā'):

> The Samyaksambuddha has obtained an awareness which is not obscured by the constituents of reality.

And in the twenty-first chapter of the same work:

> There is unsurpassable Samyaksambuddha spirituality, the turning of the Dharmacakra and the perfection of sentient beings.

In other Sūtras there are also many passages in which a Buddha's transcending awareness is mentioned.

According to the Śāstras: in the 'mDo.sde.rgyan' ('Mahāyāna-sūtrālaṅkāra' IX, 31):

> Just as with the rising of the sun
> Light spreads everywhere,
> So also know that the Buddhas'
> Transcending awareness spreads everywhere.

And (in IX, 67):

> The Ādarśajñāna is unshakable;
> Three other types rest on it:
> Samatā, Pratyavekṣaṇa and
> Kṛtyānuṣṭhāna.[5]

A Buddha's spirituality is also dealt with in other Śāstras.

(a) Relying on the authority of these texts (118b) some scholars assert that a Buddha has transcending awareness. They are termed 'existence-mongerers'.[6] This transcending awareness is, in brief, an awareness which sees Reality as it is (*ji.lta.ba mkhyen.pa'i ye.śes, yathābhūtaparijñāna*) and an awareness of Reality as it becomes manifest (*ji.sñed.pa mkhyen.pa'i ye.śes, yathāvad vyavasthānaparijñāna*). The former is ultimately real. As has been stated above, as soon as Vajropamasamādhi is attained and the closest attention is given, speech stops and thoughts no longer flow. Since Dharmadhātu and transcending awareness are both beyond speech, they are on the same level. They are inseparable as water after it has been poured into water or oil into oil. Anything seen seems like the vast expanse of a clear sky. This awareness is without deceptive appearance and the basis of all the precious qualities of deep spirituality. As is stated:

> Like water poured into water
> Or oil dissolved in oil,
> Spirituality has blended indivisibly

With that which is ineffable.
This is called the real Dharmakāya
Of all Buddhas.

And[7]

Seeing the sky,—is what people say.
How to see the sky?—find out what it means.
To see things in this way is the teaching of The Buddha.
He cannot find another simile for this seeing.

The awareness which sees Reality as it becomes manifest is relative and presentational. It is to know causal characteristics. It is a spirituality in which every conceivable veil has been destroyed in and by Vajropamasamādhi. Through this awareness the infinite variety of knowables in the three dimensions of time (past, present, future) are known and seen like a fresh olive in your hand (119a).

This relative knowledge is also mentioned in the Sūtras, as for instance:[8]

There are many causes for
A single eye in a peacock's tail.
But they cannot be known without universal knowledge,
And this is the power of relative omniscience.

And in the 'rGyud.bla.ma' ('Uttaratantra' II, 53):

With Great Compassion the Knower of the world
Looks at the whole universe.

This looking with knowing compassion is not like believing in the existence of that which is seen; it is looking at it and knowing it to be a (passing) magic spell. As is said in the 'Chos yaṅ.dag.par bsdud. pa'i mdo' ('Dharmasaṅgītisūtra'):

Just as a conjurer
Tries not to get caught up in his illusions
And therefore by his superior knowledge
Is not attached to magic forms,
So also the wise in Perfect Enlightenment
Know the three worlds to be like a magic show.

And in the 'Yab.sras mjal.ba'i mdo' ('Pitāputrasamāgamanasūtra'):

If you wish to see the illusions
Of a magician as magic
You must not allow yourself to be fooled by them.

Look at all beings in this way.
Praise to Him who sees everything (as it is).

(b) Others declare that the so-called ultimately real knowledge is in a Samyaksambuddha, but not the so-called relative knowledge. Their argument runs: There is understanding of what can be understood, but as the latter is relative, there must be relative knowledge (and yet the relatively valid no longer exists for a Buddha). Moreover, in so far as relative knowledge is caused by perceptions sullied by conflicting emotions, it is active in ordinary sentient beings. When, however, it is caused by perceptions unsullied in this way it is active in the three types of spiritual people (Śrāvakas, Pratyekabuddhas and Arhants). It is like a person with bad eyesight who thinks that he sees hairs and mist when they are not there (119b). A Buddha, however, has thrown off all ignorance in Vajropamasamādhi and sees reality without seeing it as a certain thing (that is, he does not conceptualize). The bewilderment of what may be called the relatively valid, does not exist for him, just as the hairs and mist are no longer seen after the diseased eyes have been cured. Therefore, since the appearance of that which is relatively valid, is only due to ignorance, it obtains exclusively in this world. Since it does not obtain for a Buddha (who is beyond the world), relative knowledge (which is linked up with the relatively valid) cannot also be present. If a Buddha had a mind affected by appearance, he would be bewildered by the presence of anything confusing, and this is contrary to the assertion that he is forever in a concentrated state of mind.[9]

The adherents of the view that a Buddha has relative knowledge state that it is wrong to talk of bewilderment on the mere appearance of something confusing. Knowing better that this bewilderment is due to the intellect taking objects as real, they consider this knowledge to be the cause of life in the heavens, of enlightenment and liberation. Therefore they assert:

When one knows objects as mere bewilderment
They are grasped as non-bewilderment.[10]

Others, however, affirm that there is no harm in making the relatively valid, if it is not claimed to be reality, an object of knowledge. That there is no harm in it (120a) means that a Buddha does not become confused when he regards the relatively valid in this way. Therefore those who hold that a Buddha possesses relative knowledge affirm that he has the so-called relative awareness, but that it is subsequent (*rjes, pṛṣṭhalabdha*) to ultimate spirituality. They say:

The awareness which sees Reality as it is,
Is without bewilderment, is concentration and not mentation.
The awareness of Reality as it becomes manifest
Is bewilderment, subsequent knowledge and mentation.

Those who consider that a Buddha does not possess relative knowledge follow the authority of the ''Phags.pa sGo mtha'.yas bsgrub.pa'i mdo' ('Anañtamukhasādhaka-nāma-dhāraṇī'):

A Tathāgata after having become perfectly enlightened no longer conceives. Why? Because there is nothing to conceive.

There are still other scholars who say:

Some Tīrthikas say that
You who talk of approaching liberation,
Become more than just ashes
After passing from this world.

This concludes my discussion of the various opinions about a Buddha's transcending awareness.

The view of my spiritual friends[11] is as follows: The nature of the Samyaksambuddha is Dharmakāya, the end of all error and natural harmony. But such statements are mere words. In reality Dharmakāya is unborn (so does not stand for any conception at all) and is ineffable. Venerable Mi.la.ras.pa used to say that transcending awareness is not discursive. It is beyond any predication such as existence or non-existence, eternalism or nihilism, and beyond the realm of intellect. Whatever name it is called does not alter its nature. This is particularly true of the word 'transcending awareness'. It was coined by a numskull, so that even if a Buddha were to be asked to explain it, he could not do so. When it is stated that Dharmakāya is beyond the intellect, unborn and ineffable, or such that one can only say 'do not ask me, look into your own mind', the statement is not true of reality (120b). As is written in the 'mDo.sde.rgyan' ('Mahāyāna-sūtrālaṅkāra' IX, 3):

Liberation (is) merely the end of error.

Therefore since the Buddha is Dharmakāya and since Dharmakāya is unborn and ineffable, it is not *a* transcending awareness. If you object that this contradicts the statement in the Sūtras about the two types of spiritual awareness, you must know that it does not. It is like saying that we see blue when we are merely conscious of an appearance of blueness.[12] In other words, to that which (in a process of symbolic transformation) becomes Dharmadhātu and which is transcending awareness we attribute the name 'awareness which sees

Reality as it is' and call it ultimate knowledge, while we speak of it as relative when it (the process of symbolic transformation) concerns those who have to be brought to spiritual maturity. This interpretation (of transcending awareness) is a good one. By means of it we can say that the most excellent renunciation and spirituality are the essence or the nature of a Buddha. This is confirmed by the 'rGyud. bla.ma' ('Uttaratantra' II, 4):

> In Buddhahood (there is) no differentiation;
> It is brought about by true elements of reality.
> (Bright and illumining) like the sun and the sky,
> It is characterized by renunciation and transcending awareness.

And in the 'mDo.sde.rgyan' ('Mahāyāna-sūtrālaṅkāra' IX, 12):

> Where the fog of conflicting emotions and primitive beliefs about reality,
> Though present for a long time
> Has been dispersed by very great renunciation
> The most excellent virtues and positive qualities are obtained. This is Buddhahood.

II. The meaning of the word Buddha.

We say Bud.dha (*saṅs.rgyas*) because we have awakened (*saṅs*) from sleep-like ignorance and acquired wide understanding (*rgyas*) of the two types of spirituality. As is said in a verse:

> Because of having awakened from the sleep of ignorance
> And acquired wide understanding He is Buddha.

Here 'having awakened from the sleep of ignorance' means most excellent renunciation (121a), while 'wide understanding of the two types of spirituality' is most excellent transcending awareness. Both have been explained above.

III. The classification.

A Buddha has Three Kāyas: Dharmakāya, Sambhogakāya and Nirmāṇakāya. As is stated in the 'mDo gser.'od dam.pa' ('Suvarṇaprabhāsottamasūtra', p. 201):

> All Buddhas have Three Kāyas: Dharmakāya, Sambhogakāya and Nirmāṇakāya.

You might point out that in certain works two, four and even five Bodies[13] are spoken of, but they are all included in the Three Kāyas. The authority for this is the 'mDo.sde.rgyan' ('Mahāyāna-sūtrālaṅkāra' IX, 65):

> You must know that Buddhakāya
> Is Three Kāyas.

IV. The definition of the Three Kāyas.

(i) Dharmakāya is the essence of Buddha(hood). As is affirmed in the ''Phags.pa brGyad.stoṅ.pa' ('Aṣṭasāhasrikā-prajñāpāramitā'):

> Do not consider the Tathāgata as the two form (gestalt) Kāyas. The Tathāgata is Dharmakāya.

And in the 'mDo tiṅ.'dzin rgyal.po' ('Samādhirājasūtra'):

> Do not look at the Victorious One from the viewpoint of the two form Kāyas.

(ii) These two form Kāyas are (a) obtained by the sustaining power of Dharmakāya and (b) are formed for the purpose of leading people to maturity; (c) they stem from former resolutions. They derive from this trinity.

(a) If the form Kāyas were due to the sustaining power of Dharmakāya (Dharmadhātu) alone, all sentient beings would obtain liberation without any efforts on their part, because Dharmadhātu permeates all sentient beings; or the latter would meet the Buddha face to face. Since this is not the case, the two form Kāyas do not derive from the sustaining power of Dharmadhātu alone (121b).

(b) If the two form Kāyas merely appeared for beings to be taught, all of them would be Buddhas because a thing which appears without having a reality of its own is error, and, since sentient beings have been living in that state since beginningless time, Buddhahood would be based on error. Since this is not so, the two form Kāyas do not merely appear for the instruction of beings.

(c) If the two form Kāyas were due to former resolutions alone, is Perfect Buddhahood so due or not? If there are no resolutions there will be no omniscience, and if there are, whether they were made recently or in the past, it would mean that beings are liberated without any efforts on their part. Since this is not so, the two form Kāyas are not due to resolutions alone.

Hence the two form Kāyas derive from this trinity.

V. There are three Kāyas because each is necessary, (i) Dharmakāya for its own purpose, and (ii, iii) the other two for the benefit of others.

(i) How, then, does Dharmakāya serve its own purpose? After it has been attained the basis for all qualities is present, because the powers, intrepidities and other virtues[14] are gathered as if they had been summoned. But there is more to it than just attainment. Its qualities are graded, being slight, greater, rich and infinite. (They are attained respectively) according to the devoted interest shown to a little, partial or general understanding of it.

(a) Meditative absorption below the point of highest worldly experience,[15] supersensible cognitions and all the other sublime powers (on the lower levels of spirituality) are the qualities resulting from devoted interest in Dharmakāya.

(b) The renunciation of Śrāvakas and Arhants (122a), their supersensible cognitions and wondrous manifestations are the qualities of the little understanding of Dharmakāya.

(c) The meditative absorption and renunciation of Pratyekabuddhas and Arhants and their supersensible cognitions are the qualities of a partial understanding of Dharmakāya.

(d) The renunciation, meditative absorption and supersensible cognitions of the Bodhisattvas are the qualities of the general understanding of Dharmakāya.

(ii) The two form Kāyas serve the needs of others.

(a) Sambhogakāya is for those who require teaching but are already purified (of the grossest ignorance).

(b) Nirmāṇakāya is for those who need to be taught but are not yet purified. Hence there are three types of Buddhakāya.

VI. The characteristics of each of the Three Kāyas.

(i) After Dharmadhātu has been recognized as being Śūnyatā, Dharmakāya is spoken of as the end of all error or the disappearance of bewilderment. But 'Dharmakāya' is a mere name. Since neither it, its primary characteristics, nor their basis can be found, my Guru Mi.la.ras.pa has spoken in terms of non-existence.[16]

Dharmakāya, when considered from various angles, may be said to have eight characteristics: (a) sameness, (b) depth, (c) everlastingness, (d) oneness, (e) harmony, (f) purity, (g) radiance and (h) enjoyment.

(a) 'Sameness' because the Dharmakāyas of all Buddhas are not different from each other.

(b) 'Depth' because ineffable and so difficult to comprehend.

(c) 'Everlastingness' because it has no beginning (does not stand for any conception) and is devoid of origin or end in any of the three possibilities of beginning, middle and end (122b).

(d) 'Oneness' because indivisible, since Dharmadhātu and Transcending Awareness are not different from each other.

(e) 'Harmony' because not in discord, being beyond the positive and negative poles.

(f) 'Purity' because of its freedom from the three types of mental-spiritual fog.[17]

(h) 'Possessing enjoyment' because with its wealth of qualities it is the basis of all enjoyments.

This is stated in the 'rGyud.bla.ma' ('Uttaratantra' II, 38):

> The real nature of Dharmadhātu
> Is seen by yogis in meditative concentration (to be)
> Without beginning, middle or end, indivisible,
> Non-dual, triple-free, stainless and without thought forms.

And in the 'mDo.sde.rgyan' ('Mahāyāna-sūtrālaṅkara' IX, 62):

> The Svābhāvikakāya[18] is the same throughout,
> Subtle and endowed with all enjoyments.

(ii) Sambhogakāya also has eight characteristics: (a) surroundings, (b) field, (c) body, (d) marks, (e) doctrine, (f) activity, (g) spontaneity and (h) without a nature of its own.

(a) The 'surroundings' in which it is enjoyed are the Bodhisattvas living on the ten levels of spirituality.

(b) The 'fields' where it is enjoyed are the pure Buddha-realms.

(c) The 'body' by whom it is enjoyed is Vairocana and the other Buddhas.[19]

(d) The 'marks' accompanying the enjoyment are the thirty-two major and eighty minor characteristics of a Buddha.

(e) The 'doctrine' through which it is enjoyed is the Mahāyāna teaching exclusively.

(f) The 'activity' resulting from its enjoyment is the instruction by the Sons of the Victorious One (123a).

(g) Its 'spontaneity' is its effortlessness. It is as if the king of jewels (the Wish-Fulfilling Gem) were present.

(h) 'Without a nature of its own' means that though it appears in different forms it does not possess different qualities like colours, which can only be known discursively.

As is stated in the 'mDo.sde.rgyan' ('Mahāyāna-sūtrālaṅkāra' IX, 61):

> Sambhogakāya is in all spheres characterized by
> Surroundings, fields, marks,
> Body, doctrine, enjoyment
> And activity.

And in the 'mṄon.rtogs.rgyan' ('Abhisamayālaṅkāra' VIII, 12):

> Because of possessing thirty-two major
> And eighty minor marks

And enjoying the teaching of Mahāyāna
One speaks of the Sambhogakāya of the Sage.

(iii) Nirmāṇakāya also has eight characteristics: (a) basis, (b) cause, (c) fields, (d) time, (e) nature, (f) inducement, (g) maturation and (h) liberation.

(a) Its 'basis' is the unshakable Dharmakāya.

(b) Its 'cause' derives from Great Compassion which desires the well-being of all people and creatures.

(c) Its 'fields' are the pure and impure realms.

(d) 'Time' is its continuity as long as the world exists.

(e) 'Nature' is its triple form of emanation:

(1) as artistic, being well-versed in many fine arts such as playing the lute and other instruments;[20]

(2) through birth, taking upon itself many low forms of life such as a hare;[21]

(3) as sublime when leaving the Tuṣita heaven, entering the mother's womb, passing into Nirvāṇa and so on.

As is stated in the 'mDo.sde.rgyan' ('Mahāyāna-sūtrālaṅkāra' IX, 64):

Since it always manifests
Artistry, birth, enlightenment
And passes into Nirvāṇa,
This Nirmāṇakāya of The Buddha
Is an important means for liberation (123b).

And in the 'rGyud.bla.ma' ('Uttaratantra' II, 53–6):

As long as the world exists
It manifests in various ways
Seeking birth
In the impure realms,
Entering a womb and being born,
Being versed in art,
Amused by the company of women,
Leaving home, practising austerities,
Sitting under the Bodhi-tree,
Conquering the armies of Māra,
Turning the Dharmacakra of Enlightenment and
Passing into Nirvāṇa.

(f) 'Inducement' instils a desire for the three types of Nirvāṇa into all ordinary beings.

(g) 'Maturation' ripens to the full all the merits and the spiritual awareness acquired by those who have entered the Path.

(h) 'Liberation' frees from the fetters of existence those whose good deeds have brought them to spiritual maturity. As is recorded in the 'rGyud.bla.ma' ('Uttaratantra' II, 58–9):

> This Kāya starts beings in the world along the Path to peace,
> Teaches them and brings them to maturity.

Such are the eight characteristics of the Nirmāṇakāya. They are summed up in the 'mŃon.rtogs.rgyan' ('Abhisamayālaṅkāra' VIII, 33):

> The very active Kāya of the Sage
> Is that by which, as long as the world exists,
> He performs equably
> Various useful deeds for human beings.

VII. The peculiarity is threefold: (i) sameness, (ii) everlastingness and (iii) appearance.

(i) The peculiarity of sameness is that
(a) the Dharmakāya of all Buddhas is the same, because it is not different from its basis or Dharmadhātu;
(b) so is their Sambhogakāya, since it does not differ from the intentions for which it is meant; and likewise
(c) the Nirmāṇakāya of all Buddhas, because it does the same things.

As is stated in the 'mDo.sde.rgyan' ('Mahāyāna-sūtrālaṅkāra' IX, 66):

> They are (124a) the same in basis, intention
> And activity.

(ii) The peculiarity of everlastingness is that
(a) the Dharmakāya is by nature ever-lasting, because it is the quintessence of freedom from origination and annihilation in the ultimate sense of the word;
(b) so is the Sambhogakāya, since the stream of enjoyment is not interrupted; and likewise.
(c) the Nirmāṇakāya, because even if it has disappeared it ever and again shows itself and works in its own time even if the stream of life and consciousness has stopped.

As is stated in the 'mDo.sde.rgyan' ('Mahāyāna-sūtrālaṅkāra' IX, 66):

> By nature and uninterruptedness
> They are forever ever-lasting.

(iii) The peculiarity of appearance is

(a) when the fog produced by all that can be known about Dharmadhātu[22] has been dispersed, Dharmakāya appears;

(b) when conflicting emotions have vanished, Sambhogakāya is there and

(c) when the storm clouds of Karma[23] have passed over, Nirmāṇakāya is seen.

The twentieth chapter, dealing with the Result or Perfect Buddhahood, from
The Jewel Ornament of Liberation or
The Wish-Fulfilling Gem of the
Noble Doctrine.

NOTES TO CHAPTER 20

1. See Chapter 1, p. 2.

2. See Chapter 19, p. 252.

3. *sñoms.'jug sgrib.pa, samāpattyāvaraṇa.* This is the incapacity of mind to function properly with regard to the successful attainment of meditative concentration. See 'Abhidharmakośa' VIII, 53, and 'Bhāṣya' (p. 207).

4. *rnam.par rtog.pa, vikalpa.* See Chapter 1, note 19.

5. These are four types of spiritual awareness. Various interpretations have been given by various schools of thought. A detailed discussion is found in 'Vijñaptimātratāsiddhi', p. 681. On the whole the names are explanatory: Ādarśajñāna is an awareness which realizes that the constituents of reality are not independent entities but rather like reflections in a mirror and consequently sees them in this way. Samatājñāna is the awareness of the equality and basic sameness (identity) of all the elements of reality. Pratyavekṣaṇajñāna is a surveying and investigating awareness, while Kṛtyānuṣṭhānajñāna is an awareness which works in the performance of a Buddha's duties. It must always be noted that Buddhahood is no soporific state but activity, though not in the sense of 'doing things'.

6. The followers of this view are in line with the 'realists' who assume that existence is a predicate and that even enlightenment is an entity that exists as such. The Mādhyamikas, who have no thesis of their own and on logical considerations reject both existence and non-existence as well as the possibilities that result from a combination of these extremes, naturally do not share this view. Neither does sGam.po.pa, who mentions it because it was held in several circles.

7. 'Prajñāpāramitāsaṃcayagāthā', fol. 16b.

8. The Sanskrit original is given in 'Abhidharmakośa' I, p. 2.

9. Bewilderment (*'khrul.pa, bhrānti*) is a state of distraction in the sense that mind and its functions have strayed from the initial state of rest or concentration. The latter must therefore be understood as a state of infinite possibilities rather than as a state laboriously brought about.

10. That is, they are perceived without the beliefs about them.

11. *bśes.gñen.pa.* The spiritual friends to whom sGam.po.pa refers are those by whom he received his instruction. They were in particular the followers of the bKa'.gdams.pa school which was founded by Dīpaṅkara Śrījñāna (Atīśa). Their contention is that words must not be taken for the thing and that 'the thing' cannot be conceptualized. To avoid any concretization or conceptualization, Mi.la.ras.pa, sGam.po.pa's teacher at some later time, also spoke of non-existence in the sense that ultimate reality or transcending awareness cannot be defined by positive terms. Non-existence certainly does not mean subsistence as is assumed by certain realistic schools of thought, ancient and modern. Non-existence is only a verbal device intended to free our minds from limiting conceptions. The view which sGam.po.pa offers here is the one found in the Tantras on which the Mahāmudrā philosophy is based.

12. As so often Buddhism has anticipated certain findings of modern philosophy. Until recently (and in many cases even now) philosophers have been handicapped by the dualism of body and mind and the attempts to resolve this into the one or the other have proved abortive. Buddhists of Tantric Mahāyāna did not face this difficulty because they understood what abstract terms meant and as far as psychological problems were concerned they carefully avoided any pseudoproblems. If we assume with modern logicians that 'mind' is an abbreviation denoting a bodily state that shows certain kinds of reactions, but avoid conceiving of 'body' in the ordinary naïve form and assume that it *is* mind as well, we can rephrase the Buddhist idea in Hans Reichenbach's words ('The Rise of Scientific Philosophy', p. 273): 'Another pseudoproblem is

presented by the question: if light rays hit the human eye and nervous impulses are transmitted from the retina to the brain, how and where are the impulses transformed into the sensation *blue*? This question is based on a mistaken presupposition. Nowhere are the impulses transformed into a sensation. The impulses generate a physiological state of the brain; the person whose brain is in this state sees *blue*, but the *blue* is neither in the brain nor elsewhere in the body. "Seeing blue" is an indirect way of describing a bodily state; this state is the causal product of the light rays and the subsequent nervous impulses, but there is no causal product *blue*.'

13. The two Kāyas are the Real Body (*bhūtakāya*) and the Created Body (*nirmāṇakāya*). See 'Vijñaptimātratāsiddhi', p. 787. The four Kāyas are Dharmakāya, Sambhogakāya, Nirmāṇakāya and Svābhāvikakāya. The five Kāyas are these four and the Mahāsukhakāya (Body of Great Bliss).

14. These are the Buddhadharmas. See Chapter 1, note 39.

15. On this see Chapter 17, note 34, and 18, note 10.

16. See above, note 11.

17. They are conflicting emotions, primitive beliefs about reality and the incapacity of mind to function properly with respect to the attainment of meditative concentration.

18. The Svābhāvikakāya has often been counted as a fourth Kāya. However, in the Tantras and in sGam.po.pa's view it is a term for pointing out the unity of the Three Kāyas. See my 'The Psychology of the Three Kāyas', Uttara Bharati, 'Journal of Research of the Universities of Uttar Pradesh', vol. ii, pp. 37 seq.

19. There are five Buddhas as symbols of the various aspects of transcending awareness: Vairocana, Ratnasambhava, Amitābha, Amoghasiddhi and Akṣobhya.

20. This is a reference to the Kusa-Jātaka, where among other arts the Buddha as a Bodhisattva displays his skill in playing the lute to win the heart of his bride.

21. This is a reference to the Sasa-Jātaka, where the Buddha as a hare illustrated the ideal of the Buddhist way of life. It resulted in his image being painted on the moon (similar to our man in the moon).

22. See Chapter 1, note 19, for an explanation.

23. See Chapter 1, note 19.

21
BUDDHA ACTIVITY

(f) 'The activity is working for the benefit of others without preconceived ideas.'[1]

ONE SHOULD ADOPT an attitude towards enlightenment, then follow the Path and finally aspire for Buddhahood solely to burn up the misery of sentient beings and help them to attain happiness. When a man becomes a Buddha, habit-making thoughts and forced effort cease for him. Therefore whatever is, or is thought to be, necessary for sentient beings happens all the time of its own accord, as is the case with Buddhas. How this comes about is indicated in the couplet:

> The Body works for sentient beings without habit-making thoughts,
> So do Speech and Mind.
> These three factors (124b) outline Buddha-activity.

The working for the benefit of sentient beings by Body, Speech and Mind without habit-making thoughts is illustrated by similes in the 'rGyud.bla.ma' ('Uttaratantra' IV, 13):

> Like Indra, a drum, a cloud, Brahmā,
> The sun, a jewel,
> Like an echo is the Tathāgata;
> Like sky and earth.

(I) The vision of Indra is a simile illustrating the activity of Body for sentient beings.

Indra, king of gods, surrounded by a crowd of goddesses stays in his palace, which is pure and transparent as beryl, and outside it his reflection appears. Men and women living on the earth then see that reflection, perceive his enjoyments and resolve soon to be like him. To that end they strive for the good and wholesome and when they die are reborn in the heavenly world. The vision of Indra is not premeditated and cannot be shaken. It is the same with us. Having approached the Great Meaning of Reality, developed confidence and seen the Body of the Samyaksambuddha adorned with all attributes; having witnessed how variously he sits, rises, moves and goes out; having listened to the Dharma and concentrated on it, we gain confidence by this vision and long to attain this splendour. We then adopt an attitude towards enlightenment as the cause of the Buddha state and in the end realize Buddhahood. In this vision of the Body there is nothing of premeditation, it is something unshakable. So also it is said:[2]

Just as the body of the king of the gods
Is reflected on the polished surface of a beryl (125a),
So in the polished mind of sentient beings
The reflection of the Body of the Buddha appears.

In this way the Body works for the benefit of others without premeditation.

(II) The drum of the gods is a simile illustrating how Speech acts for the benefit of sentient beings.

The drum 'Holding the Power of the Dharma' appears in the palace of the gods as a result of their good deeds and without premeditation proclaims the transitoriness of all that is created[3] thereby admonishing the care-free gods. As is said:[4]

Through former good deeds
Of gods and goddesses
Without exertion, location, intention
And premeditation
The drum of the gods admonishes
The care-free gods ever and again,
By its voice proclaiming
Transitoriness, misery, non-individuality and peace.

In the same way without effort or discursiveness the Buddha's Voice proclaims the Dharma simply because it is good for those so fortunate as to listen to it. As is stated:[5]

Without exerting itself
The Buddha Voice encompasses
All sentient beings
And teaches the Dharma to the fortunate.

In this manner Speech works for the benefit of others without premeditation.

(III) The cloud is a simile illustrating the unpremeditated working of Mind.

In summer the sky is covered effortlessly with clouds and rain falls without premeditation so that it is said:[6] (125b)

In summer clouds
Are the cause of excellent crops

And rain falls
Effortlessly on the earth.

In the same way the working of Mind without premeditation causes the rain of the Dharma to fall and so brings the crop of the good and wholesome to fullness. As is said:[7]

Out of the cloud of Compassion
The rain of the Doctrine of the Victorious One
Falls without premeditation
As a continuous harvest for all.

In this manner Mind works for the benefit of others without premeditation.

(IV) Just as Brahmā, king of gods, without leaving his own world shows himself in all those of the gods, so also The Buddha without moving from his Dharmakāya displays the twelve events in his life[8] and other wondrous manifestations for those who have to be taught. As is stated:[9]

Just as Brahmā
Not moving from the Brahma world
Without effort appears
In all spheres of gods,
So without moving away
From the Dharmakāya, The Buddha
Without exertion in all realms
Shows his manifestations to the fortunate.

(V) Just as the rays of the sun without premeditation simultaneously open the buds of numberless flowers, so the rays of The Buddha's Dharmakāya, without premeditation and effort, open the buds of white lotuses which are the minds of an infinite variety of individuals with different interests and waiting to be taught. As is said:[10]

Just as the sun without premeditation
By the direct spreading of its rays
Opens the lotus flowers (126a)
And ripens others,
So the rays of the sun-like Dharma
Of the Tathāgata
Enter without premeditation
The minds of beings to be taught.

Or, just as the sun is reflected simultaneously in all clean vessels, so is The Buddha at one and the same time in all beings to be taught. As is stated:[11]

Therefore in water vessels and
In individuals to be taught,
The reflection of the sun, the Tathāgata,
Appears simultaneously in infinite forms.

(VI) Just as a Wish-Fulfilling Gem, after being prayed to, without premeditation grants any wish, so through reliance on The Buddha the various aspirations of Śrāvakas and others are fulfilled. As is written:[12]

Just as the Wish-Fulfilling Gem
At once and without premeditation
Grants every wish of
Those who live in this world of Karma,
So also in relying on the Wish-Fulfilling Gem
(The Buddha), the various aspirations
Are fulfilled without premeditation
By hearing the Dharma.

In the same way the similes of echo, sky and earth are used to illustrate a Buddha's working without premeditation, for the benefit of all sentient beings.[13]

The twenty-first chapter, dealing with the Buddha-Activity, from
The Jewel Ornament of Liberation or
The Wish-Fulfilling Gem of the
Noble Doctrine.

This explanation of the stages in the Mahāyāna Path, The Ornament of Liberation
or the Wish-Fulfilling Gem of the Noble Doctrine, has been written by the doctor (*lha.rje*) bSod.nams rin.chen at the request of the Venerable Dar.ma.skyabs.

NOTES TO CHAPTER 21

1. See Chapter 1, p. 2.
2. 'Uttaratantra' IV, 14.
3. Four topics are proclaimed: Everything composite (created) is

transitory; the whole of reality has no individuality of its own; everything imperfect is misery and Nirvāṇa is highest peace.

4. 'Uttaratantra' IV, 31–2.

5. ibid., IV, 33.

6. ibid., IV, 42.

7. ibid., IV, 43.

8. The twelve events are the departing from Tuṣita heaven, entering the mother's womb, up to the passing into Nirvāṇa. See Chapter 20, p. 266.

9. 'Uttaratantra' IV, 53–4.

10. ibid., IV, 58–60.

11. ibid., IV, 62.

12. ibid., IV, 67–8.

13. These similes have been elaborated in 'Uttaratantra' IV, 71–6, reaffirming that Buddhahood is without premeditation in its operation.

PRONUNCIATION GUIDE

ONLY THE BAREST OUTLINE of the intricacies of the pronunciation of the Tibetan language can be given here. While the Western dialects have preserved much of the original pronunciation and approach the written form fairly closely, it is the Lha.sa dialect which is considered most elegant, although its pronunciation deviates most from the written form. In the following the Lha.sa dialect is taken as the standard.

The Tibetan language has five vowels,

a i u e o

which are pronounced like their Italian equivalents, but always short; and thirty consonants:

	surd	aspirate	sonant	nasal
guttural	*k*	*kh*	*g*	*ṅ*
palatal	*c*	*ch*	*j*	*ñ*
dental	*t*	*th*	*d*	*n*
labial	*p*	*ph*	*b*	*m*
palatal-sibilant	*ts*	*tsh*	*dz*	
	w	*ź*	*z*	'
semivowels	*y*	*r*	*l*	
	ś	*s*	*h*	*a*

k is pronounced like English *k* in *king* without the slightest admixture of aspiration.

kh is an aspirated *k*, pronounced in one breath, like *ink-horn.*

g is pronounced like English *k*, but low toned, unless 'protected' by the following consonants: *d* (*dg-*), *m* (*mg-*), ' (*'g-*), *r* (*rg-*), *l* (*lg-*), *s* (*sg-*), *br* (*brg-*), and *bs* (*bsg-*), when the pronunciation becomes like English *g* in *good*, the 'protecting consonants' not being spoken.

ṅ is pronounced like *ng* in *ring.*

c is spoken like *ch* in *chill*, but without the slightest aspiration.

ch is an aspirated *c*, as in *touchhole.*

j is pronounced like *c*, but low toned, unless 'protected' by the consonants *m* (*mj-*), ' (*'j-*), *r* (*rj-*), *l* (*lj-*), and *br* (*brj-*), when it is spoken like the English *j* in *Jack*, the 'protecting' consonants remaining silent.

ñ is spoken like *n* in *new* or *nuisance.*

t is a purely dental sound, pronounced with the tongue between the teeth and without aspiration.

th is an aspirated dental *t*, NOT to be confused with the English *th.*

d is pronounced like *t*, but low toned, unless 'protected' by *g* (*gd-*), *b* (*bd-*), *m* (*md-*), ' (*'d-*), *r* (*rd-*), *l* (*ld-*), *s* (*sd-*), *br* (*brd-*), and *bs* (*bsd-*), when it is pronounced as a soft dental *d* (tongue between the teeth).

n is like the English *n* but with the difference noted under *t* and *d*.

p is pronounced like *p* in *pat*, without the slightest aspiration.

ph is an aspirated *p*, like in *top-hat*, but pronounced in one breath.

b is pronounced like *p*, unless 'protected' by the consonants ' (*'b-*), *r* (*rb-*), and *s* (*sb-*), when it is pronounced like English *b*. The combination *db* is silent and only the following vowel (as for instance in *dbU.ma* = *+u.ma*) or the following semivowel (as for instance in *dbyer.med* = *+yer.med*) is spoken. If *b* begins the second syllable of a word whose preceding syllable ends in a vowel or in *ṅ*, ', *r*, *l*, it is pronounced as *w*.

m is like English *m*.

ts is like English *ts* in *hats*.

tsh is an aspirated *ts*, like in *hits hard*, but spoken in one breath.

dz is pronounced like *ts*, unless 'protected' by *m* (*mdz-*), ' (*'dz-*), *r* (*rdz-*), and *br* (*brdz-*), when it is pronounced almost like *ds* in English *words*.

w is like English *w* in *water*.

ź is pronounced like English *sh*, but low toned.

z is almost like English *s*, but low toned.

' has no pronunciation of its own. It either carries a vowel or 'protects' the following consonant.

y is like English *y* in *yawn*.

r is like English *r* in *run*.

l is like English *l* in *light*.

ś is pronounced like English *sh*, but more sharply and through the teeth.

s is like sharp English *s*.

h is like English *h* in *hut*.

a is initial *a*, and also carries like ' the other vowel signs (i.e. *i*, *u*, *e*, *o*).

The following consonants and groups of consonants, *g*, *d*, *b*, *m*, ', *r*, *l*, *s*, *br* and *bs* (the so-called prefixed and superscribed letters) are not pronounced before any other consonant. Thus:

gduṅ	*+duṅ*	'bone'
dgu	*+gu*	'nine'
bka'	*+kā*	'order'
mgo	*+go*	'head'

'di	*+di*	'this'
rkaṅ	*+kaṅ*	'marrow'
lṅa	*+ṅa (nga)*	'five'
spu	*+pu*	'hair'
brda	*+da*	'sign'
bsgom	*+gom*	'meditation'.

The following combinations, *kl, gl, bl, rl,* and *sl* (and also *brl* and *bsl*) are all pronounced as *l.* Thus:

klu	*+lu*	'serpent'
glu	*+lu*	'song'
blo	*+lo*	'intellect'
rluṅ	*+luṅ*	'wind'
brla	*+la*	'thigh'
sla	*+la*	'easy'
bslab.pa	*+lap.pa*	'doctrine'.

Only *zl* is pronounced as *d.* Thus:

zla.ba *+da.wa* 'moon'.

The following groups of consonants, *kr* (*skr, bskr*), *tr, pr* (*dpr, spr*) are pronounced like the Sanskrit cerebral *ṭ*, which is approximately the English *t* in *tongue.* Thus:

krog.chen.po	*+ṭog.chempo*	'durable'
skra	*+ṭa*	'hair on the head'
pra	*+ṭa*	'token'
dpral.ba	*+ṭä.wa*	'forehead'
sprin	*+ṭin*	'cloud'.

Similarly the combinations *khr* (*'khr, mkhr*) and *phr* (*'phr*) are pronounced as an aspirate *ṭ*. Thus:

khrag	*+ṭha(g)*	'blood'
'khruṅ.ba	*+ṭhuṅ.wa*	'to be born'
phra.mo	*+ṭha.mo*	'thin'
'phro.ba	*+ṭho.wa*	'to emanate'.

The combinations *gr* (*dgr, bgr, mgr, 'gr, sgr, bsgr*), *dr* (*'dr*), and *br* (*dbr, 'br, sbr*) are all pronounced like Sanskrit cerebral *ḍ*, approximately English *d* in *dog*, when 'protected', otherwise as low toned *ṭ*. Thus:

gri	*+ṭi*	'knife'
dgra	*+ḍa*	'enemy'
bgraṅ.ba	*+ḍang.wa*	'to calculate'

mgrin	+*ḍin*	'neck'
'gro.ba	+*ḍo.wa*	'to walk'
sgra	+*ḍa*	'voice'
dri.ma	+*ṭi.ma*	'impurity'
'dri.ba	+*ḍi.wa*	'to ask'
braṅ	+*ṭang*	'breast'
'briṅ	+*ḍing*	'mediocre'
sbraṅ.bu	+*ḍang.bu*	'fly'.

sr is pronounced as *s*. Thus:

sraṅ.'gag	+*sang.ga*	'narrow lane'.

The combinations *py* in *dpy* and *spy*, and *by* (*'by*, *sby*) are pronounced like *c* and *j* respectively. Thus:

dpyod.pa	+*cö.pa*	'to examine'
spyaṅ.ki	+*cang.ki*	'wolf'
bya	+*ja*	'bird'
'byuṅ.ba	+*jung.wa*	'to originate'
sbyor.ba	+*jor.wa*	'to unite'.

phy and *'phy* are pronounced like *ch*. Thus:

phyir	+*chir*	'again'
'phyi.ba	+*chi.wa*	'to be late'.

db in *dby* is silent. Thus:

dbyer.med	+*yer.me*	'indivisible'.

In all other combinations such as *ky*, *khy*, and *gy*, both consonants are spoken distinctly. (In the Mongolian pronunciation of Tibetan, however, these combinations also are spoken as *c*, *ch*, and *j* respectively.) An exception is the pronunciation of *bka'.'gyur* as Kanjur and *bstan.'gyur* as Tanjur.

my (*dmy*, *smy*) are always spoken as *ñ*. Thus:

myu.gu	+*ñu.gu*	'sprout'
smyu.gu	+*ñu.gu*	'reed-pen'
dmyal.ba	+*ñǟ.wa*	'hell'.

mr (*smr*) is pronounced either as *m* or *mar*. Thus:

smra.ba	+*ma.wa*, *mar.wa*	'to speak'.

lh is distinctly spoken as *l* and *h*.

The following ten consonants, *g*, *ṅ*, *d*, *n*, *b*, *m*, ', *r*, *l*, *s* and their combinations *gs*, *ṅs*, *bs*, and *ms* occur at the end of a syllable. Of these *g* is pronounced so slightly as hardly to be heard and shortens the preceding vowel. Thus:

mig	+*mi*	'eye'
lug	+*lu*	'sheep';

but when it is followed by another consonant in a second syllable of the same word it is clearly pronounced. Thus:

lug.pa +*lug.pa* 'shepherd'.

gs preceded by the vowel *a* has the effect of lengthening the *a*.

' also lengthens the preceding vowel.

The consonants *d*, *n*, *l*, and *s* modify the value of the preceding vowel. There *a* becomes *ä* (like French *ê* in *bête*), *u* becomes *ü* (like in French *mûr*), and *o* becomes *ö* (like in French *bleu* and *neuf*). Apart from effecting this change in the quality of the vowel, *d* leaves the preceding vowel short and itself becomes silent. *l* and *s* lengthen the changed vowel and also become silent. *n* is itself pronounced, but becomes *m* before a following labial. Thus:

lud	+*lü*	'manure'
gad.mo	+*gä.mo*	'laughter' (see pronunciation of *g* above)
'dod.pa	+*dö.pa*	'desire'
lan	+*län*	'answer'
dgon.pa	+*göm.pa*	'monastery'
kun.rtog	+*kün.to*	'imagination'
bal	+*bǟ*	'wool' (see pronunciation of *b* above)
lus	+*lǖ*	'body'
las	+*lǟ*	'work'
chos	+*chȫ*	'Dharma'.

Often for the sake of euphony the pronunciation is modified. No fixed rules can be given for such cases. Therefore it seems unnecessary to enumerate them in this short guide. Similarly the three tones of the Tibetan language, viz. high, medium and low, may be mentioned but not discussed in detail.

INDEX OF BOOK TITLES

A. TIBETAN

Kg = bKa'.'gyur. Tg = bsTan.'gyur. Works marked by * are not found in either collection. The numbers refer to the sDe.dge edition catalogue.

'dKon.mchog ta.la'i gzuṅs', 21
    (Kg. mDo.sde, 145; gzuṅs.'dus, 847)
'dKon.mchog.sprin'
    vide ''Phags.pa dKon.mchog.sprin'
'dKon.mchog.brtsegs.pa'
    vide ''Phags.pa dKon.mchog.brtsegs.pa'
'sKu'i mdzod 'chi.med rdo.rje'i glu', 228
    (Tg. rGyud, 2269)
*'sKul.byed.kyi gẓuṅs', 127
'bsKal.ba bzaṅ.po'i mdo', 130
    (Kg. mDo.sde, 94)
'Kye.rdo.rje', 221
    (Kg. rGyud.'bum, 417)
*'Kye.rdo.rje lha.dgu'i mṅon.rtogs dkyil.'khor.gyi cho.ga daṅ bcas.pa dṅos.grub.kyi gter.mdzod, 231
'kLu'i rgyal.po rgya.mtshos žus.pa'i mdo', 203
    (Kg. mDo.sde, 153–5)
'sKyes.rab', 242
    (Tg. skyes.rab, 4150)
'Khyim.bdag Drag.śul.can.gyis žus.pa'i mdo', 153, 191
    (Kg. dKon.brtsegs, 63)
'Khyim.bdag dPa'.sbyin.gyis žus.pa'i mdo', 43, 121, 134
    (Kg. dKon.brtsegs, 72)
*'mKhas.grub.kun gyi gtsug.brgyan paṇ.chen Na.ro.pa'i rnam.thar ṅo.mtshar smad.byuṅ', 228
*''Khor.ba thog.ma.med.pa'i mdo', 93
*''Khor.lo bcu.pa'i mdo', 223
'Ga.ya.go.ri'i mdo', 204
    (Kg. mDo.sde, 109)
'Gaṅ.pos žus.pa'i mdo', 181
    (Kg. dKon.brtsegs, 61)
'Go.cha bkod.pa bstan.pa'i mdo', 184
    (Kg. dKon.brtsegs, 51)

B. SANSKRIT

C. PĀLI

INDEX OF TECHNICAL TERMS

A. TIBETAN

kun.tu rtog.pa, 12
kun.tu reg.pa, 64
rkyen, 11, 200
lkugs.pa, 24
sku, 13
skye.ba'i bsam.gtan, 89
skyes.bu byed.pa'i 'bras.bu, 88
bskyed.rim, 221, 231

kha thur.du lta.ba, 65
khva lcags.kyi mchu.can, 59
khyi bsre.po, 59
'khor gsum rnam.par dag.pa, 110
'khyil.bar byed.pa, 64
'khrul.pa, 9, 10, 227, 269

gaṅ.zag, 51
gaṅ.zag.gi bdag.med, 51
go.ba, 53
dga'.ba, 90
dge.ba, 84
dge.ba'i chos.la 'dun.pa, 13
dge.ba'i rtsa.ba, 13
'gog.pa'i bden.pa, 89
rgyas, 262
rgyu, 11, 29, 200
rgyu mthun.pa'i 'bras.bu, 85
rgyud, 27
rgyun.du žugs.pa, 70
sgom.pa, 38, 51
sgom.spaṅs.kyi ñon.moṅs.(pa), 234, 252
sgom.lam, 113, 237
sgyu.ma lta.bu, 162
sgyu.lus, xiii
brgyud.pa'i bla.ma, 9
bsgrub.pa, 37, 38

B. SANSKRIT

arbuda, 64, 65
alakṣaṇa, 254
avidyā, 9, 11, 84, 140
aśaikṣa samyagjñāna, 235
aśaikṣī samyagvimukti, 235
asaṃjñin, 22
asādhāraṇa, 108

ākāra, 9
ākāśānantyāyatana, 80, 90
ākiṃcanyāyatana, 81, 90
ātman, 27, 51, 70, 226
ātmādivikalpavāsanā, 70
ādiviśuddhi, 254
ādhāra, 11
ānantarya, 89
ānantaryamārga, 238
āniñjya, 84
ānimitta, 255
āneñjya karman, 28
ārūpya, 90
āloka, 229
āśraya, 11
āsrava, 83, 140

indriya, 237

utpannakrama, 221, 231
utpala, 61
utsada, 57, 59
upa, 110
upapattidhyāna, 80, 89
upādāna, 70, 226
upādānaskandha, 70, 226
upāya, 11, 147, 225, 226
upekṣā, 90, 139
uṣmagata, 229, 236

ṛddhi, 52
ṛddhipāda, 233

ekāgratā, 199

bodhimaṇḍa, 141
Bodhisattvayāna, 109
bodhyaṅga, 237
brahmacaryāvāsa, 89

bhava, 84, 140
bhāva, 226
bhāvanā, 38, 51, 84
bhāvanāmārga, 113, 201, 237
bhāvanāheya kleśa, 234, 252
bhāvābhāvādvaya, 254
bhāsvara, 10
bhūtakāya, 270
bhūtārthapraveśa, 89
bhrānti, 9, 227, 269

mati, 11
matimān, 11
manas, 140, 198, 199, 201
manaskarman, 84
manojalpa, 229
manomayakāya, 12
manovijñāna, 201
mantra, 221
mahākaruṇā, 13
mahāpadma, 61
mahāyānagotra, 12
mahāsukha, xiv
māyāsvapnapratibhāsapratiśrutkodakacandrapratibimbanirmāṇa, 254
māyopama, 162
mārga, 237
mārgasatya, 89
mithyādṛṣṭi, 23
mīmāṁsā, 138
muditā, 90
mūrdhan, 229, 236
maitrī, 90
moha, 9, 199, 252
maula, 89

INDEX OF NAMES AND SUBJECTS